AF522040

THE DRAWINGS OF
Picasso

THE DRAWINGS OF

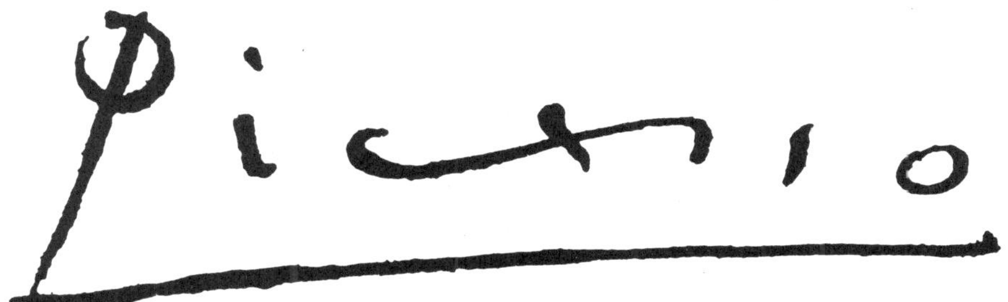

Georges
Boudaille

HAMLYN

First published in the U.K. in 1988 by
The Hamlyn Publishing Group Limited
now a Division of The Octopus Publishing Group plc
Michelin House, 81 Fulham Road
London SW3 6RB

ISBN 0 600 55278 0

Printed in Czechoslovakia

2/02/14/51-01

CONTENTS

I	Picasso's Drawings	6
II	Picasso's Style	13
III	The First Period	25
IV	Cubist Drawing	35
V	The Twenties and Thirties	57
VI	Guernica	85
VII	After the Civil War	99
VIII	The Last Period	119
IX	The Smokers	129
X	The Musketeers	135
XI	Eros Eternal	155
XII	Confronting the Present	185
	Chronology	193
	Select Bibliography	197
	List of Colour Plates	203
	List of Black and White Reproductions	204

I

PICASSO'S DRAWINGS

The work of Picasso has been the subject of countless studies, some devoted to his life, documented or fictionalised biographies, others to certain periods within his work and to some of the painter's favourite themes: the *Déjeuners sur l'herbe*, War and Peace, the Theatre and so on. All these studies concentrate on his painting and sculpture which are indeed major aspects of his work, but few are devoted entirely to the drawings. This is an enormous lacuna given the importance of drawing in Picasso's life and art.

The sheer volume of Picasso's graphic work imposes limits on the subjects covered, and it would be impossible to examine every aspect of Picasso's drawings without running into several weighty tomes. It is therefore with conscious bias that the author has selected the series and groups of drawings that he considers of particular significance in various periods. Efforts have been made to accentuate the originality of this book with the inclusion of unpublished material, notably the series of colour drawings known as the *Fumeurs* (Smokers), from spring 1964, which has never before been reproduced. There were choices that were logical, not to say unavoidable, in relation to the artist's beginnings, to Cubism or to his return to classicism in the Thirties. Illuminating comparisons are also made in connection with the famous protest painting, *Guernica*.

In the body of work after the Second World War, there is such a wealth of famous series that choices are not so much born of logic as of emotion. Hence the series taken from the sketchbooks, studies for the chapel at Vallauris transformed into a Temple of Peace, studies of couples embracing, wash silhouette studies, dozens of male and female heads, the portraits of *Musketeers* from 1967, highly erotic linear compositions and more, the only limit being that of space.

This iconographic selection is justified when one compares Picasso with the great artists of the past: he is so totally unlike them. His utter originality bursts forth from his drawings no less than his paintings – even when he is parodying the Old Masters.

There is some confusion about what drawing actually is. Everyone knows where it begins: often on the lined page of a school exercise book with a mere stub of a pencil, and there is much drawing of this kind in Picasso's work, but with the artistic licence that creative minds grant themselves, it is impossible to say where it ends or what its limitations are.

It is important at the outset to define as clearly as possible the terms that are used to describe the work.

There are two approaches to drawing: one by its *function*, its role and the significance of the artist's intentions; the other strictly *technical*.

First of all, let us simply say that drawing is the representation and/or suggestion of an object or a being. It may simply be a sketch, outline, draft or diagram or it may develop into a perfectly finished work of art. (This excludes many other forms of drawing: geometric, industrial, decorative, scientific, ornamental, etc.)

Picasso's drawing is often at the same time both a 'diary' and a kind of logbook in which he entered all his ideas and his visions. Therein lies a difficulty for the author. With Picasso, everything began with drawings; so in practice, a study of the drawings involves the whole of his life's work, notwithstanding the gaps and omissions that there may be in this selection.

However, the author was fortunate enough to be allowed access to the treasures held in the archives of a publishing company established some forty years ago which specialised in Picasso's art and was committed to the presentation of his works and research for the benefit of all art lovers. The friendship between the artist and the publisher,

Charles Feld, has its place in the history of art.

Let us try nevertheless to limit the range of our survey by attempting to define what is a drawing and what is not.

What we call drawing is differentiated from other artistic techniques by the medium and the material used, although the latter can be of almost infinite variety.

Drawing proceeds by strokes and lines. The line is a visibly or virtually continuous stroke. A line, theoretically, has only one dimension, length. Only a stroke may be thin or thick. The difference between line and stroke is reflected by many expressions in everyday use: you can sketch with 'bold strokes', but you are 'out of line'.

The most commonly used medium is pencil; charcoal and chalk have similar properties and offer different shades. But one does not only draw with pencil or chalk; one can also draw with a brush like the Chinese, or in pen and ink. One can use wash or sepia. (These have nothing to do with gouache and watercolour – they consist of blobs of colour and belong in the painter's domain.) However, the borderline between gouache or watercolour on the one hand and wash on the other is a subtle one, since both are blobs from a brush, the former using all the colours of the palette, the latter restricted to black and white, whence all its severity and dignity. But drawing has its colour too, with coloured pencils, pastel (chalk), or the relatively recent oil pastel, developed in the laboratories of the colour manufacturers and sometimes known as greased chalk. And drawings indeed may be retouched with watercolour.

A study of drawing materials through the ages would entail years of work: the traditional material is paper and there are hundreds of different kinds and makes of paper. But a drawing can be made on practically any surface, plaster, linen, glass, marble, and even, as in the dawn of mankind, on the rock surface of a cave.

As far as Picasso is concerned, his indifference to material details is well known. He drew on whatever happened to be to hand, for example, restaurant napkins, with whatever medium was at his disposal. This happened in moments of inspiration or of pure fantasy, for the amusement of friends. The same applies, whether he was drawing or sculpting, when he assembled heterogeneous objects that happened to take his eye and corresponded to the shape he needed. Witness his *Goat* or that monkey with the miniature Renault for a head. One extreme example reported in the press of the day was that of a drawing in lipstick on the breast of an overzealous admirer. Picasso was also particularly fond of medium- or large-sized sketch pads with spiral bindings in which he would make his sequences of drawings on a single theme, repeating and repeating them until he was satisfied – or simply exhausted. And yet when he wanted to, he would spend much time and trouble choosing the right quality of paper.

This comparison between drawing and 'assemblage' – sculpture made up of pre-existing objects – goes further than might at first appear. One has to go back to the heyday of Cubism and to the first collages. One of Picasso's many acts of audacity was to compose in two dimensions, drawing in pencil but also sticking on scraps of newspaper, or the wrapping from a packet of tobacco, the only constant being the material, paper! Can collage be seen as part of this panorama of Picasso's drawing work? Why not, since collage is really an embellished form of drawing. In collage, the effect is reinforced by the material, be it wallpaper, printed paper, old bus tickets or whatever, which is sometimes ridged or creased to add relief and to catch the light.

But *papier collé,* which Aragon distinguishes from Surrealist 'collage', was not born of fantasy, chance or whim, but of necessity. The necessity lay in introducing not merely another material but another dimension, a point of reference, a scrap of reality in a work of fiction, or to give an idea of scale where there was none, since it is practically impossible for a reproduction to convey the dimension of a drawing, except in the case of Cubist *papier collé*. This is achieved by the instantly recognisable size of the newsprint characters or the famous 'packet of shag' which Picasso sent straight from the tobacconist's shop into a museum.

Paradoxically, here was a man whose creative power knew no bounds who applied himself to showing the bounds of the world and to giving it a precise definition.

The comparison between Picasso and Degas, and especially between certain of their drawings, is a significant one. Intellectually they were diametrically opposed, one conservative, not to say reactionary in his views, the other a communist, a fervent advocate of progress in all spheres, social as well as artistic; yet they came together when they drew the form of a woman on paper. And it would seem at certain times that Picasso, when he was in Rome rehearsing the ballet *Parade* and living among ballerinas, had his illustrious predecessor in mind. In the wings of the theatre, both of them banished reality.

Degas (according to Paul Valéry) said that 'drawing is not form but the way one sees form'.

Picasso (according to Hélène Parmelin) said that 'what is needed is to NAME things. They have to be called by their name. I NAME the eye. I NAME the foot . . . ' Which confirms yet again that the result is not the object itself, but its translation into another universe — art transcendent.

Commenting on Degas's thinking, Valéry writes: 'Therefore here you have to *will* to be able to see and drawing is both the *end* and the *means* of this *willed* sight.' Picasso had that will too, ever present, face to face with all his subjects.

Of the nude, beloved of both Degas and Picasso, Valéry said that it was to artists of form what love had been to the storytellers and poets. This was, and remained, more true of Picasso than of any other artist.

Further comparisons could be made. In Degas one finds the need for perfection to the highest degree and a noble idea of art which are only found in the greatest artists. Ingres said that drawing was the probity of art, a statement which has been the object of countless interpretations. As for Degas, 'since the true believer answers only to God . . . , so he remained untouched and constant, submitting only to the absolute idea that he had of his art. He wanted nothing other than that which he found most arduous to obtain for himself' (Valéry).

Once again, if one excludes the reference to religious faith, the sentence could equally well apply to the exigency of the painter of Notre-Dame-de-Vie.

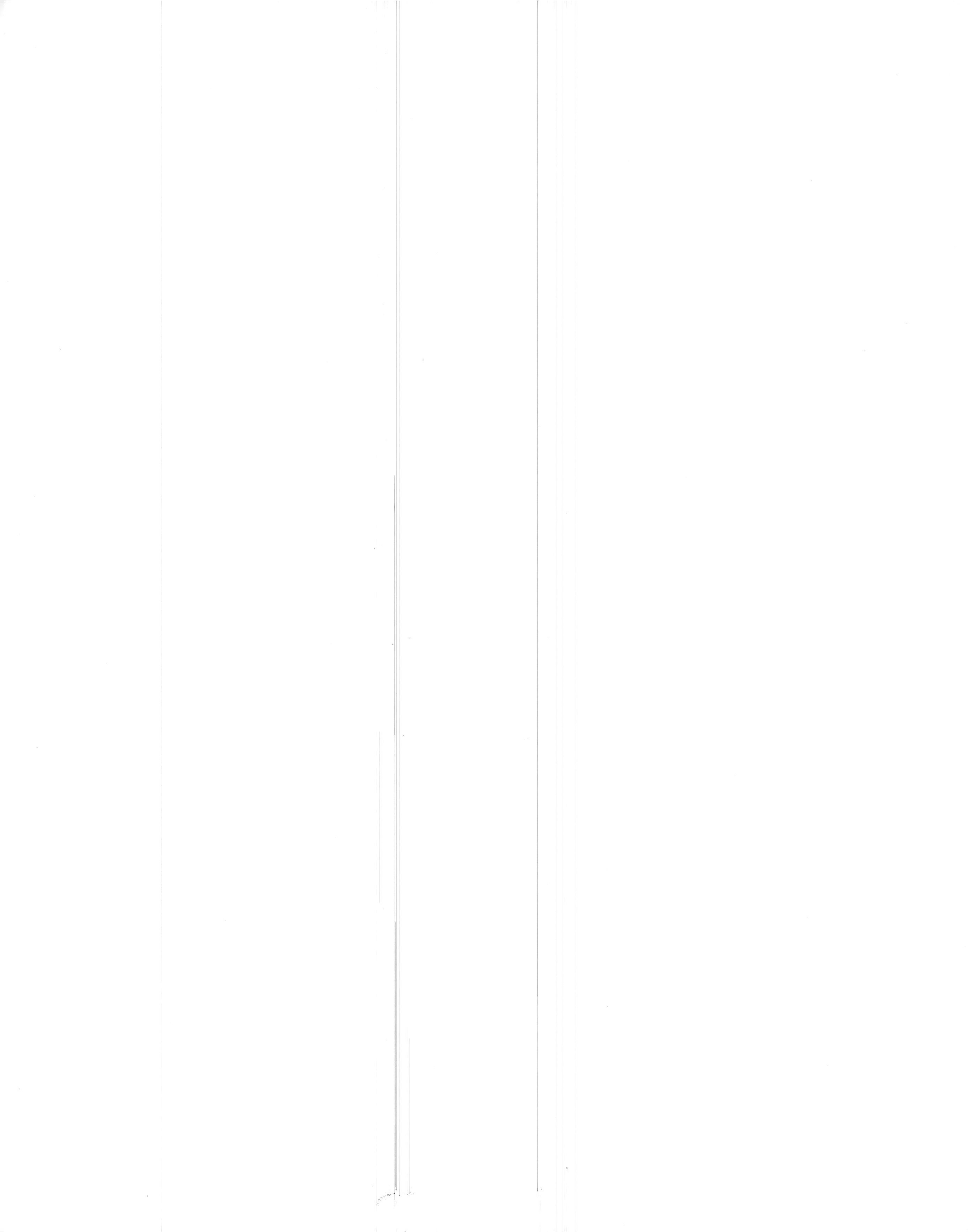

II

PICASSO'S STYLE

One of the accusations commonly levelled against Picasso is to be found within the customary reference to his 'virtuosity', a double-edged compliment, the origin of which needs to be clarified by an analysis of the creative process. How many private views have rung with words like 'talent', 'speed' or *fa presto* as the Italians say, with comments on precision of line and, most of all, virtuosity? All these are merely qualifying terms related to technique and say nothing at all about quality. With the word 'virtuosity' so-called art-lovers blind themselves to everything that formed the genius of Picasso, his behaviour, his attitude towards the world and towards society, his regard for truth, his passionate, not to say vital, need to translate on to canvas or paper a vision which professes to be realistic. And the realistic vision of Picasso is more truly realistic than the appearance of reality itself, because he also presents us with the underside of beings and of objects; he shows us the submerged portion of the iceberg.

One senses this truth throughout Picasso's work without being able to explain it. It results from a complex mechanism which, going from the eye to the hand, owes everything to the mind. With the exception of the Cubist period (from 1909 to 1921), what first strikes one about a Picasso drawing is the suppleness of the line, its fluidity, its freedom. It appears to be guided only by itself, by its own inherent need.

The next, natural, impression is of what this line, which has neither master nor reason, shows us. The line, the trace of an instrument held in the artist's hand, can be compared to the curve left by a recording barometer. The line itself is nothing – or next to nothing! Only the stroke has depth. A straight line is the shortest link between one point and another, but Picasso's line dawdles and meanders sinuously to draw an outline, enfold a shape to give it a life of its own, and allows him to recreate the illusion of a presence that, man or object, springs up from the paper.

The impression of truth that emanates from drawing does not result from a mechanical process. Drawing has nothing in common with photography nor with the use of the camera obscura by 15th-century artists obsessed with perspective. The inherent truth of the stroke is born of an analysis of visible reality to arrive at a two-dimensional graphic transcription which is the synthesis of volume and form, and takes account of the effect of light. Indeed, all volume, as concrete and stable as it may be both theoretically and physically, ceaselessly varies according to a number of parameters which include intensity of illumination and the angle of the light rays.

It is impossible to reproduce volume perceptibly by purely technical means, however proficient. The most advanced of today's computers use a system of purely linear contour lines, a system that has been in use for centuries, used by Leonardo da Vinci and by our ordnance surveyors on their 1/25,000 maps. Such definition is precise and vital in a number of practical areas, particularly in geology and for military campaigning, but it has no suggestive value at all and its visual power is nil. Hence it is artistically nonexistent.

So what was happening in the art of Picasso and of some of his contemporaries in the first half of the 20th century?

Beneath a semblance of extreme simplification and of visually reductive diagrams, drawing achieves expressive power of as much, if not more, intensity as under the hand of the most famous creative artists of past centuries. Thus Picasso rivals Ingres, at a century's distance.

Such a statement gives rise to a number of questions about the power and the methods of line or, more precisely, of drawing.

The real questions, translated into everyday language, are: Where does it happen? How does it really work? It is immediately obvious that this remarkable evocative power does not reside in even the most skilful hand if it is skill alone that guides it. Therefore, it must be declared without reservation that the possession of so-called virtuosity explains nothing whatever.

What then? Is it observation? In Picasso, those deep, almost bottomless, black eyes which look out with loathing at you and at the whole world, which sometimes turn opaque as if to shut out an importunate world, have been the subject of much literature, not all of it sound. But, however bright the eye, we know that it serves only to transmit an image to the retina and thence, via the optic nerve, to the brain. Which only goes to prove what we already knew or guessed: everything happens in the brain.

Paul Valéry foreshadowed today's psychologists in his analysis of the physiological mechanisms when he wrote: 'I cannot define my perception of a thing without *actually* drawing it and I cannot draw this thing without a voluntary attention *that remarkably transforms that which at first I thought I saw and knew well.* I realise that I did not know what I knew: the nose of my best friend . . . '

This is precisely the process of Picasso. In every plate in this book, this amalgam of observation, execution and revelation is apparent. Picasso shows us what we did not know how to see, what we thought we knew best, the nose of our best friend.

To make us see it is the result of effort and self-control. Paul Valéry said that it was a 'question of direction . . . To give the hand its *visual* freedom, one must take away its *muscular* freedom; in particular, make it supple in any and all directions, which it does not like. Giotto used to draw a perfect circle with a brush, both ways'.

It is worth remembering that Paul Valéry was himself accustomed to drawing. He spoke not just as a theoretician, but as a practitioner too.

This gives the lie to the paradoxical slur that the finest artists are not intelligent. A work of art is the result of conscious reflection on the image of the outside world and the possibilities for translating it graphically in two dimensions.

It takes years, those famous years of youth, those formative years, for an artist, however gifted, to assimilate the methods of his predecessors, to modify, enrich and transform them to the point of creating his own style, a mode of reading and writing which corresponds to his personality and which may one day, many years later, ensure his fame.

The aesthetic effect appears simultaneously, sometimes even afterwards, and proceeds according to different rules, albeit more subtle ones and more difficult to analyse because they are occasional and temporal.

Therefore, every drawing, and every stroke that goes to form that drawing, is the result of at least four operations:

(a) Vision and absorption of a scene or fragment of a visible subject not merely as a whole but in each of its constituent elements and details.

(b) Analysis of the vision, selection of elements that are significant or subjectively important.

(c) Choice of the most appropriate medium for the expression and materialisation of these elements on a flat surface, including numerous decisions as to omission or accentuation.

(d) Impulse to and control of the hand. Needless to say the artist, in the heat of creative activity, does not rationalise every one of his actions and is therefore not conscious of these phases. He reacts according to the innumerable automatic responses acquired over years of experience and experimentation.

The next stage involves a critical testing of the efficiency of the methods chosen and their correction in order to achieve increased, then optimal, effectiveness. This goes some way towards explaining the long series of studies, the fat sketchbooks wholly devoted to the same subject. But the repetition of a single subject does not necessarily imply dissatisfaction. There will be many examples of the way in which Picasso used this means to study various aspects of the same object, to multiply his approaches to it, to delve into its essence in order to arrive at maximum intensity.

The methods of graphic expression are as numerous as the aspects of life that Picasso sought to capture and to make us experience, which is to say that they are too numerous to be listed within the confines of this book. However, we shall not be discouraged and shall examine as many of them as possible in the following pages.

We shall concentrate on the salient points of his style: the faces and the portraits, the figures, their shape and posture, the illusion of volume created by a systematic deformation of outline, the suggestion of movement by a similar process, the exaggeration of certain parts of the model, and other less common but no less effective characteristics.

All of Picasso's graphic work serves not only to show us what he wants us to see, but also to give us a lesson in drawing.

Through the years, periods and themes, the procedures that Picasso used evolved and diversified. The Barcelona sketches, the drawings of the Blue and Rose periods, the Cubist *papiers collés*, the neo-classical drawings inspired by the theatre and by Roman antiquities throughout the twenties and thirties, the faces torn by the sufferings of war (the Spanish Civil War and the World War of 1939–45), finally the twenty-five years of joyful or passionate improvisation in the postwar period: this indefatigable quest that was to end only with death itself constitutes a body of work so vast that its only limits are those imposed by the artist himself.

One can say that Picasso had nothing to hide and hid nothing from us of his experiments, his uncertainties, his second thoughts. On the contrary, by revealing the successive stages of his work, he helped us to see what he wanted to show us, both the subject and his way of showing it. Looking through the pages of his sketchbooks, we feel somehow obtrusive as though we were violating a secret — that of the creativity of one of the most important artists of the century – and we cannot help but experience a pleasure that is both aesthetic and perhaps a trifle morbid at the same time. This is what made Henri-Georges Clouzot's 1956 film so successful, its title *The Picasso Mystery* underlining its revelatory attraction. No one before Clouzot had been allowed to plant a camera in front of Picasso, separated from him only by a mirror which became the canvas of a drawing. No one had been able to conceive of the swiftness and sureness of the painter's hand. Equally, no one before could have imagined his qualms, his anguish, his despair when nothing that flowed from his hand seemed to satisfy him.

Thanks to Clouzot, as well as to the numerous books on Picasso's methods, people are able, if not to participate, at least to feel actively involved with the creative process.

The reader should take part in this work of analysis, comparison and consideration. He may not always agree. That is not important. On the contrary, such a reaction will be proof of an interest not only in Picasso but in this book too.

In the preceding pages, through Valéry's understanding of drawing, a parallel has been drawn between the approach of Degas and that of Picasso. We could, in the pages that follow, pursue other parallels with other great masters of drawing. First and foremost, there was that old painter who was 'mad about drawing', Hokusai. Surely, the hand of Hokusai, a tireless observer, a virtuoso champion of speed, could have competed with the most advanced of today's photographic lenses and shutters – made, of course, in Japan!

Hokusai could bring a man, an animal, a plant to life with a single stroke of his brush and Indian ink. And Picasso rivalled him for speed of execution, while revealing in many ways that he knew and admired the work of the great Japanese draughtsman.

Like Picasso later, Hokusai doggedly sought to take possession of his subject in its totality and from all its aspects — witness his well-known *Thirty-six views of Mount Fuji*, which were followed by a series of one hundred! But it is in the sketching of daily life that the Japanese school of *Ukiyo-e*, 'the Painting of the Passing Scene', affirms its specificity and unfolds its splendours. It was drawing with Indian ink wash that permitted simultaneous speed and freedom of execution. In this respect, Hokusai was probably surpassed by the younger Hiroshige who, having produced a great number of famous engravings of landscapes, recorded scenes of vegetable, animal and human life with a freshness and vivacity which has lasted until the present day.

This is what Picasso shared with the Japanese, with whom he had, in other respects, little affinity.

Hélène Parmelin remarked on the process: 'Working fast, he reduces to nothing the time for thought between the canvas (or the drawing) and himself. The immense weight of artistic knowledge which he carries in both his head and his hands enables him to achieve the greatest effect with the least effort.

'This is no "automatic writing". It is with full consciousness, never for a single moment lost, that his hand seeks to convey the highest degree of reality. In fact it is the very opposite of "automatic writing". Picasso is not searching for the subconscious truth that is repressed by conscious thought. Not for him the pure (or impure) gesture that results from sweeping away clear reason. On the contrary, he brings to bear the sheer immensity of his science, of his work, of his astounding technique. He trusts in the means at his disposal, to try, in the lightning speed of his work, to clear the way for thought *alone*; that which will "stick" to the painter and his subject and tell them what they are, without art and its mannerisms interfering.' (Hélène Parmelin, *Notre-Dame-de-Vie*, Editions Cercle d'Art, 1966.)

And then there was Ingres. There is much complicity despite all that would have set them at loggerheads had they been contemporaries! Picasso with his faultless education appreciated the master of Montauban in his own way and remembered his lesson. This is particularly evident in the drawings of 1925–30 when he was using grey tints again to make the curve of an arm or a thigh, or the cylinder of a distant tower 'turn'.

When he was working on the theme of the *Harem*, as early as 1905, it is evident that he was thinking of Ingres's *Turkish Bath*. And among all the nudes that sprang from his pencil in the last period, there are many which still owed something to Ingres.

Between 1920 and 1930, Picasso occasionally ventured in a direction where so many artists had lost their way (Giorgio de Chirico and André Derain among the most famous of them) and seemed to set at stake again everything that he produced during the Cubist period. He used historical references. He showed columns, drapery and folds, that came from Rome, perhaps even from Athens, and many of them had passed through the studios of David and Ingres.

To pursue the comparison to the limits of the absurd, what dominates the parallel between Picasso and Ingres is both their concern for realism and their total independence from reality. Enough has been said about the extra vertebrae with which Ingres endowed his odalisks, but that was no isolated case. He lengthened arms, deformed thighs, in short he reconstructed woman according to his own taste. And to hell with anatomy!

As for Picasso, no one needs to be reminded of the liberties he took with nature and the human figure. His friend Max Jacob was once moved to exclaim: 'Imagine if I were to see your family arriving at the gare d' Austerlitz with faces like that!'

It is also worth remembering here Paul Valéry's quip in *Degas, Dance, Drawing* on the usefulness of a knowledge of anatomy to an artist. So many bad painters know it perfectly, he said, so let's forget it! The same could apply to perspective. It has to be reinvented, and that is what Picasso did with Cubism.

To sum up, I would not say that Ingres and Picasso asserted their total freedom from reality, but that they confirmed the predominance of art over nature.

There would also be much to say of the relationships between Picasso and Dürer, Manet, Clouet, Rembrandt, Goya and Velasquez, all brilliant draughtsmen.

When he portrayed his wife Olga, might he not have intended to please her by presenting her with a pastiche of Ingres' most typical portraits? On the other hand, when he took up the theme of the *Women of Algiers*, it was the colourist in Delacroix which fascinated him and, learning from him, he attempted to rejoin his friend Henri Matisse. In fact, in his *Women of Algiers*, Picasso retained only the idea of colour and reintroduced his rigorous composition and his need to define shapes.

So these two great masters of the 20th century, Picasso and Matisse, were never to meet in the realm of colour, even though they were both working under the same Riviera sun, living not many miles apart and both following a similar dream. Their differences were manifest from the outset. Matisse was a Fauve, Picasso never was; Picasso created Cubism, Matisse ignored it. And yet both of them were among the greatest draughtsmen of our times!

Their styles are different, in drawing as in painting, but paradoxically, they both used similar processes, especially in conveying volume. Matisse always used a linear style, as did Picasso at certain times, to produce, for example, the admirable series of erotic drawings in this book, which are of a purity that far surpasses that of Ingres. Yet, when one thinks of the two men's ways of working, one can see that their methods not only had nothing in common, but were direct opposites. As shown in a film about his work, Matisse, face to face with his subject, began humbly with a painstaking, almost academic, charcoal portrait with many corrections. There was even a glimpse of him using an eraser. This would be the first of many drawings, successively stripped of more and more detail, purified, until after a long work session, or even several, he was able to convey his subject at a single stroke, sometimes without lifting his hand from the paper. That was Matisse, that was the achievement that dazzles us and that will dazzle generations to come!

Picasso disdained this laborious process. Picasso never retouched, never corrected: he took a new sheet and started again. He could fill a whole sketchbook in next to no time. Each drawing was different from the one before and yet almost the same, with variations, until Picasso finally drew the version that satisfied him. But the success of the final version takes nothing away from the interest of its predecessors. In fact, these sequences of drawings are a fascinating revelation of the creative process in one of the greatest artists of our time. That is why they have been faithfully reproduced here. Picasso attached great importance to them and facilitated our task by systematically dating every drawing, as he did his paintings and, when there were several on the same day, he numbered them chronologically in roman numerals. These valuable indications are preserved here.

Finally, Matisse and Picasso were, like Hokusai, 'mad about

drawing' and relentlessly hard-working. They would go over their work a hundred times in their different ways, deforming the outline, seeking the equivalence of volume, making the most extreme simplifications, including references to primitive civilisations, in order to create the style of our era, the 20th century, resolutely modern and affirming their own personality and originality throughout.

One question remains: What did drawing mean to Picasso? At first sight, there was no essential difference for him between drawing, watercolour and painting. Whatever served to convey what he wanted us to see was good enough for him, it seems, just as in his sculpture, he saw no difference between so-called 'noble' materials and others. If some of his sculptures were cast in bronze, it was primarily to ensure their preservation, as well as their wider distribution, especially when they were in demand in many of the great museums of the world.

For many artists, the drawing is a study, a sketch, the first stage in the gestation of a work of art and as such of lesser quality and interest than the finished canvas. Certainly Picasso also used drawing to collect his thoughts, to note down ideas, to seek a plastic solution to a visual problem that he would ultimately use, though perhaps in another technique. But with him the process was not systematic. The drawing existed by and for itself.

His drawing rarely pretended to perfection, to the absolute, to the quality of a masterpiece, as was often the case with other artists, Matisse, for example. Picasso used drawing as Cézanne did. It was a means to an end; he was always searching for something. Hence, as we have already noted, the series. There are exceptions, of course, such as the admirable Cubist drawings of 1911–12 and the contemporaneous *papiers collés.*

We shall attempt to show how, throughout the various periods of his work, he adapted his style and technique to fit the desired end. The task was all the more arduous and all the more impressive in that, all his life, Picasso never appeared to be an artist who gave priority to colour. Even the so-called Blue and Rose periods owe their names to nothing more than a chromatic dominant. Drawing and structure were always uppermost. The whole of Picasso's work can thus be considered as dominated by the line, or the stroke. Masterpieces like *Guernica* or *The Charnel-house* are treated as monochromes. Often, in his haste to express himself, to *Name*, to use his term during a conversation with Hélène Parmelin, he covered his surface with the expressive shade. In fact, he did not cover it entirely, he streaked it quickly, as if to say: 'you understand, this is red (or yellow)'. Thus to study Picasso the draughtsman is to study the whole art of Picasso in all its formidable diversity.

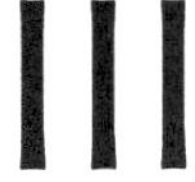

THE FIRST PERIOD

From his very early creative years, Pablo Ruiz loved to draw and displayed most of the traits common to young artists, ambition, spontaneity, impetuosity and, to be honest, dissipation. He hurled himself in many different directions, accumulating experiments and experiences in all fields.

His drawings from 1891 to 1905, that is to say from the age of ten to his aesthetic coming-of-age, reflect a certain psychological and almost physical state.

Pablo was voracious, he wanted to absorb everything, record everything, to fix everything on paper. Needless to say, at the age of ten he was merely imitating – albeit with great delicacy – the drawings he saw in the studio of his father, Don José Ruiz Blasco (Picasso was his mother's maiden name). Academic realism and caricature in the 'Parisian' spirit (Toulouse-Lautrec, but also the *miserabilist* painters Forain and Steinlein) characterise this very early period. It is no mere coincidence that the oldest drawing reproduced here is a *Woman and Child by the Sea,* muffled in their clothes as if they were suffering from the cold. This small pastel can be considered the first manifestation of the personality of the painter who was to become a symbol of his time and even of his century. Misery, drama, famine, but also the grandeur and dignity of woman, are all contained in this simple drawing, and Picasso was to come back to this theme time and again because it is full of meaning and was dear to his heart.

Thus, amid much experimentation, Picasso was already finding his own path. But one should also bear in mind all those portraits of friends 'snapped' in the taverns of Barcelona which have brought down to us the features of the poets and artists of the circle of Barcelona intellectuals that used to meet at Els Quatre Gats.

Curiously enough, if one deals in isolation with all the so-to-speak biographical sketches which make his notebook a kind of diary, Picasso's drawing activity can be divided into two parts, one Parisian, the other Catalan, one reflecting the world – and also the underworld – of Paris society, the other depicting the cruel life of fishermen's wives, peasants and workers in Catalonia.

They prefigured important paintings. Some of them were highly coloured, lit by the beacons of Fauvism even before it exploded on to the scene at the Autumn and Independents' Salons. (It is worth noting that Picasso who was the butt of critical reaction at the time of these great artistic events, did not participate in either of them.) These belong in the line of Toulouse-Lautrec and Van Dongen was a *fauve* before the Fauves. The others are bathed in a dramatic, disturbing, at times lambent light, with the ultramarines and greenish blues which preceded the Blue period.

Since the aim of this book is to show Picasso as creator, we have included only some of the major drawings and not the 'souvenir' sketches which, regardless of quality, are no more than the equivalent of a personal diary and not works of art in themselves. To rediscover the wealth of the early 1900s, one must turn to the work of Alexandre Cirici-Pellicer and to his pre-eminent book *Picasso before Picasso*. Others have devoted themselves to the subject: Palau y Fabre, who revised his evaluation several times, the last version published in 1975 under the title *Picasso in Catalonia*, and Cesareo Rodrigues-Aguilera whose lavish work *Picasso in Barcelona* explores this first, and certainly decisive, period.

In this book, we intend to show works of a high standard, studies which were the origin of some of Picasso's masterpieces, more particularly those of the watershed year of 1903. *Nude Crouching*, or more precisely 'with legs crossed', is the origin of a long series.

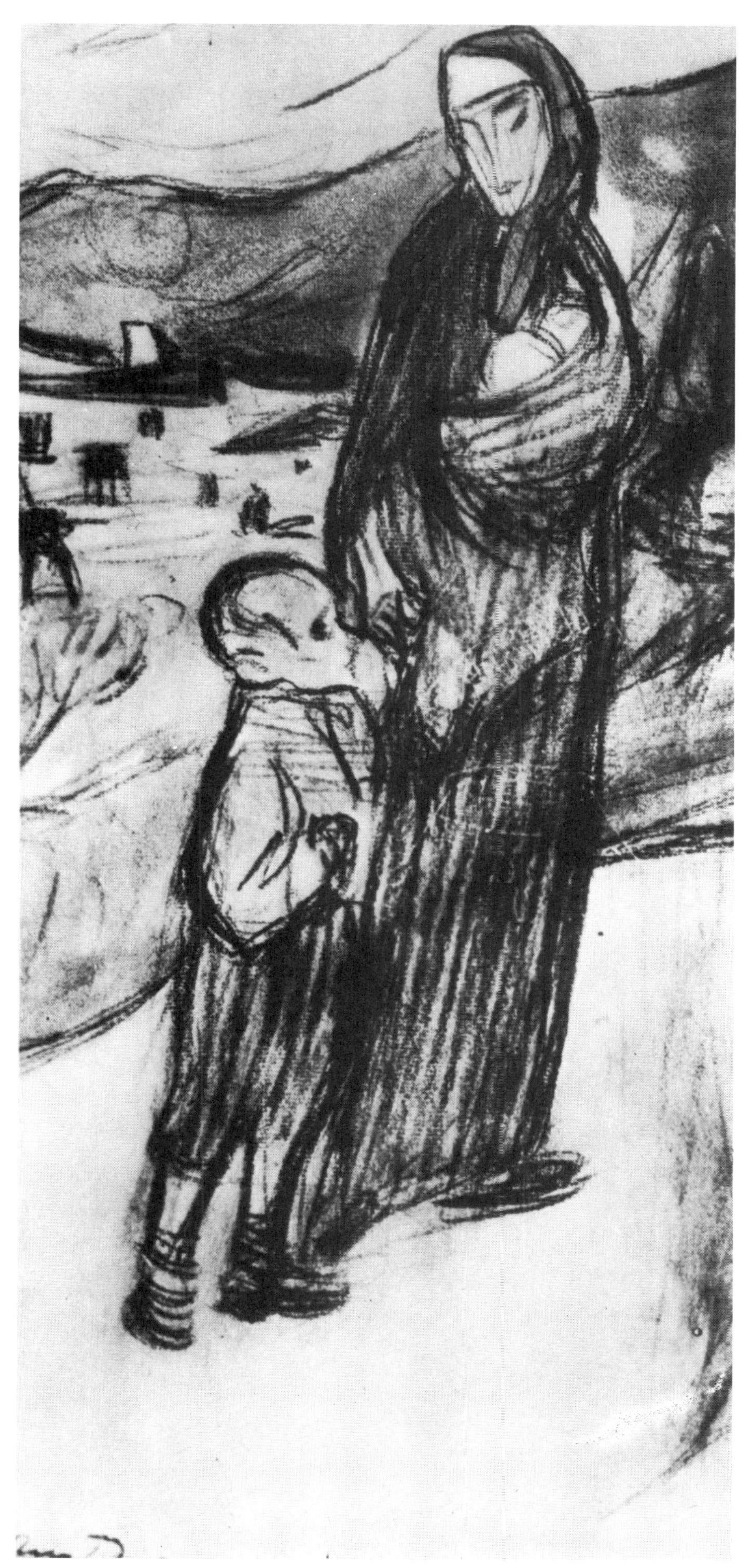

1
MOTHER AND SMALL BOY
charcoal coloured in oil
48×25.5
Barcelona 1903
private collection, New York

The *Woman and Child by the Sea* is evidence of the enormous progress Picasso made in just a few years. Finally, three *Women* from 1904, 'with helmet of hair', 'with a crow' and 'mother and child', are remarkable in that they are neither Blue nor Rose but transient, and show the painter's fascination for a certain type of woman, a slender woman with a fine head of hair (a woman, it is worth mentioning, noticeably different from Fernande Olivier who burst into his life at about this time). These drawings are part of a 'Parisian' phase. They have none of the sinister light of the Blue period; they precede, and herald, the moody and equally famished-looking lighting of the Rose period.

2
NUDE WITH LEGS CROSSED
pastel 60×46
Barcelona 1903

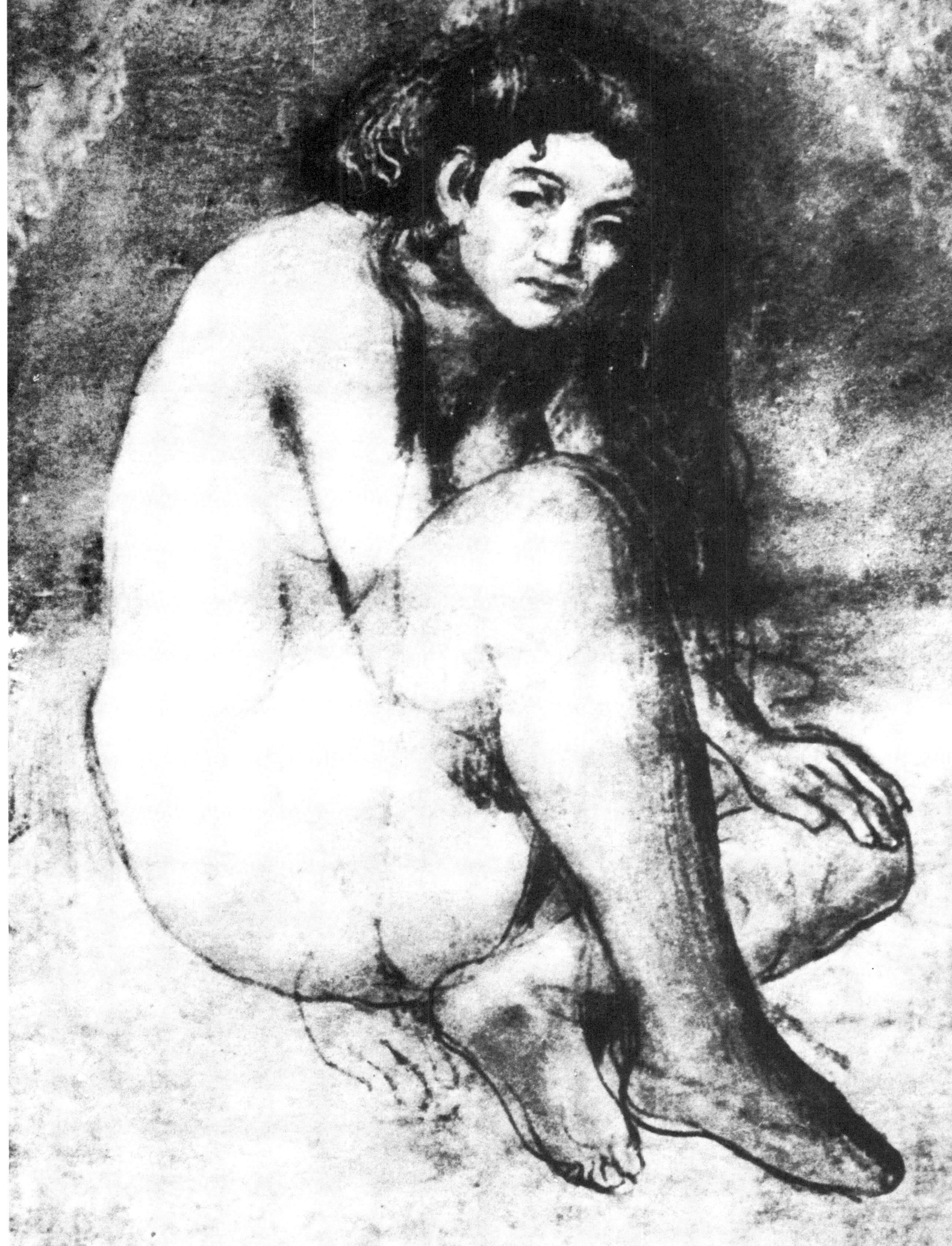

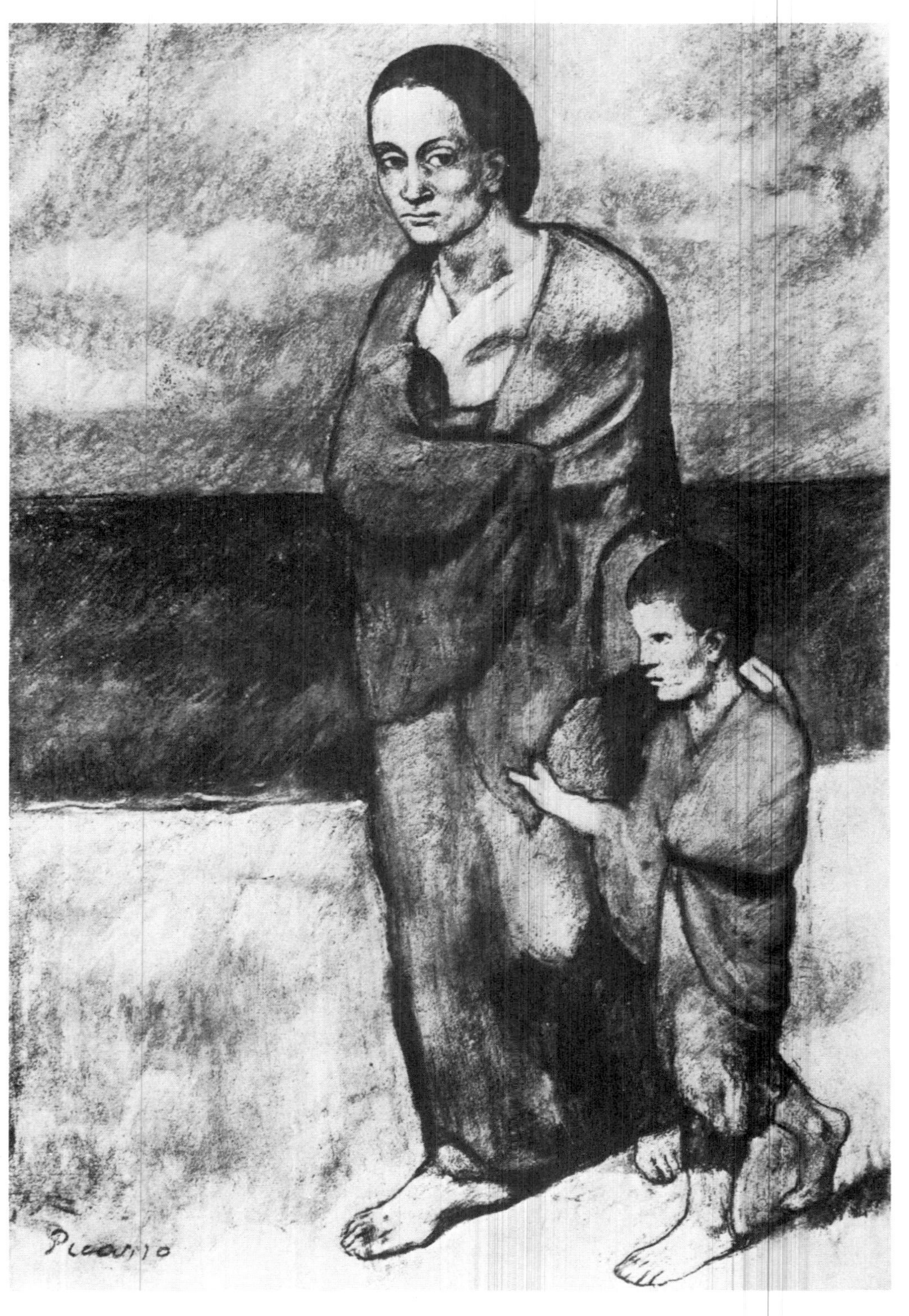

3
WOMAN AND CHILD BY THE SEA
pastel, 1903
private collection, Paris

4
WOMAN WITH A CROW
charcoal, pastel and watercolour
Paris 1904
The Toledo Museum of Art, Toledo, Ohio

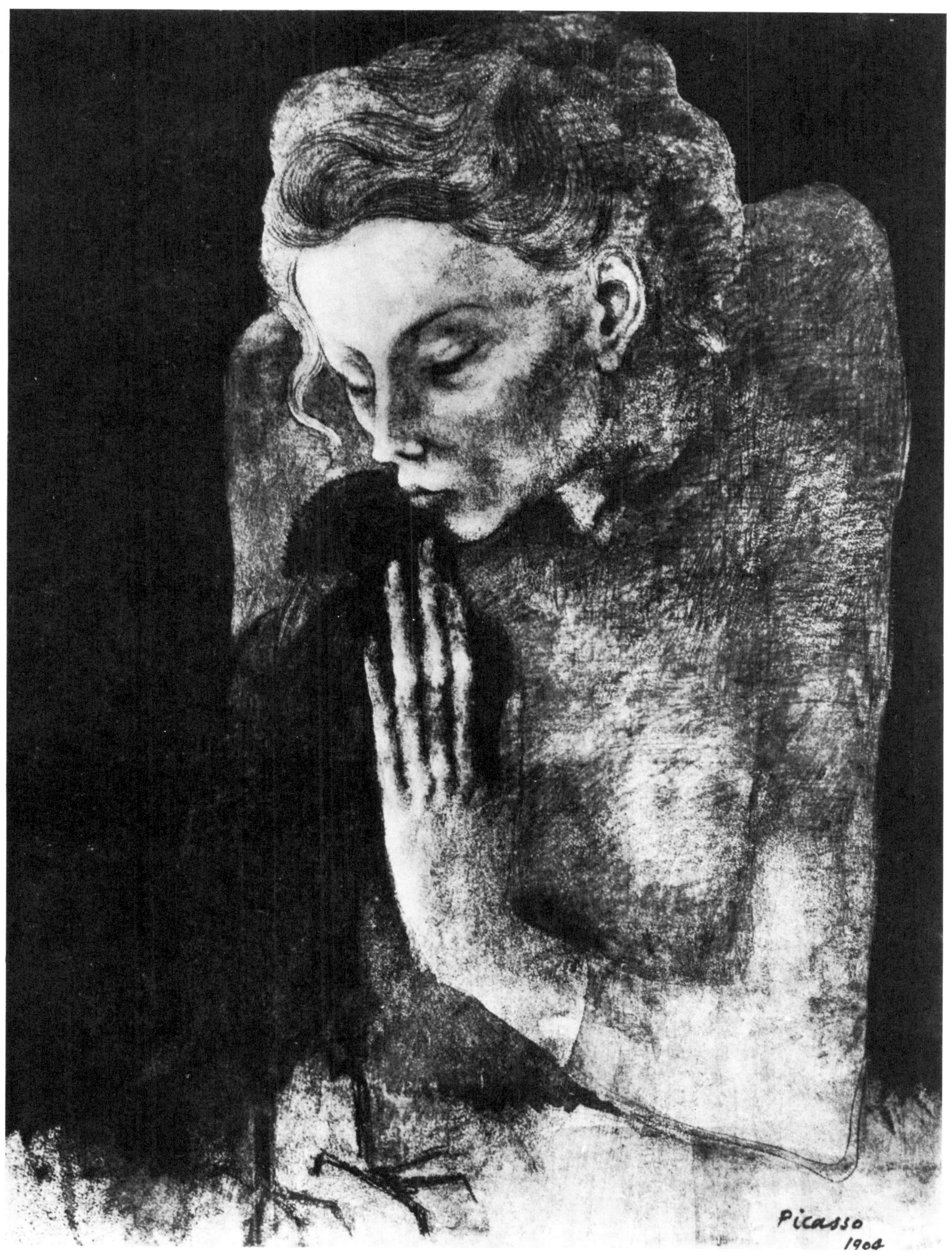
Picasso
1904

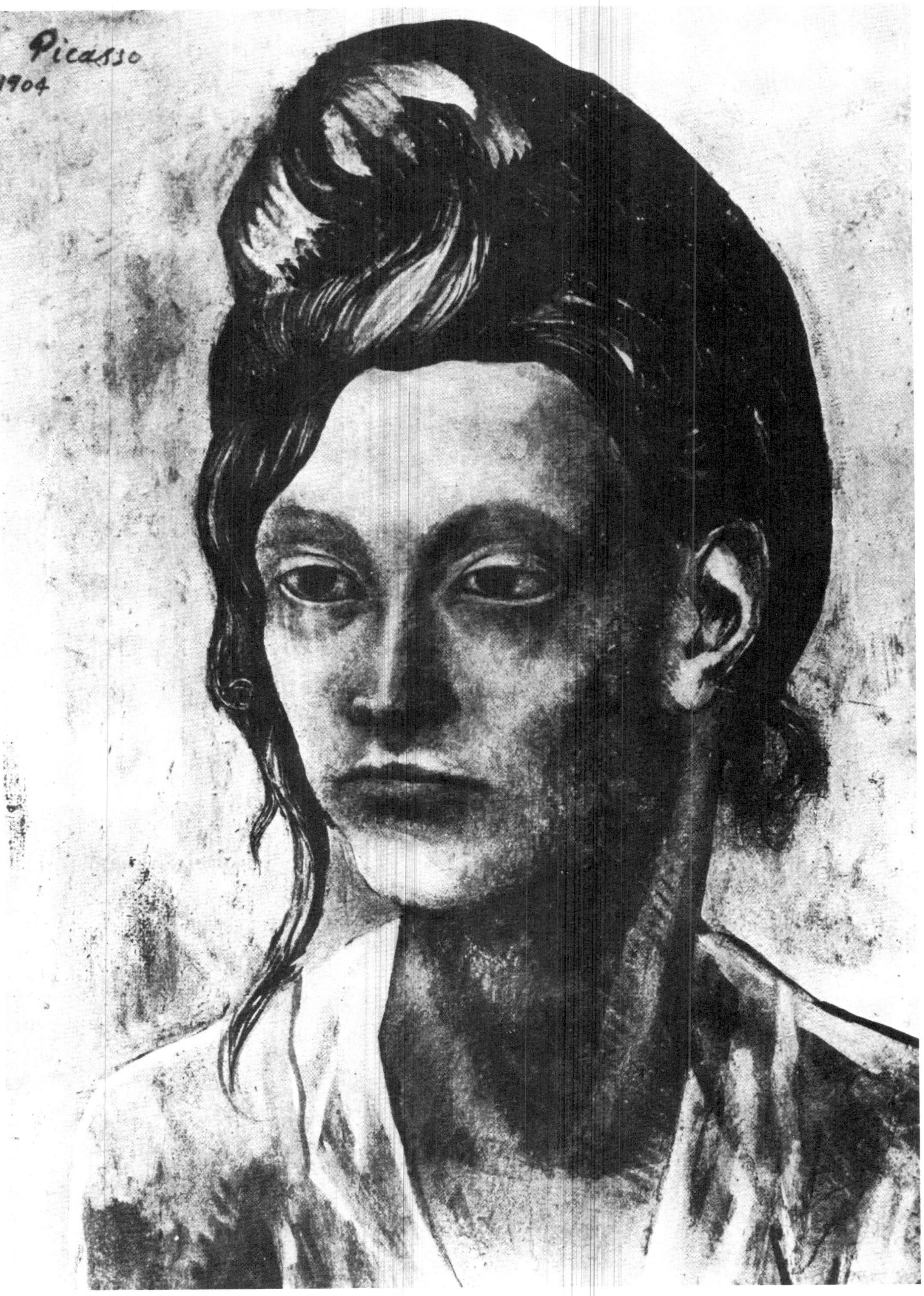
Picasso
1904

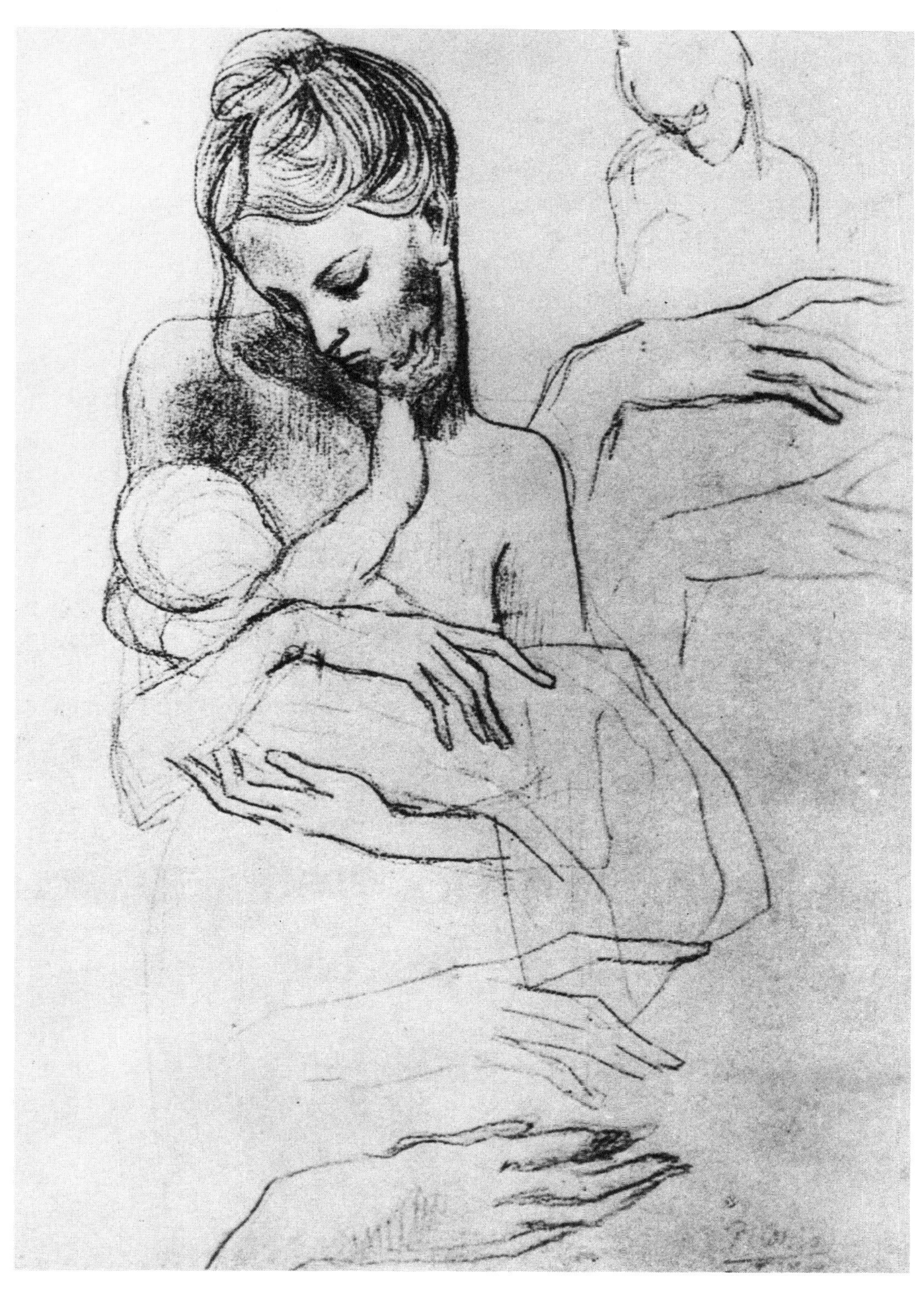

6
MOTHER AND CHILD (studies)
black crayon 36×26
Paris 1904
The Fogg Art Museum, Cambridge

5
WOMAN WITH HELMET OF HAIR
gouache 42×30
Paris 1904
Art Institute, Chicago

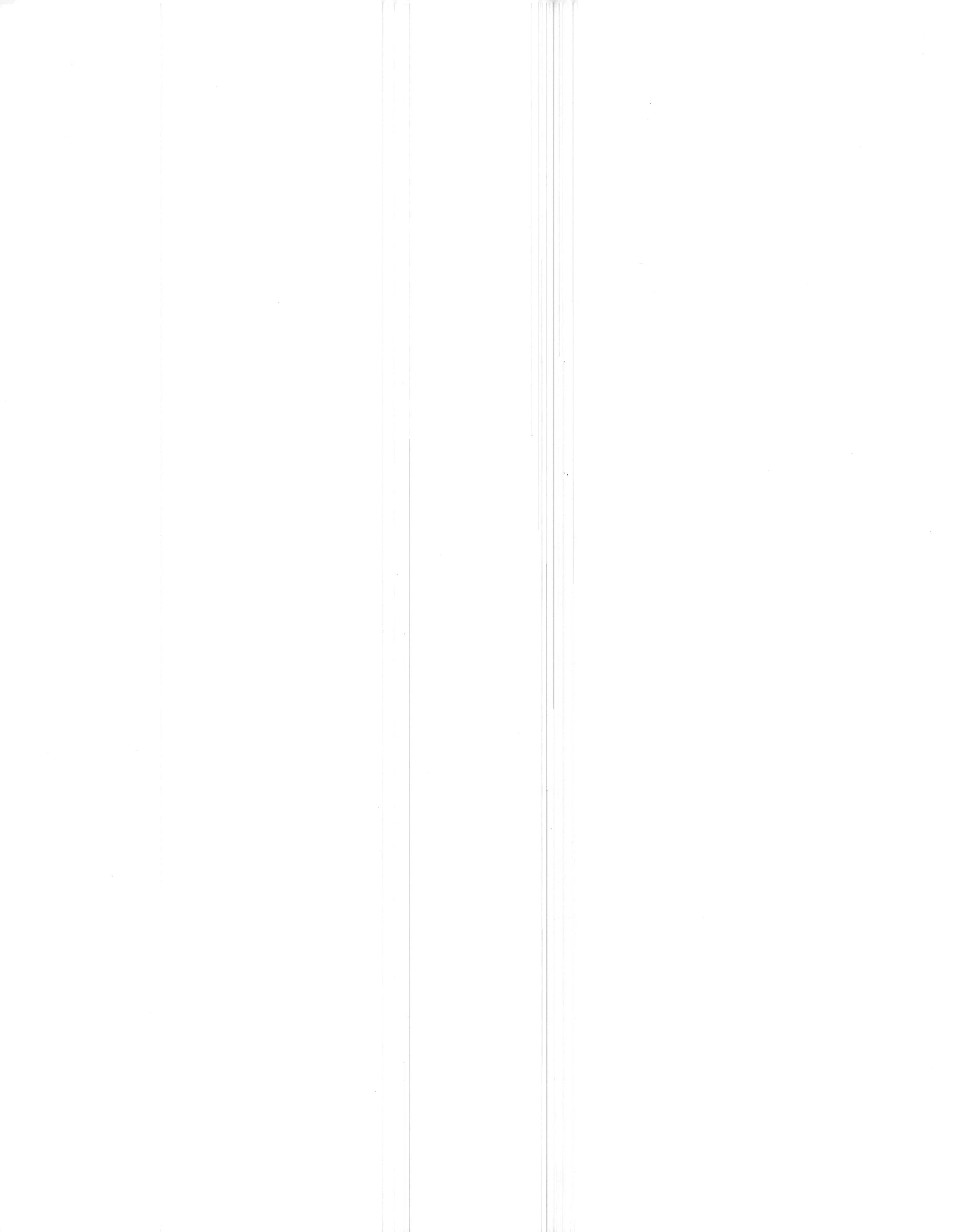

IV

CUBIST DRAWING

The drawings of the Cubist period differ fundamentally from traditional drawings and from those of Picasso's preceding period, just as the Cubist paintings differ from those of the Red period. But, brutal though they may be, revolutions, whether aesthetic or social, are not born overnight and one can foresee them in many precursory signs. The same is true of Picasso and Cubism.

The drawings reproduced here are important not only for their quality, but because they serve to illustrate the new preoccupations of the artist and his decisive passage to another way of transcribing space and even to another form of art.

What is apparent first of all, and denotes a clear change, is the interest in volume and how to render it. From this point of view, the *Coiffure* of 1905 is visibly an extended study for a sculpture, worked in relief with a fine, sharp lead, with hatching, which suggests the work of a chisel in stone or marble. It belongs to a sequence which leads to the *Standing Figures* of 1906 and to the *Demoiselles d'Avignon*.

There was an early glimpse of that desire for monumentality which sprang from his study and love of primitive Catalan sculpture, examples of which can be seen at the Catalan Museum in Barcelona. Already the extreme simplification of shapes and exaggerations of contour tend to create a sense of volume. The rigour of the positioning and the rigidity of the limbs accentuate the verticality of the composition. But relief and volume are still conveyed in textbook fashion, with hatching. To join the *Demoiselles d'Avignon*, these figures have to divest themselves of everything that still binds them to an academic past.

The lesson of Cézanne is there, as Picasso began to cut up his figures, if not into geometric shapes, cones, spheres and cylinders according to Cézanne's principle, at least into clearly defined planes that can be read, even at this early stage, as signifying volume. A series of frenzied experiments throughout the spring of 1906 resulted in some masks, the origin of which some experts were to attribute to the influence of African art. They were the subject of a lengthy debate between William Rubin, Director of Paintings at the Museum of Modern Art in New York, which owns enough of his work to constitute a prestigious Picasso museum on its own, and Pierre Daix, the question being whether or not Picasso had had any contact with African art when he composed the *Demoiselles d'Avignon*. He had almost certainly seen some examples, at Braque's studio perhaps, but definitely at those of Matisse and Derain. The exhibition 'Primitivism in 20th-Century Art' at the New York Museum of Modern Art in 1984 defined the influence of the arts of Africa and Oceania.

His visit to the old Trocadero Museum was far more decisive, and he recalled it in the souvenirs that he confided to Dor de la Souchère, curator of the museum at Antibes, since renamed the Picasso Museum. It was a revelation and 'there he found his defenders'.

It is worth taking time to try to understand Picasso's thinking. When he spoke of 'defenders', he did not mean that he had found new ideas, but that he had found what one might call referees, that is to say respectable and respected artists who had, long before him, worked along the same lines, used similar methods. Thus the methods that Picasso employed were not only viable, but worthy of esteem, whether they were effective or not. It also justified his approach among artist friends and more hesitant admirers. Wouldn't it also have served to give him confidence?

Be that as it may, the *Demoiselles* is a hybrid work and some critics have even described it as unfinished. Indeed, at the last moment the painter gave two of the five figures faces with planes as sharp as blades – they are the shape of blades as well. The cutting-up work can be

7
LA COIFFURE
drawing
Paris 1905

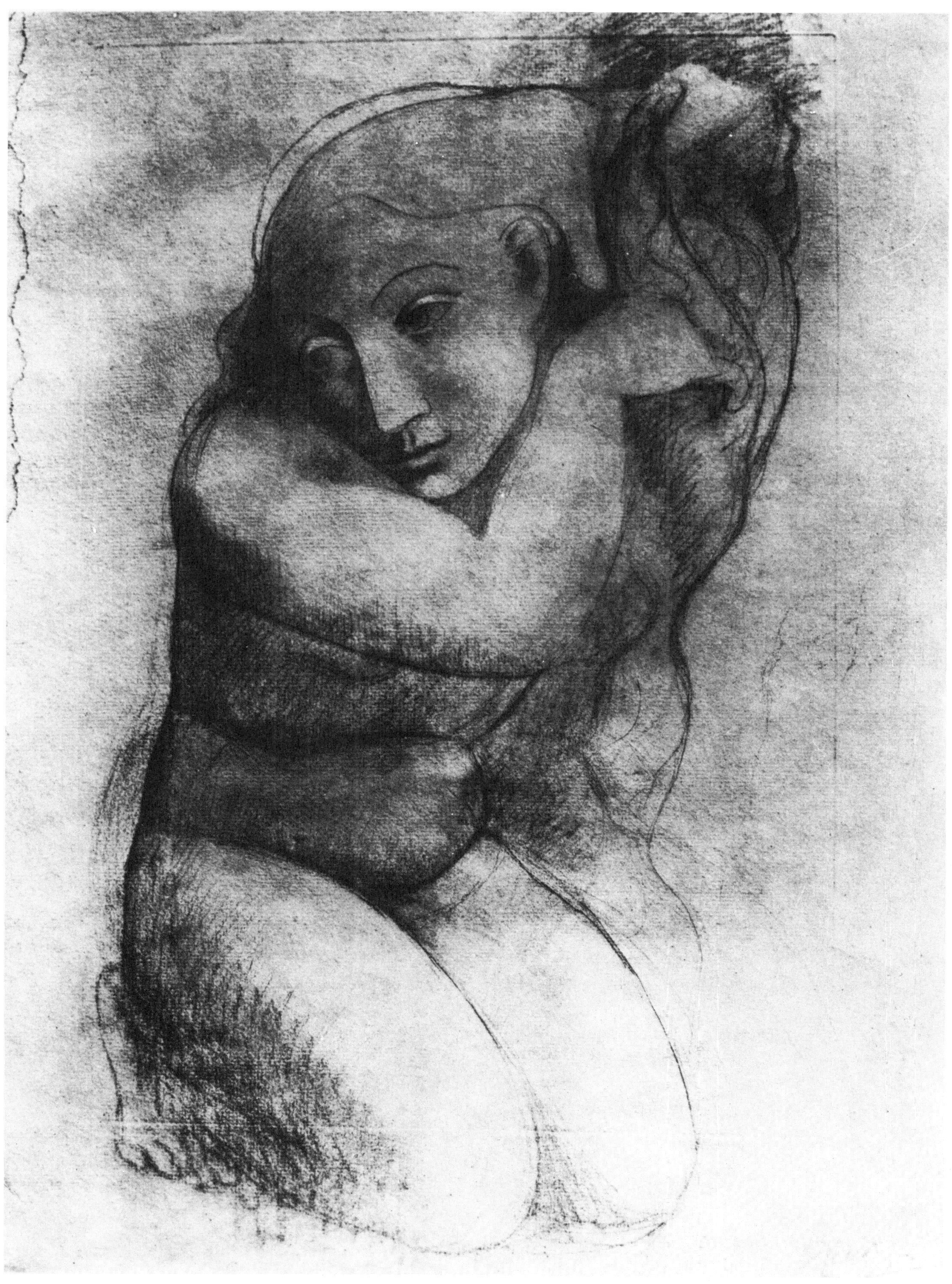

clearly seen in the studies reproduced here. The shapes become more elongated, the lines fit into the surface of the sheet and the hatching no longer purports, as in classical drawing, to suggest volume, but to signify the passage from one plane to another. In the painting, Picasso 'over-signified' the cutting up with brightly coloured streaks reminiscent of the tribal scars on the faces of some African tribesmen or simply of the ribbing on certain masks which is, in fact, no more than the trace of the sculptor's tool.

However great one's admiration for the painting, the critic and historian cannot resist the temptation to examine the sketches closely. What one finds is that there is no trace in these 1907 drawings of the 'virtuosity' that the journalists had so fulsomely praised in previous exhibitions. On the contrary, what strikes one is the reworking of the doubled, tripled, multiplied, over-laden strokes to satisfy his own exacting demands, to reduce volume to a juxtaposition of tight shapes, of taut lines, until it would have been impossible to have a single one without destroying the balance of the whole.

This obsessive quest for perfection knew no pause until Picasso had attained it and, after the paroxysm of 1907–1914, was to continue into 1921, the year of the *Harlequins*, one of his last strictly Cubist canvases. To be able to 'read', to understand and appreciate the finest examples of pure Cubist drawing, it is useful to remind oneself of the main structural principles of this aesthetic movement. It is, of course, easy to simplify Cubism as the painting of Picasso and Braque between 1909 and 1914. But that does not tell us a great deal without direct access to the works themselves. On a more theoretical level, Cubism is defined by a certain number of features which are unique to it: collage, the use of characters, and printing characters in particular, control of colour and its use outside the bounds of any realist connotation; finally an attempt to express a fourth dimension, that of time, by means that may vary but all

8
TWO NUDES
Paris 1906

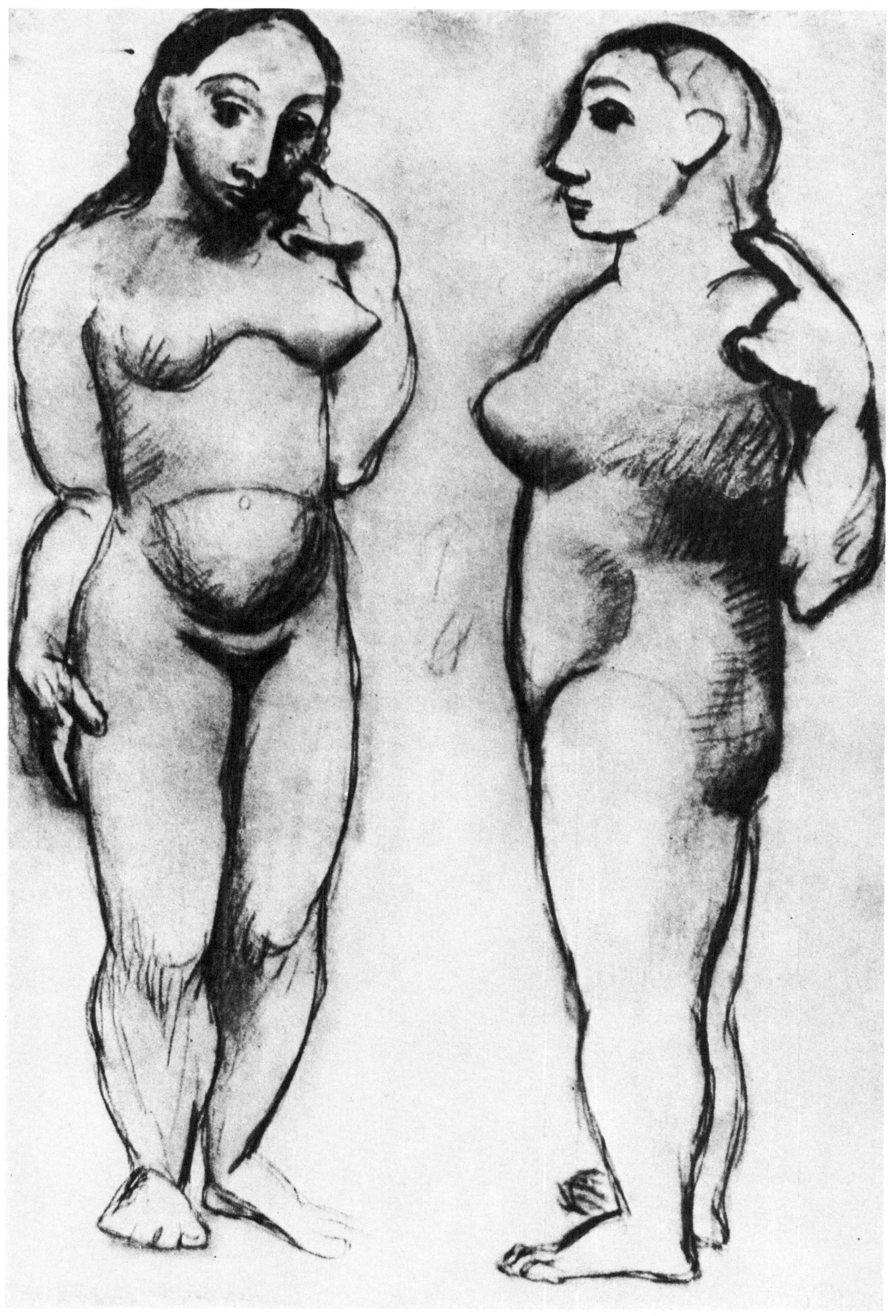

lead in the same direction. It is apparent, in the first place, that the figure fixed on to the canvas or paper results from the superimposition of several images of the same subject, either in time (the subject has moved), or in space, as if it had been captured from different viewpoints and not from a single predetermined angle.

Another technique is the impression of transparency, the use of which allows several visions of the same model to coexist on one and the same surface.

In this case, the effect is comparable to what a photographer sees when focussing his lens: fuzzy-clear-fuzzy, all conveyed on the same palpable surface. The four drawings chosen here belong to the period known as Analytical, the purest form of Cubism. The Cubism of Cézanne, which preceded it, was still tainted with a kind of Impressionism, with trees rising up as rigidly as the columns of a Gothic cathedral. It was a beginning. Analytical Cubism which followed did away with excess rigidity to knit forms together, to entwine them in an elegant and expressive arabesque, for all the formal rigour that was still adhered to. The last phase of Cubism, while preserving the strictness in drawing, differed fundamentally in painting, with a return to often bright and cheerful colour, speckled and stippled, in Impressionist fashion, yet somehow rendering the density of space concrete.

The Cubist drawings, the *papiers collés*, by both Picasso and Braque, are compelling in their grandeur, their monumentality, their haunting silence. The formal repertory is reduced to a minimum: rectilinear lines and very few curves, most so regular that they could have been drawn with a compass. And then, from time to time, an almost provocative realistic detail, a smoking pipe, an eye, a packet of tobacco.

The 1910 *Nude Woman* in its purity and elegance could almost have been conceived to illustrate a study of Picasso's method during this first stage of Analytical Cubism. The body volumes are analysed and cut up

9
WOMAN SITTING AND WOMAN STANDING
drawing 61 × 46.4
Paris 1906

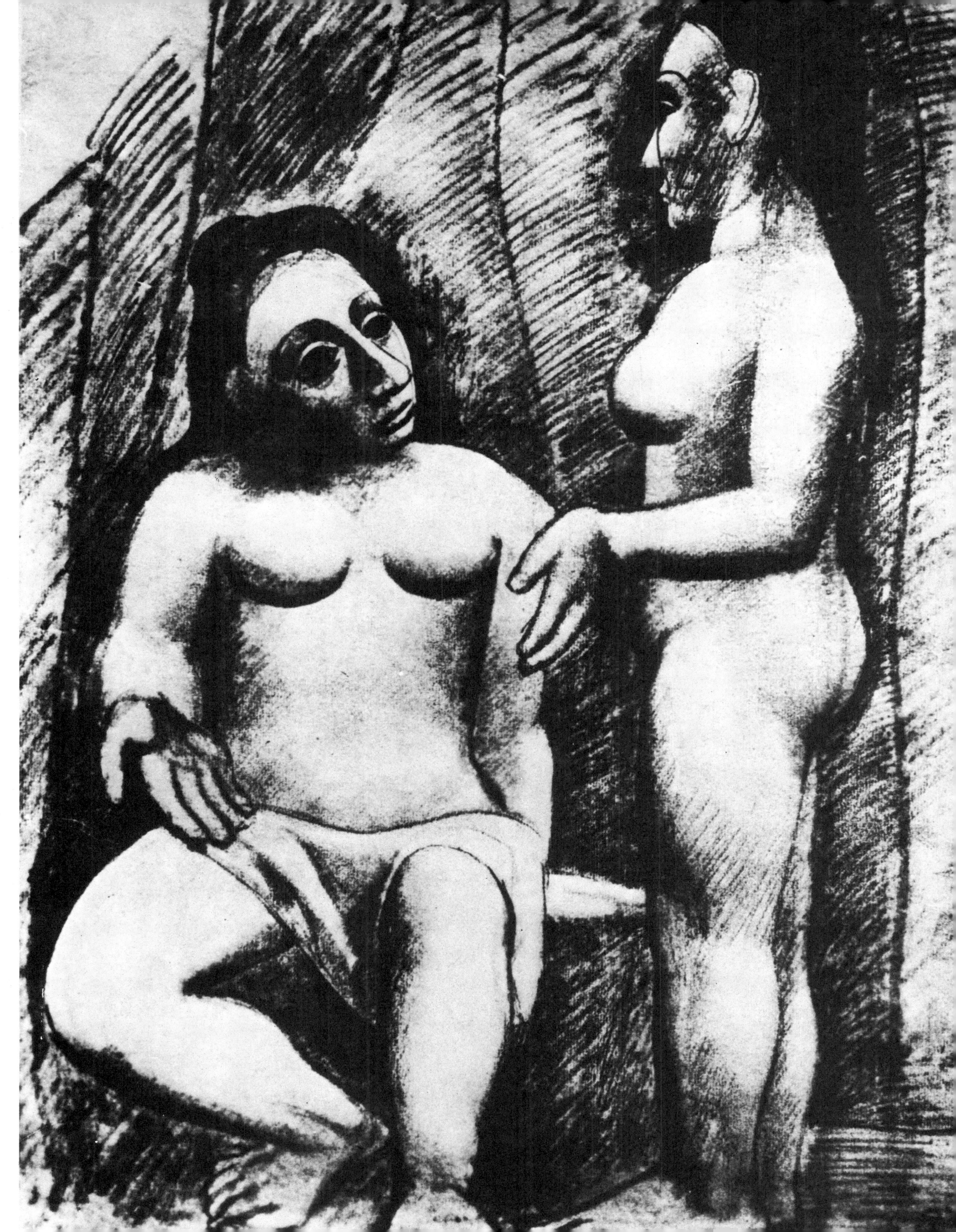

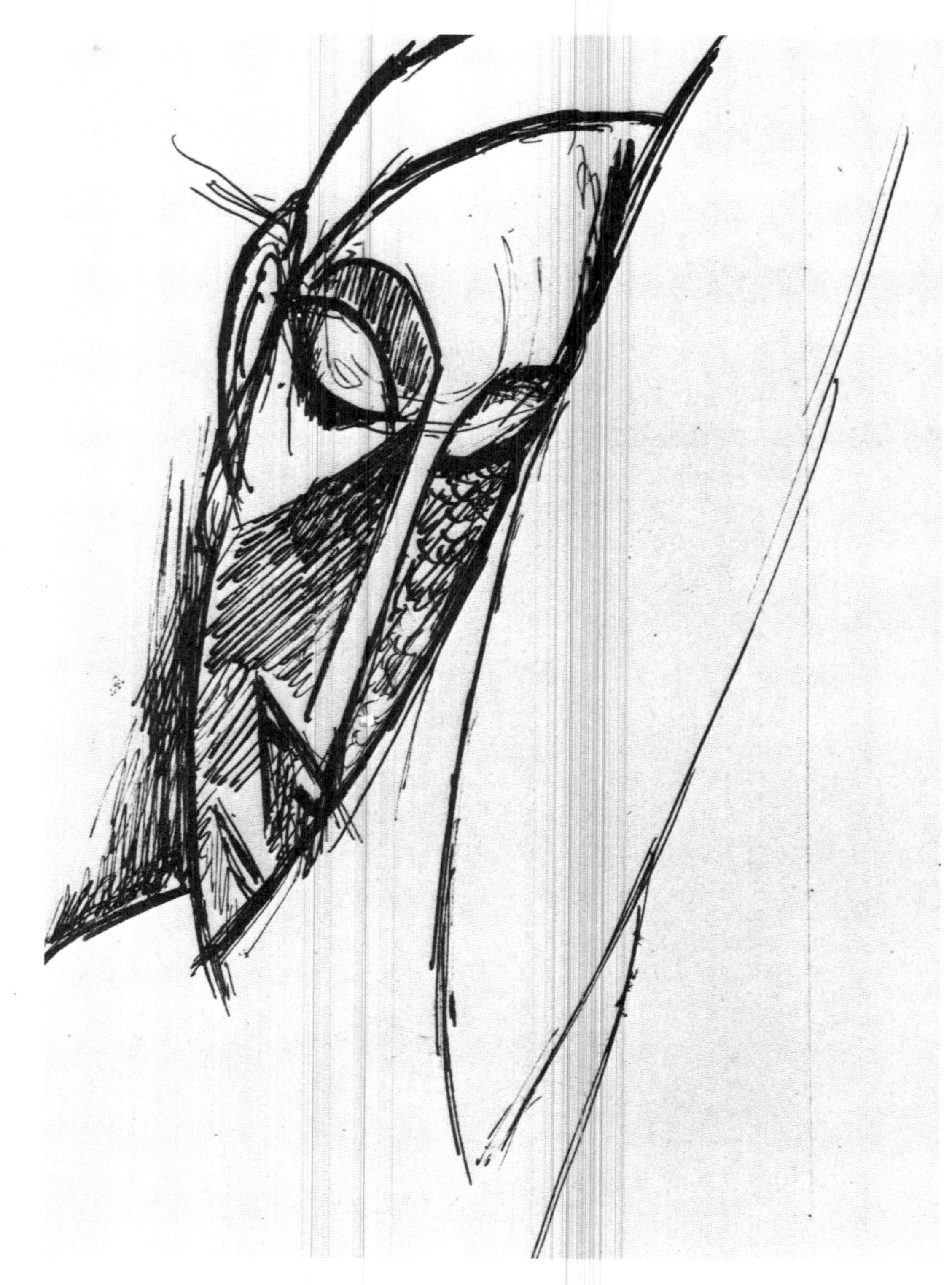

10
STUDY
drawing 22.5×17.5
Paris 1907

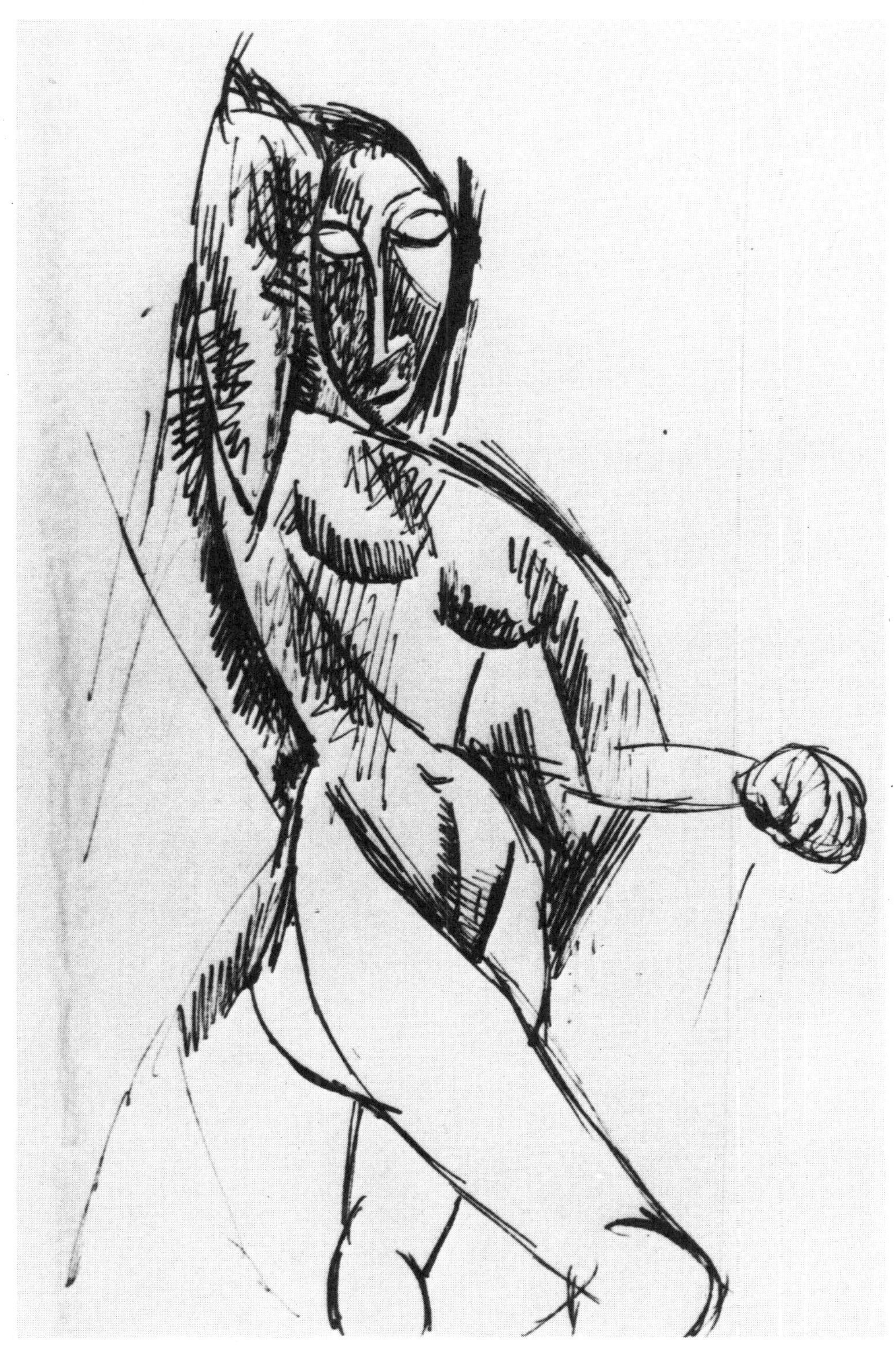

11
STUDY FOR NUDE WITH DRAPERY
(Moscow linen) 22.5×17
1907

into geometric planes. From the base to the top where three curves suffice to allow us to imagine a head, perhaps even a face, breasts, thighs, there is a strict sequence of straight lines and arcs. The former denote volumes, the latter the axes of movement, the joints at the approximate level of knees, hips and shoulders. Everything is in its proper place, everything suggests a rather ghostly human figure, a being reduced to a graphic symphony. The generous, rather greasy, texture of the fusain (a form of charcoal crayon) attenuates the severity of the drawing and gives it a human density.

Can one see it as a stele, a caryatid or a syncopated rhythm measuring out space? Should one see it as proof of a theory devised by Cézanne who was never able to confirm it himself? It probably required a few more years (Cézanne died in 1906) and another generation for his prophecy, ambition and fantasy to become reality.

A drawing such as this is the logical outcome of the portraits of Fernande in 1909. The wide, generous, rather fleshy face is broken up into minuscule facets, exploded into rectilinear planes and curves. The painter, in his obsession to verify that his vision, even his reasoning, were exact, had become a sculptor, kneading the clay, powdering it, structuring it with his palette. And proof was at hand: the system worked! The traditional model could be replaced. Picasso could substitute for it a collection of lines to signify planes. Bronze was endowed with dramatic dignity and grandeur which reflected the shadowy character of the figure.

The 1912 *Head of a Man* results from the same system but accentuates its rigour and above all its frontality. It creates relief by multiplying the planes. The face is not only situated on the plane of the paper, but cut up at different levels suggested by the rectangles formed by two or three lines at right angles. Thus the face is almost exclusively composed of rigid lines. Even the curves are geometric, and volume, or rather the

12
STUDY FOR THREE WOMEN
drawing 62×47
Y. Zervos collection

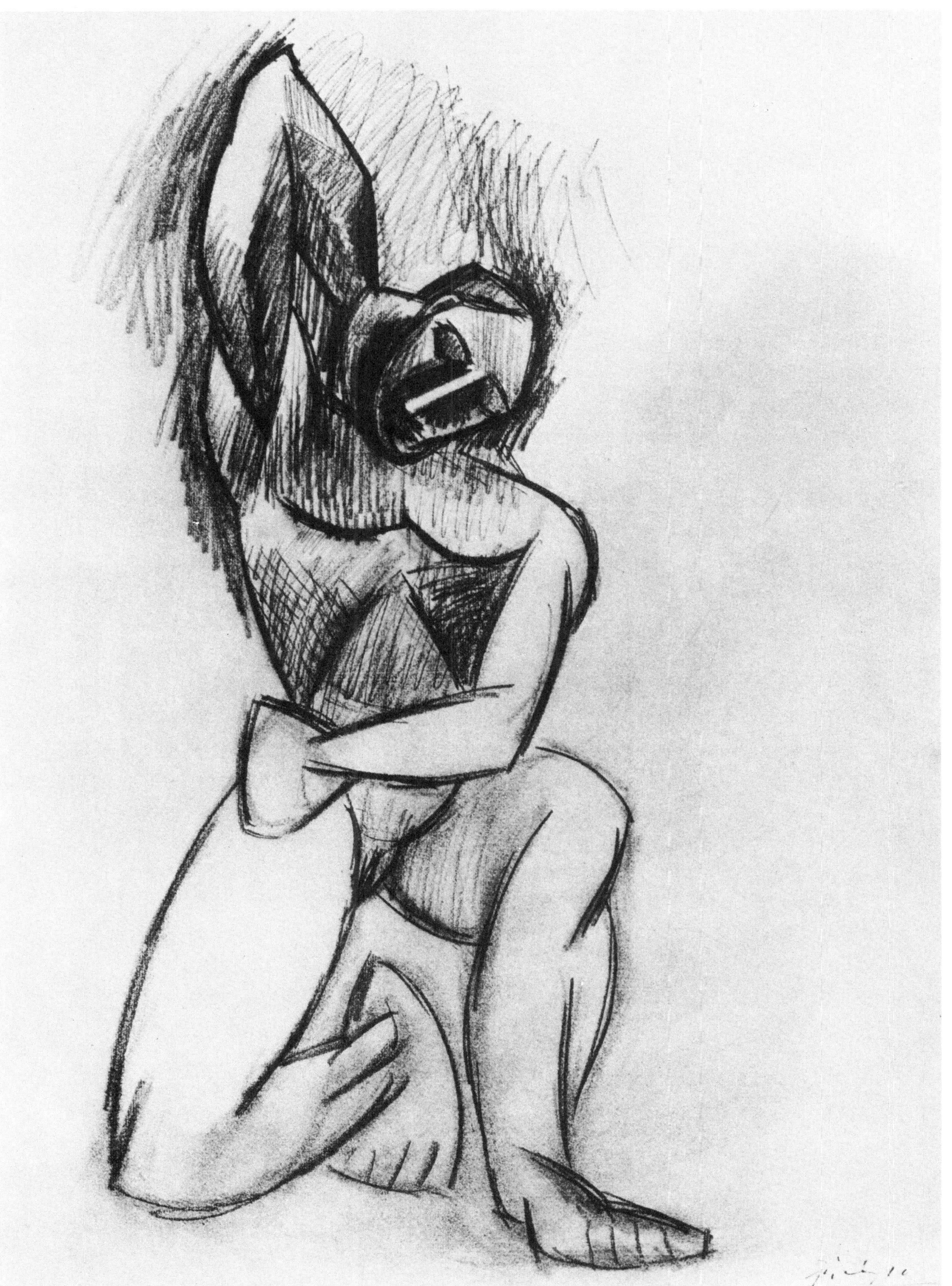

illusion of it, is born of this artifice. The effect has a monumental and somewhat theatrical character. It shows the dominance of the concept over any form of naturalism and *trompe-l'oeil*.

However, all Picasso's Cubist portraits are individualised. Not only do they not resemble one another, they always represent clearly visualised people. There are, of course, the famous portraits of Clovis Sagot, Ambroise Vollard, Wilhelm Udhe or Daniel-Henry Kahnweiler, but there are also all those faces with titles that respect their anonymity but which assert their personalities nonetheless. Be it *The Poet*, the *Man with Pipe* or *with Guitar*, or the *Woman with Fans* they are not just anyone. He saw them and drew them and all of them recognised themselves just as we recognise them without ever having met them.

The verisimilitude of Cubist portraits, the sparest portraits possible not only in Picasso's work but probably in the whole history of art, does not hang on the detail that allows one to identify them and give them a title. No, it is not the moustache, nor the guitar (of which there are dozens) which impart character, but the authentic features of each face, its volume, the width of the jaw, the protuberance of the brow ridges, the length of the nose, the thickness of the lips. As early as 1911, Picasso had his own Cubist vocabulary which allowed him to say, or rather to show, everything he wanted. When one examines the long series of drawings from this period, one is led to realise that the accessories with which Picasso endowed his subjects were not so much symbols as plastic signs of an aesthetic value. Picasso loved the shape of the guitar, which has its own perfection, and the guitar probably evoked for him the music of Spain. It was a subject, a theme, a pretext for painting and drawing. The work of art found its *raison d'être* in its harmony, in what it suggested, in the same way as a Mozart sonata or (closer to home) an Albéniz concerto. Indeed, there is something musical about the beauty of these drawings. Certainly what first meets the eye is their surface, but they are also symphonic and need to be perused. The contemplation of them and the pleasure one derives from it presuppose the idea of time. The eye has to wander, scale the curves, slide down abrupt rectilinear lines, pause on the well-punctuated horizontals to penetrate a universe where all is peace, beauty and perfection.

Contrary to so many other aspects of Picasso's work which spring from passion and immediacy, the Cubist drawings (and paintings) demonstrably required patience and stubborn perseverance. Many were probably destroyed before they were finished. That is what confers their particular intensity on those that have come down to us and assures their value in such an abundant body of work.

When looking at the 1912–13 *papier collé* entitled *Bottle, Cup, Newspaper*, I see not a cup, but a kind of beer glass which seems to be crowned with a thick head of foam, but I could be wrong. Curiously enough, the formal detail which contributes to the balance of the composition can lend itself to commentary and to the attribution of an anecdotal value. Who would presume to disagree? Even during this period of severity, Picasso remained Picasso and no one could begin to guess what was going through his mind, what provocative detail he may have slipped into the most austere of his works.

The appearance of a scrap of newspaper stuck on to the paper, a bit of the headlines of one of the popular dailies of the time, brings us to an original art form which could almost be regarded as personal to Picasso and Braque, although the same technique was employed by others a little later. Certainly, purists could argue that the introduction of a foreign element changes the nature of a drawing to the point where it no longer qualifies as a drawing at all. Certainly, there are painted works in which the role of painting is hidden behind an accumulation of heterogenous material, transforming them into a new art form which can no longer, by any stretch of the imagination, be qualified merely as relief. But, leaving aside controversies of definition, there is a subtler distinction, as made by Aragon, between *papier collé*, which was typically Cubist, and collage, which was specifically Surrealist.

Aragon wrote that 'collage as we understand it today is something entirely different from the *papier collé* of Cubism. But the latter was already posing certain questions that the former is still asking'. And further on in this preface to an exhibition in 1930, Aragon prophetically wrote: 'One can imagine a time when painters who, already, do not bray their own colours any more will consider it infantile and beneath their dignity to apply the paint themselves and will see in this personal touch upon which the merit of their pictures depends today no more than the documentary interest of a manuscript or an autograph.

' . . . Collage is a foretaste of that time.'

If Aragon's hypothesis has proved true, if some of today's artists have renounced traditional techniques, others remained faithful to the old craftsmanship and Picasso, to his last breath, gave it the lie. Picasso never gave up his brushes, even when he used acrylic or vinyl instead of oil paints, and he always drew with a lead or Conté pencil.

The introduction of a piece of newspaper, a packet of tobacco, was something quite different.

The first example came when Picasso stuck a piece of linoleum on to a painting, *Still Life with Chair Caning*. The scrap of something real torn from the world gives a new reality to the canvas. It seems to act as a reference and suddenly the painting, which appeared to imitate the visible world, was admitting its deceit, confessing that it was nothing but illusion, simulation. The artifice is all the more powerful for its admission.

Having said that, there are two distinct categories of *papiers collés*, depending on their purpose. In the first kind, the 'real' material is used for itself, for its plastic value or its suggestive power. Its presence

13
NUDE WOMAN
charcoal 48.5×31.5
spring 1910
private collection, New York

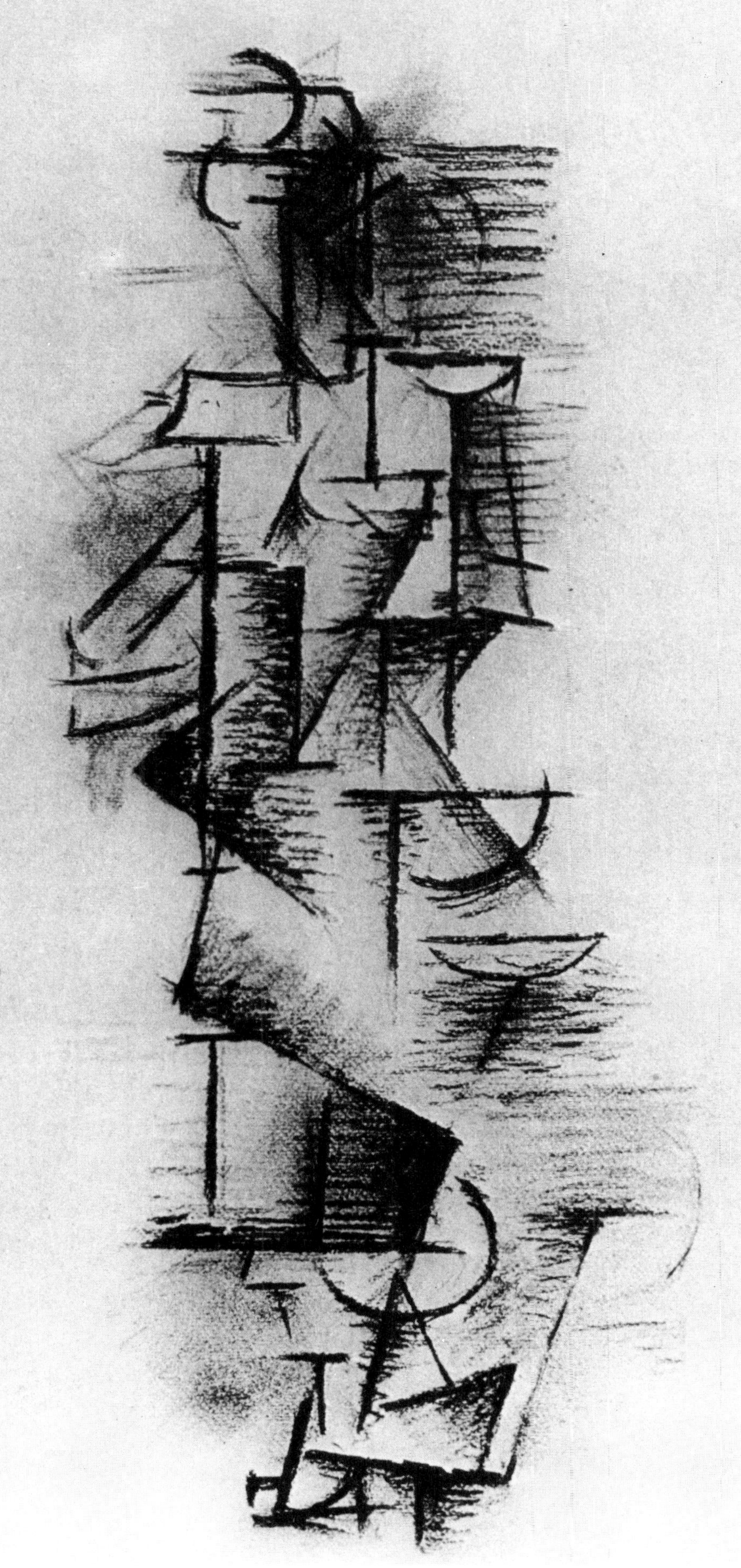

aesthetically conditions the work. This aspect of Cubism brings it close to future aspects of Surrealism. In the second kind, the *papier collé*, be it newspaper or a scrap of wallpaper (often employed by Braque), has no independent existence. It is like any other pictorial material, like a touch of paint or an area blackened with charcoal or coloured with wash. The effect is all that matters and the unusual technique can almost be ignored.

Aragon was saying the same thing in 1930: 'Two quite distinct categories of work came out of these first collages, one in which the pasted-on element was added for its form, or more precisely for its representation of the object, the other in which it was there for its substance.'

Georges Braque's *papiers collés* were the subject of two exhibitions in 1982, one at the Centre Georges Pompidou, the other at the Galerie Maeght, both in Paris, and of a remarkable book by Jean Laude. Those of Picasso, which are related to them albeit, Braque and Picasso being so different, with their own specific character, merit scientific study that would be the subject of a book as long as this one, whatever their general importance in the catalogue of Cubist works.

Certain historians in the world of art pay enormous attention to dates, which is natural, and to problems of antecedence, which are not always as important as one might believe. From a historical perspective, quality always triumphs over petty squabbles about antecedents. One such squabble arose immediately after the Second World War when the chronology of the first appearances of abstraction in painting was the subject of heated debate. Honourable and honoured widows haggled over a year, even over a few months. It was said that some of them went so far as to predate pictures! What did Kandinsky, Otto Freundlich, the wonderful Klee have to do with these Byzantine quarrels? As Aragon wrote in 1930, 'I do not know whether it was

14
HEAD OF A MAN
Conté pencil drawing 62.5×47
Paris 1912
private collection

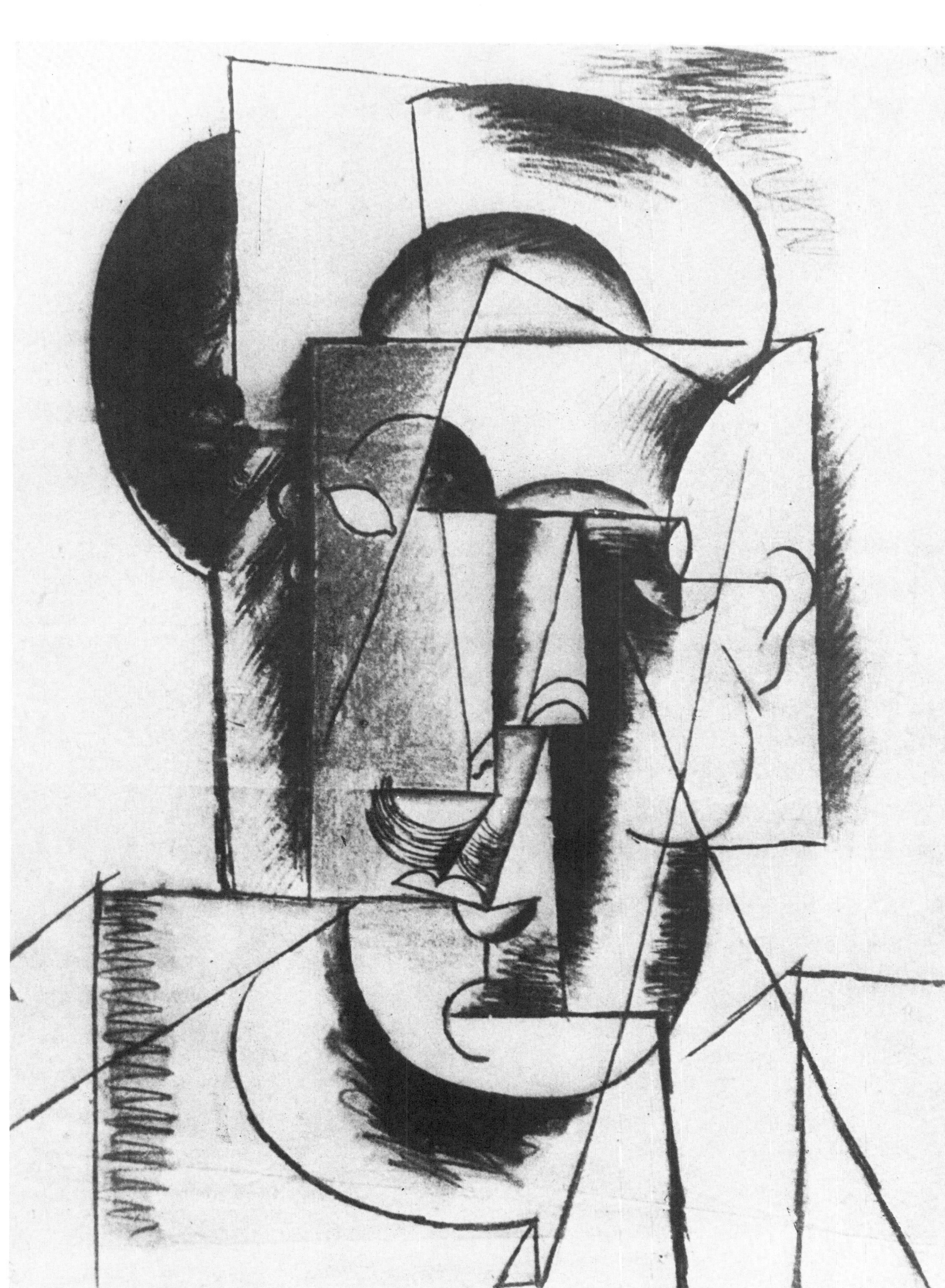

Braque or Picasso who was the first to use, as if in desperation, a ready-made wallpaper, newspaper or stamp, to complete or to begin a picture which must have made art lovers jump, or even if it was really in desperation. It would probably be useless to ask these two contemporaries about a priority which is less important than the spirit in which they originally had recourse to glue and to borrowed reality. Would they even remember it?'

Today, alas, neither of these two giants of modern art is here to answer the question, but, as Aragon said, their replies should now be devoid of interest.

In this art which is all allusion and suggestion the purity of the drawing triumphs over all other requirements and its power is manifest. Above all others in the early years of this century, Picasso and Braque succeeded in discovering what a line could suggest and in showing it.

Let us look once more at the *Man with Pipe*. It is a symphony of successive curves and straight lines. They scale the space suggested by the paper to culminate in the form of a jaunty sort of hat (which is to say that it doesn't look like the sort of hat a very serious man would wear). It has many elements, including the pipe and an inverted column that comes from the top right-hand corner. Nothing, according to traditional realism, is in its place and yet everything is, plus an aesthetic joy close to that which music brings. Is this not the synthesis of Cubism?

15
BOTTLE, CUP, NEWSPAPER
papier collé with drawing
Paris 1912–13

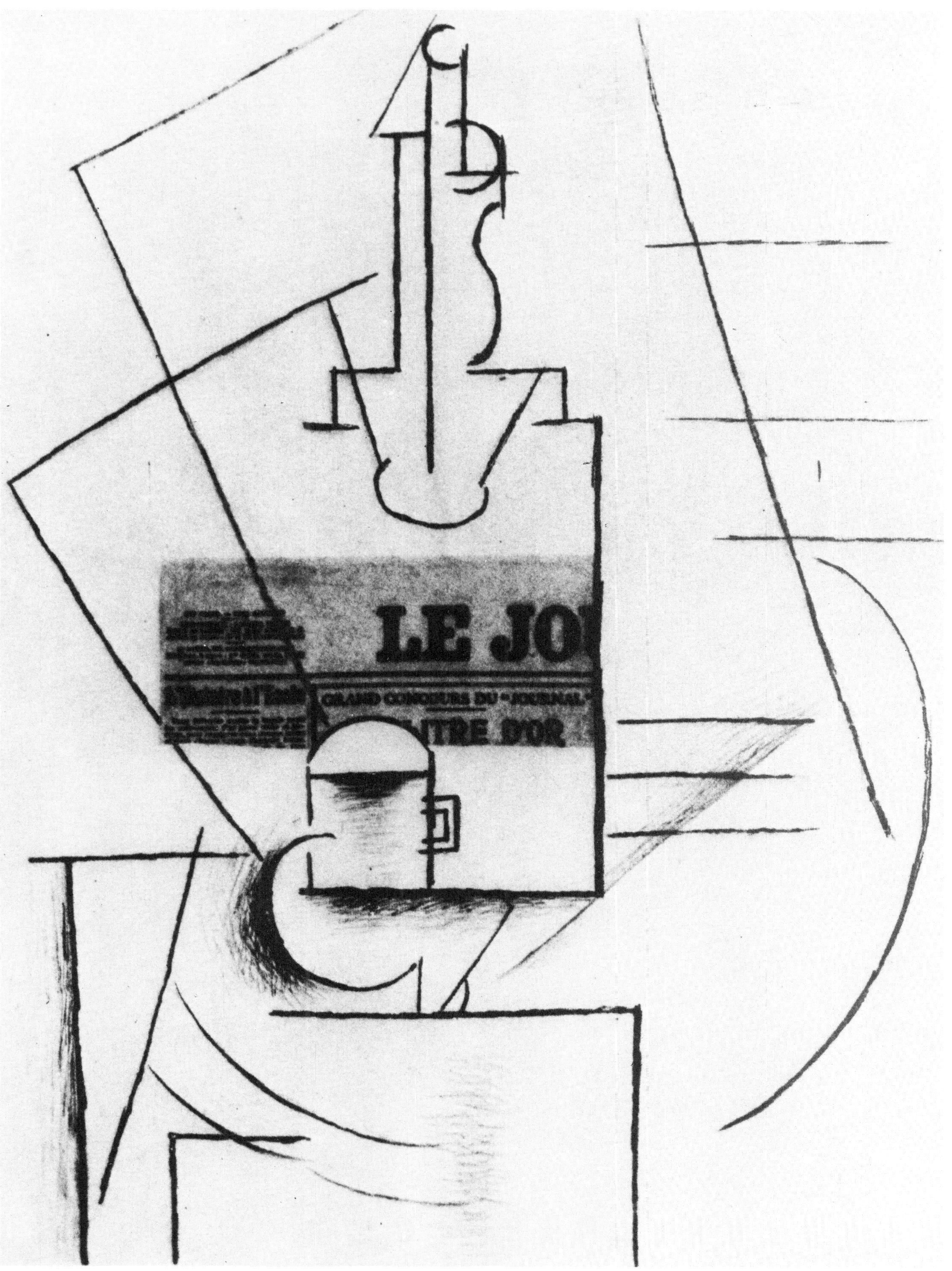
LE JO
GRAND CONCOURS DU "JOURNAL"
TRE D'OR

16
MAN WITH PIPE LEANING ON A TABLE
drawing 32×24
Paris 1914

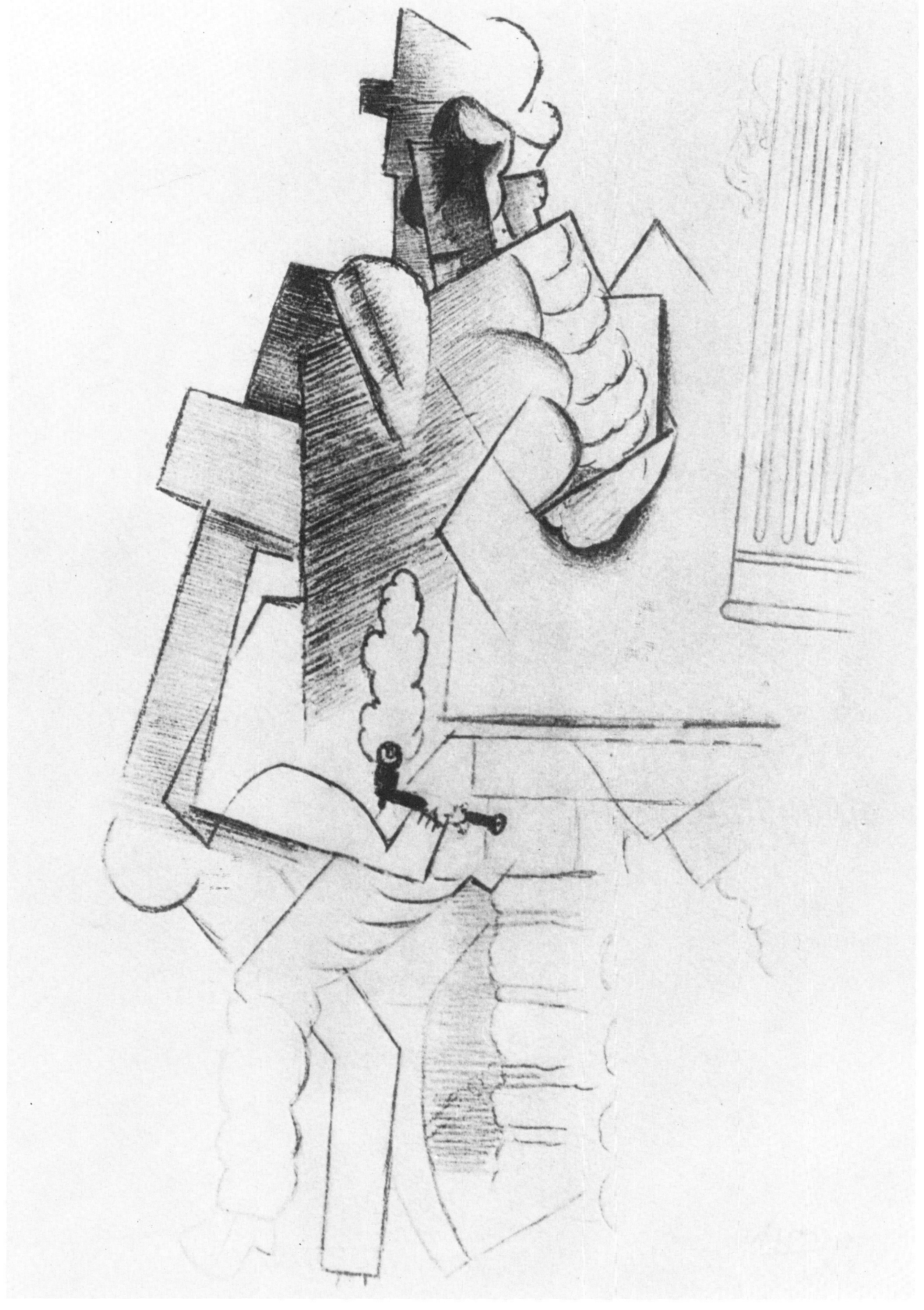

V
THE TWENTIES AND THIRTIES

To speak of 'the Thirties' as a period in relation to the art of Picasso means absolutely nothing whatsoever. It must be recognised that for Picasso, that 'protean' and 'many-sided' artist – to use just two of the standard clichés about him – the period that followed the First World War marked several important turning points in his work and in his life. This explains why there is no unity, either of style or of themes generally, in the period between 1920 and 1936.

There are works inspired by love, there are works inspired by the theatre, there are many family portraits and portraits of friends, there are corridas, bulls and Minotaurs, there are the dream fantasies admired by André Breton and the Surrealist poets and, at the end of this period, there is the horror and indignation provoked by the civil war that was to ravage his country.

Let us look first at images touched with tenderness, poetry and sensuality. It was almost as though, after the years of Cubist discipline, Picasso needed to refresh himself at the springs of life, love and friendship.

The change of direction probably originated in his meeting with Jean Cocteau. Picasso agreed to participate in the ballet *Parade* as set and costume designer, and in February 1917, having scarcely travelled at all since the Barcelona-Paris shuttles of his early youth, he left for Rome with Cocteau. There he met a dancer of Russian extraction named Olga Kokhlova and one could be forgiven for wondering whether his passion for the Russian ballet might not be explained by his attraction to the woman who was to become his wife the following year.

Leaving aside all biographical or anecdotal considerations, consider *Sleeping Peasants*, a watercolour drawing executed in Paris in 1919. Antiquity and rusticity mingle in equal parts. There is something of

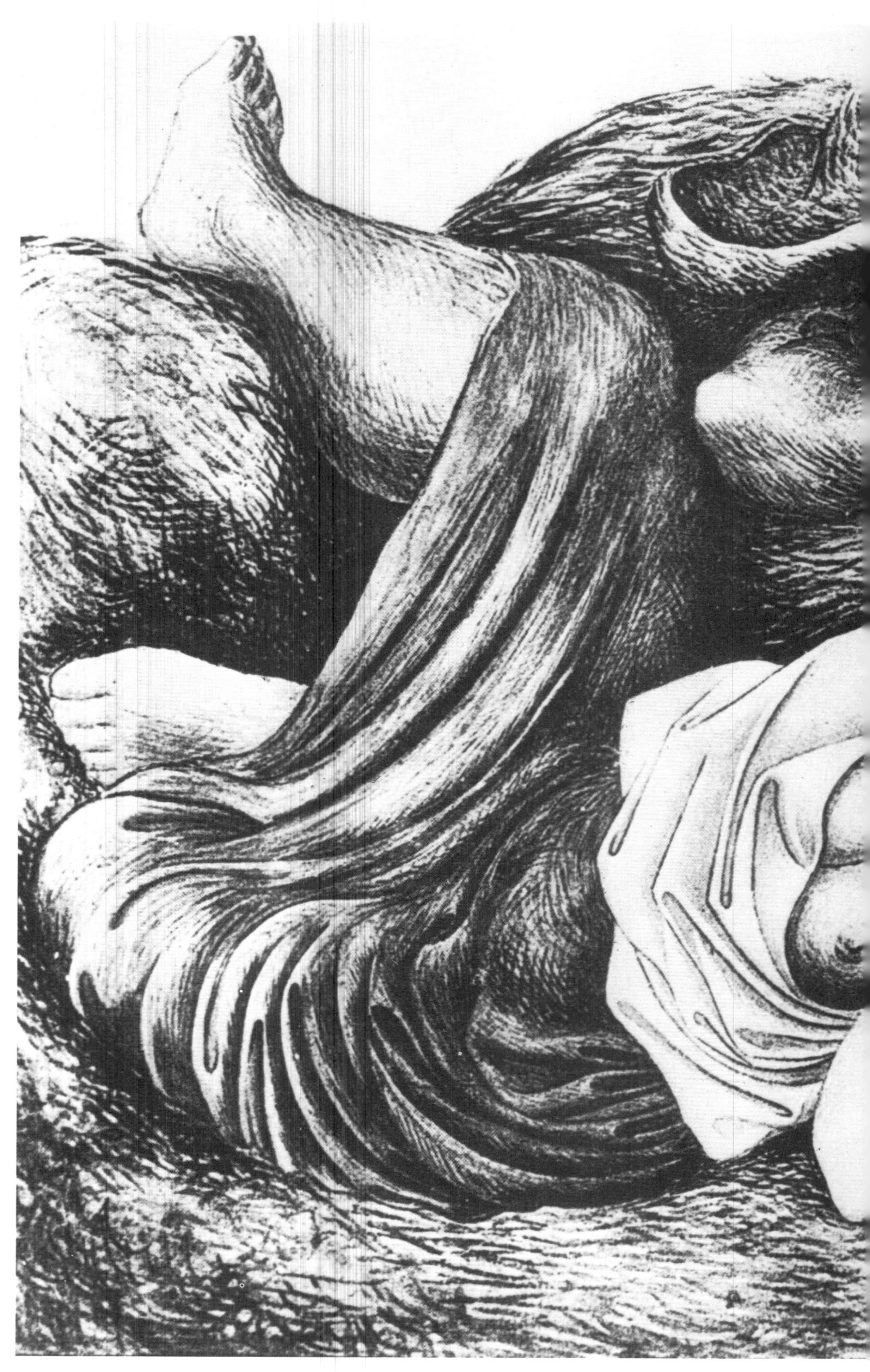

17
SLEEPING PEASANTS
tempera, watercolour and pencil
31×48
Paris 1919

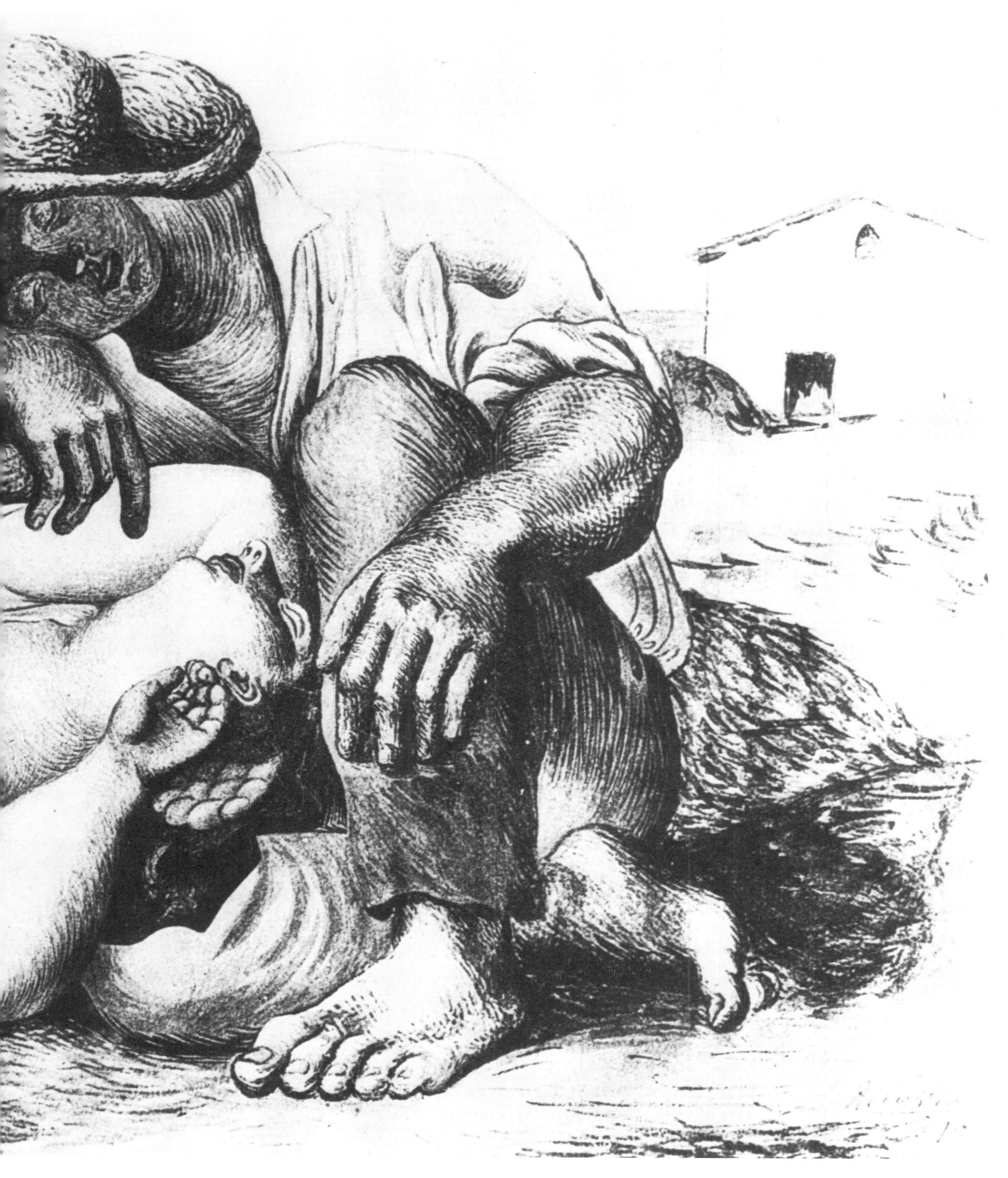

antiquity in the woman's anatomy and in her pose, of rusticity in the young man's misshapen straw hat, and also in his hands and feet, which are too real, too human. The composition is harmoniously balanced, like a ballet figure. The outline of a barn in the distance and the straw in which the bodies seem to roll strengthen the feeling of quietness and sunshine. One is led to think that this might be a remembered scene from Picasso's journey to Naples during the rehearsals for *Parade*.

The first thought that springs to mind in analysing the style for this piece is that Picasso had come a very long way from the rigour of his Cubist compositions. Had he renounced his past? Should this be seen as a kind of 'return to order', such as Giorgio de Chirico was to make?

No one should believe any such thing, nor should he see here the influence of Jean Cocteau and his entourage, which several commentators have rather hastily proclaimed. The proof of this lies in the catalogue of Picasso's work produced by Christian Zervos, which shows that Picasso, in that same year (1919), painted several Cubist canvases. This phenomenon recurred several times in his work. Periods and styles often overlapped for years at a time. In any case, whatever the aesthetic adventure upon which he had embarked, he considered himself totally free and did not hesitate to use a technique or style which is almost shocking in its strangeness in order to perfect a work, because he needed to. Each drawing and painting had its own existence, particularly when it was a relatively isolated piece in his work generally, but even when it was not.

In this instance, Picasso came back to grey tints to render the scene, but he escaped academicism by giving them roughness, breadth and vigour, which serve to corroborate the atmosphere of the whole and the character of the subject. There is something rustic about the colour too: you can almost smell the hay.

18
HEAD OF A WOMAN
pastel 75×60, 1921
collection of Madame Cuttoli

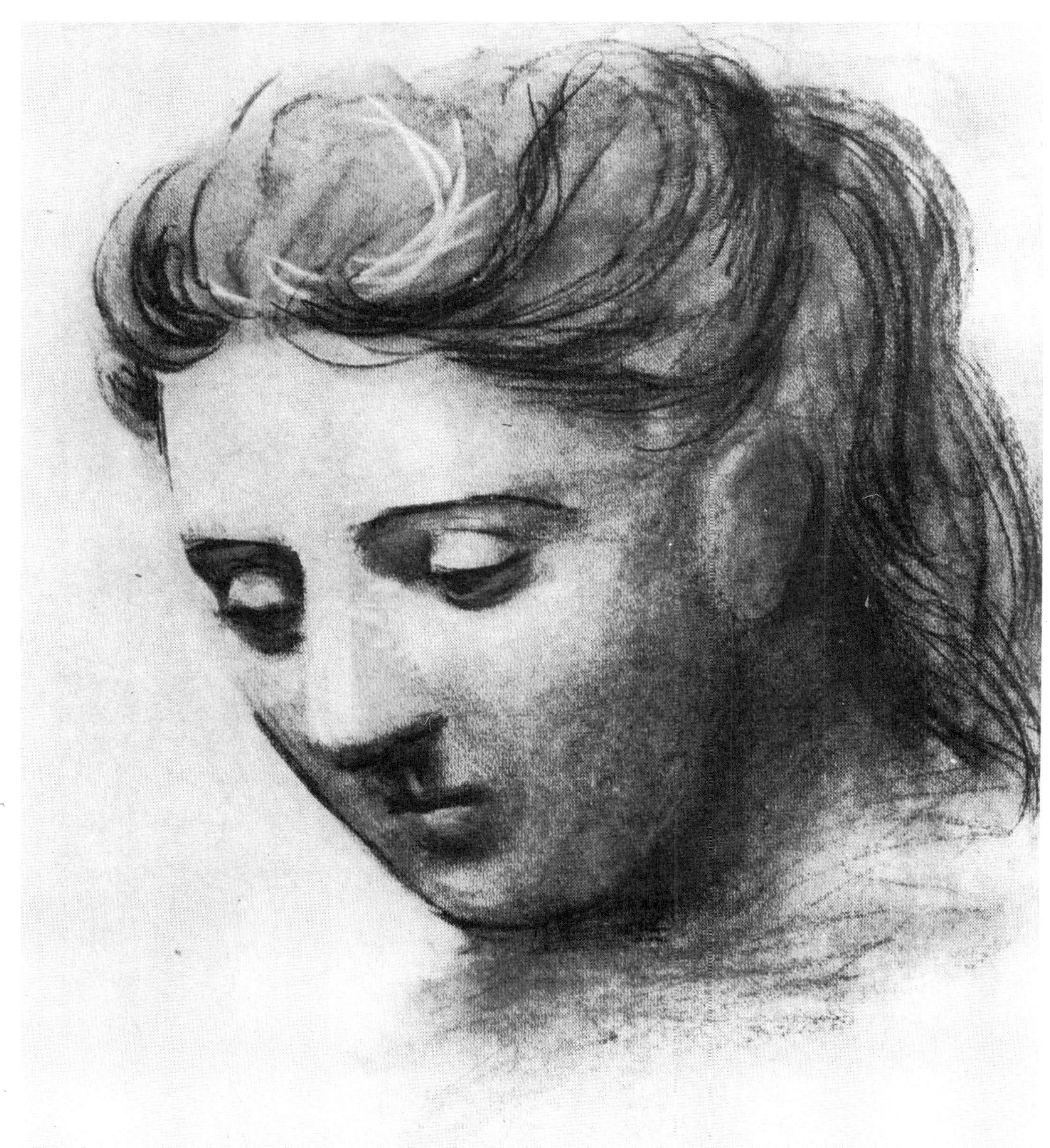

This wish to render volume stripped to its essential purity is apparent in two very fine heads, of a woman and of a young man so angelic that one might mistake him for a woman or for one of those androgynous angels of *quattrocento* art. Here, the relative dryness of pencil is enough to lend precision to an outline, to emphasise the line of a nose and the firm shape of lips, the shadow of the ridges of a brow which accentuates the far-away, almost absent, gaze. Some hatching defines volume. But usually, out of affinity with his subject, Picasso preferred a softer medium, crayon or pastel, with their velvety blurred strokes and dream-like quality. Gradually the features become indistinct and the face, drawn entirely in pastel, is made up of large areas of light and shadow in the manner of an ancient plaster cast. We are touching here on one of the characteristic features of this period. These faces drawn from very human models have points in common: the aggressive shape of the nose which juts out of masks of great softness as if to deny that very softness, and the absent gaze in those beautifully drawn eyes. Was Picasso thinking of the Greek and Roman busts which he had studied in their hundreds in Spanish museums? A few years later, he was to display the monumental forms of his Pompeian period giantesses

Grandeur and monumentality were already visible in embryonic form in the charming pastel *Two Women with Hats*. The amplitude of their limbs (muscular arms, crushing thighs) was perhaps inspired by the deformations that the Baroque painters visited upon their figures to compensate for perspective and the distortion of curves in the vaulting of the churches they decorated. Be that as it may, there are disturbing similarities.

Once again, Picasso avoided the trap of academicism by adopting the ochre tone of frescoes.

Sometimes Picasso seemed to be simply having fun, sketching his friends, but the Barcelona days were long gone. There was precision in

19
HEAD OF A MAN
pastel 77×60, 1921
collection of Madame Cuttoli

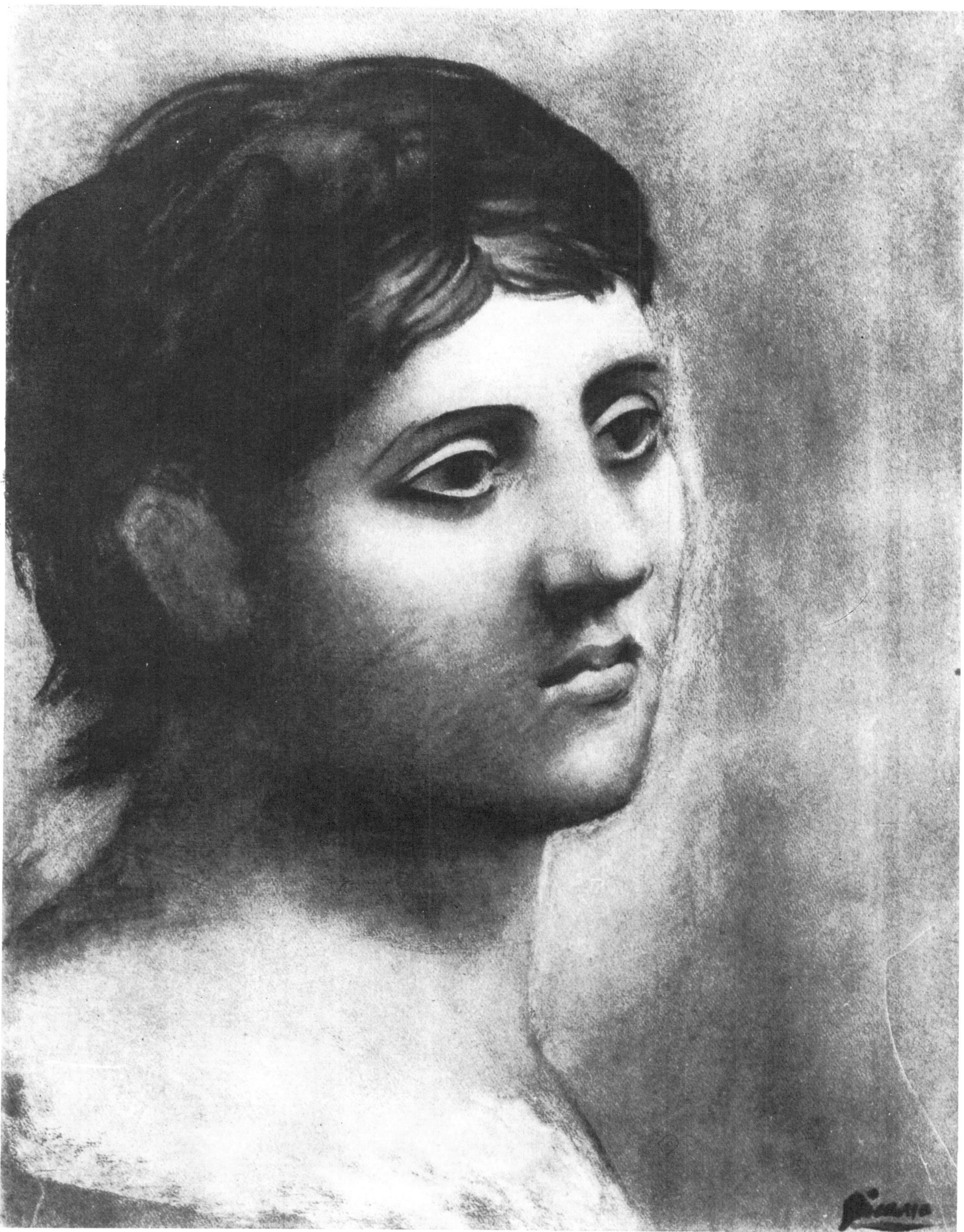

the line that fixed on paper for all time the profile of Stravinsky, Cocteau, Ernest Ansermet, or his compatriot Manuel de Falla.

The drawings are extremely clear, almost dry, and fascinating. We see the subject in front of us, alive, with none of his personality lost. They are marginal to Picasso's graphic work in general but, few as they are, they deserve their place in this overview.

Much could be said about Picasso's purely scenographic work, and first that, as always, Picasso bowed to the practices of the profession. His sketches set out to be *technical* and they were. For a discussion of this subject, the reader should consult *Picasso and the Theatre* and Douglas Cooper's study.

This same period saw many dancers and Harlequins, and also the first of the *Women Running along the Beach*. They are giantesses in Roman tunics which leave their breasts free. Movement is accentuated and the theme anticipates other women running along other beaches, those of Biarritz and of Dinard a few years later, which were to become sculptures.

As so often with Picasso, reproductions are misleading: a picture that one imagines to be enormous turns out to be tiny when one actually sees it in the gallery; the reverse is true of another. Size is not a question of dimension, but of intent. Science plays a part too and sometimes the sheer cunning of the artist who knows how to exploit all the resources of his craft.

Picasso was in transition between a unitary, homogeneous space and a simultaneous and multiple vision. The same subject can be considered from several points of view, as in *Three Bathers*, or it can be deconstructed into what seem to be quite arbitrarily juxtaposed fragments. Picasso was pleasantly pointing out, they say, that 'everything is there', everything that traditionally and anatomically represents a nude. The spectator is free to use his imagination and to put the diverse

20
HEAD OF A WOMAN
pastel 62×46
Fontainebleau 1921

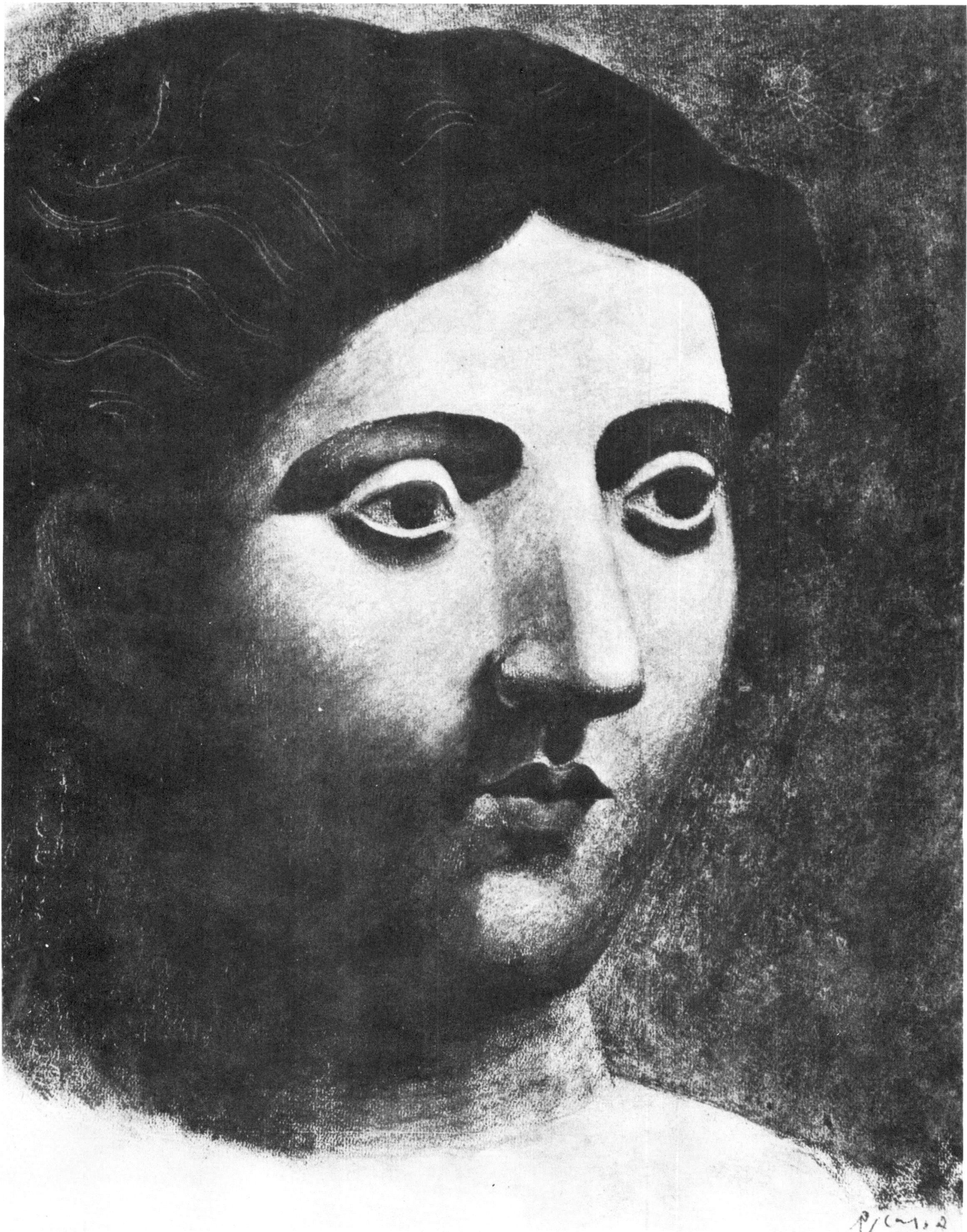

elements back into place, if he wants to.

However, concern for truth moves us to say that reality is not like that at all and that, from a strictly aesthetic point of view, things don't happen that simply. There is nothing gratuitous in Picasso's work and he was at his most serious when he was drawing the most disconcerting of his figures. If he appeared provocative at times, it was never on a whim but of necessity. It was his self-imposed demands, his need to pursue his perpetual quest for expressiveness that led him to create these surprising figures with their unusual beauty.

In his works of the years 1927–28, Picasso allowed observation to take second place to an exploration of realms unknown, realms that were essentially of form. This is not to say that his investigations were gratuitous; on the contrary, he was working towards the strongest and most powerful expression possible.

Two obsessions in his work are evident: the translation of volume and the rendering of movement. The diversity of his experiments illustrates the scale of his field of research. However, two methods predominate and both are to be found in the drawings reproduced here.

First of all, he divided the plan of the work into several spatial areas. He thus created a new dimension and succeeded in making actions, or people acting in different places, coexist on the same sheet of paper or the same canvas.

Then, with a daring simplicity so extreme that it ought to appear primitive but in Picasso's hands acquires a convincing efficacy, he grossly enlarged the elements in the foreground or, at all events, those closest to the spectator. The rendering of relief is exaggerated, the perspective breathtaking.

This audaciousness gave us those enormous thighs surmounted by bodies in diminishing perspective which end in tiny arms. He also used the reverse procedure. Add to that the systematic elongation of limbs in

21
TWO WOMEN WITH HATS
pastel 105×75
Fontainebleau 1921

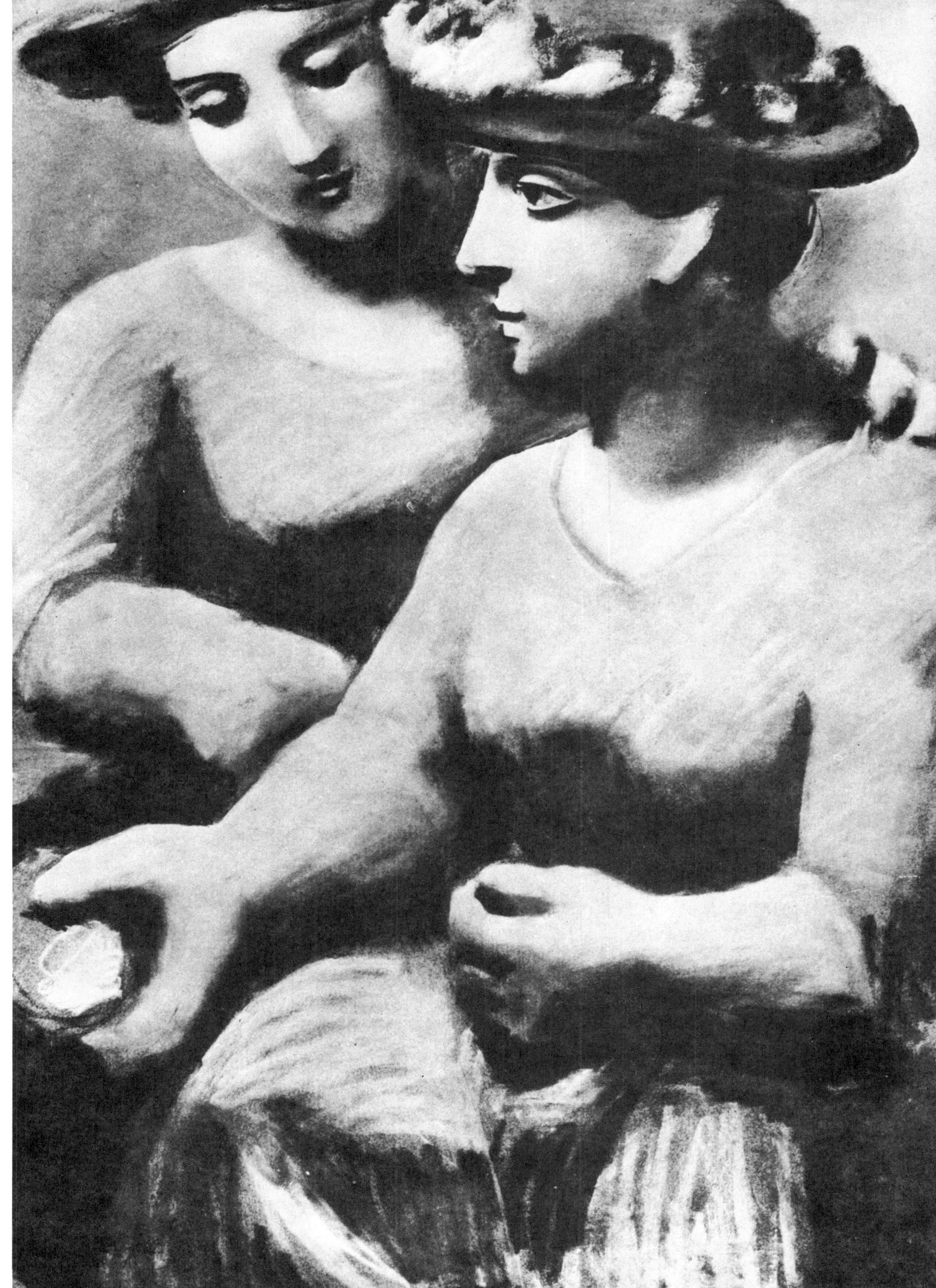

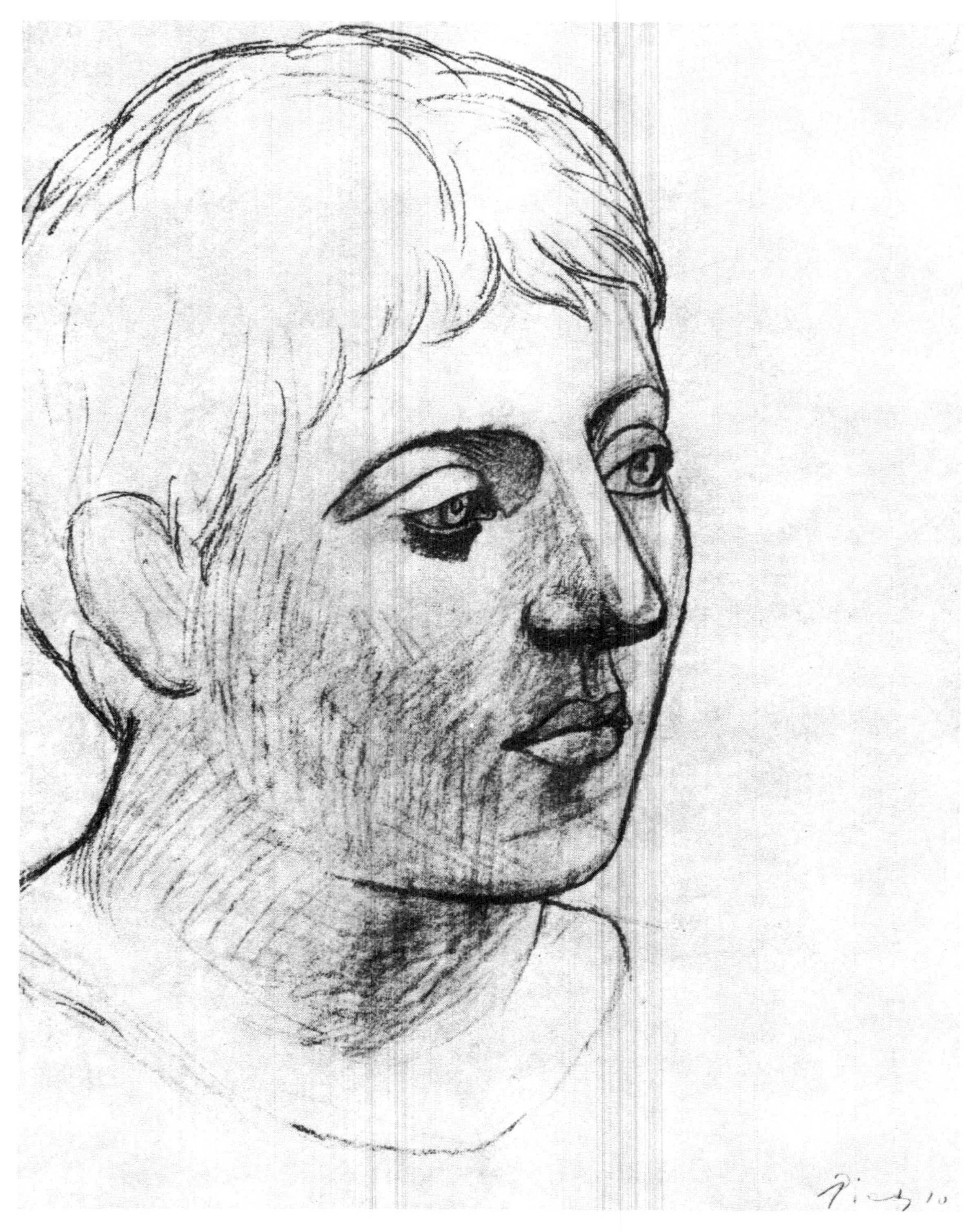

22
HEAD OF A YOUNG MAN
Conté pencil 60×47
11–12 February 1923

motion, for example the legs if the person is running – all to accentuate the illusion of movement.

Henri Matisse used a similar process in his linear drawings: the deformation that consists of enlarging the visible form is a means of signifying volume. The classical painter blackened the inside of the outline, used grey tints and blurring in an effort to recreate real vision. He was imitating a photograph before photography was invented. Many generations of artists, from the discovery of classical perspective in the Renaissance, used this translation of space by a play on light. To the classical painter, the painting – or the drawing which prefigures it – should appear as a window open on to the world. The foreground is situated at the level of the frame, that is, of the wall on which the painting hangs. Beyond, the landscape rises in tiers to the horizon. Colour corroborates the effect of the drawing. Highly coloured foregrounds sometimes respect local colour. Then the tones get gradually lighter, until distances are drowned in bluish pallor. Thence the illusion of space, of an open window. From these beginnings, classical painting culminated in the art of Poussin and the Dutch landscape painters.

This is all standard dogma, but if one does not remind oneself of what three centuries of painting represented, one cannot appreciate the contribution of Picasso and his contemporaries to the art of our time. The break occurred in the late 19th century and came between Ingres and Delacroix, the descendants of David, and those revolutionary colourists the Romantics on the one hand, and the Impressionists on the other: first Manet, then Monet, Pissarro and the others, and above all Cézanne. From 1863 on, artists discovered that a painting could exist by and for itself and not only as a depiction of the outside world, which is not to deny that the greatest masters of earlier times knew how to convey a personal vision of the world under the guise of an objective portrayal. Yet the Impressionists were the first to assume the new creative responsibility. They knew that the picture of the world they were showing was theirs and theirs alone.

A second conquest went even further: the painting no longer had to depict another world, it had to exist in itself. It was no longer a window, it was an object, situated at the same level as the wall which held it. It renounced all traditional illustrativeness, all *trompe-l'oeil* effects. Picasso and a few others concluded that new means had to be found to express the visible.

Paintings – and drawings – are two-dimensional and the object of Picasso and his contemporaries was to stop 'cheating' by pretending they are three-dimensional. Art does not have to relay methods of reproduction; it has to find its own way. Cézanne knew this when he was reworking for the tenth time a view of the Montagne-Sainte-Victoire, suggested by a few light touches of watercolour, as if it were drowning in mist or dissolving in the warm sunlight of Provence. By his action he freed himself of any compromise, any reference to tradition and became the prophet of modern art.

Picasso understood the lesson of Cézanne, whose paintings he saw in Ambroise Vollard's studio during his first years in Paris in the early 1900s. He started by adopting Cézanne's system, whence the style of the early Cubist period of 1908–09, then he pushed his exploration of the powers of line further. Already in 1907, with the *Demoiselles* and all the studies that surrounded it, he had achieved a new transcription of the visible. In 1911, Analytical Cubism was a decomposition of volume in two dimensions. As a result of his experiments with antiquity, he regained contact with tradition and put its limits to the test. The *Giantesses*, the *Women Running along the Beach* were to be metamorphosed. They were not to remain mere reference art. They materialised in space, they demanded to live their own lives in a three-dimensional art.

23
DRAWING
charcoal, sketchbook
summer 1927

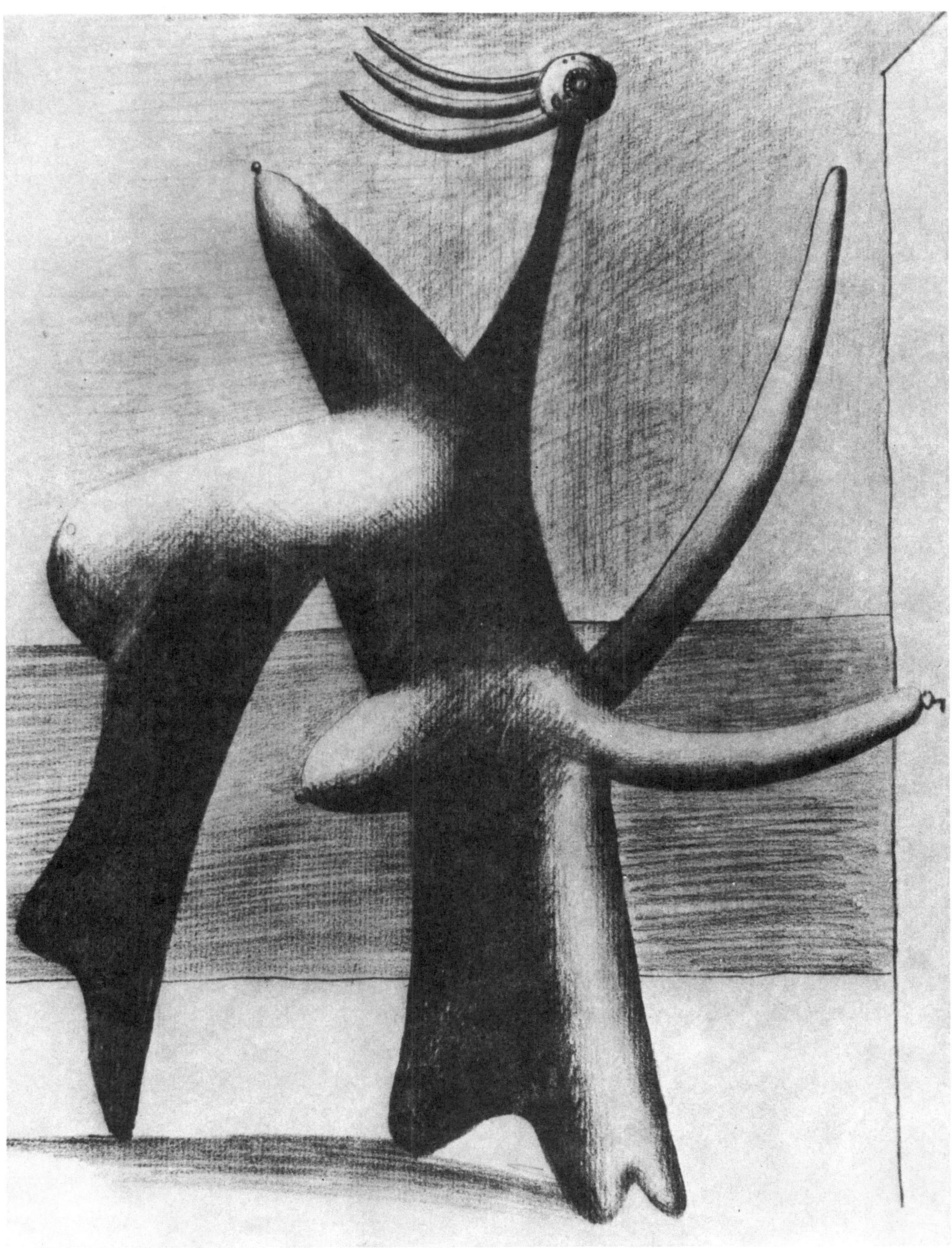

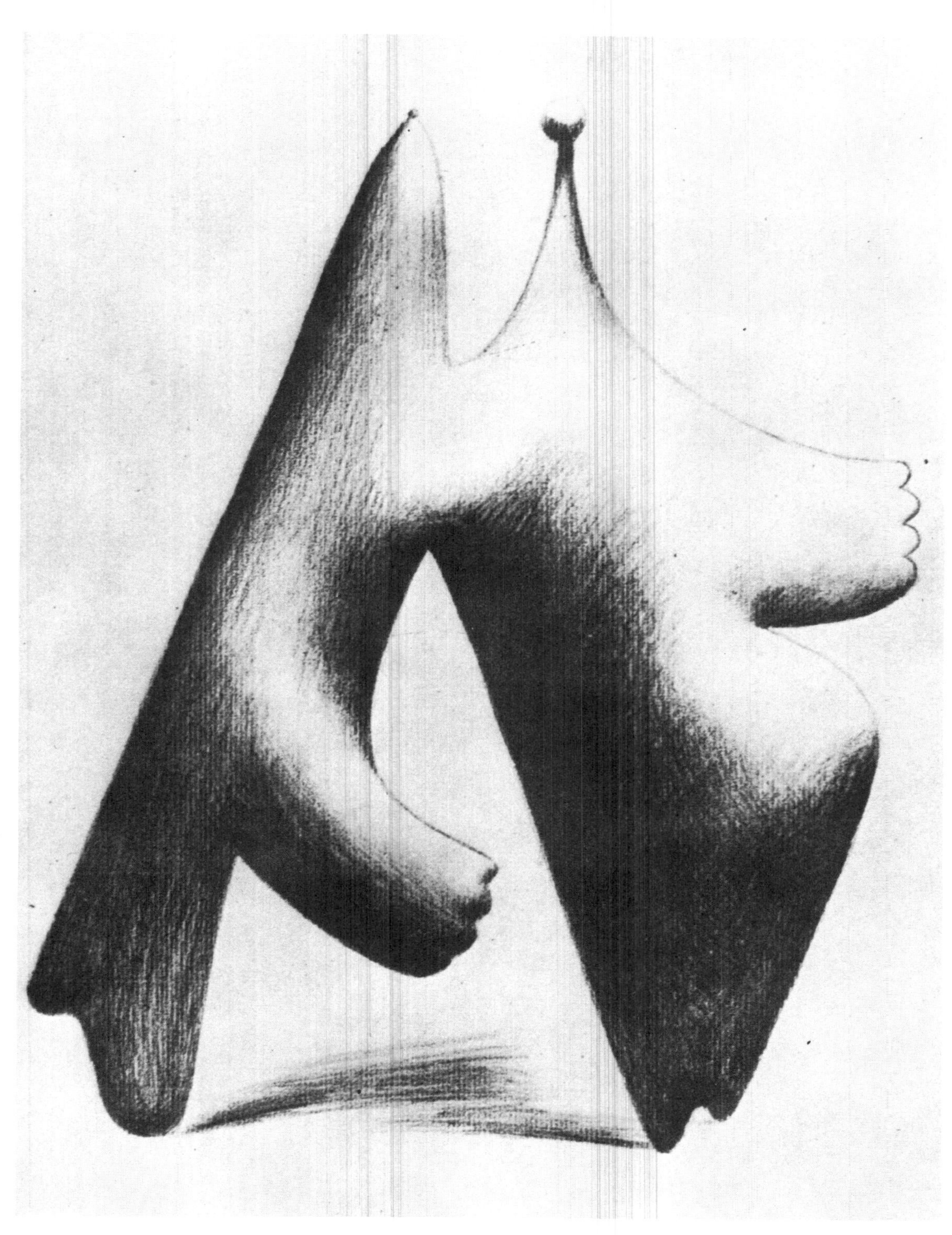

24
DRAWING
charcoal, sketchbook
summer 1927

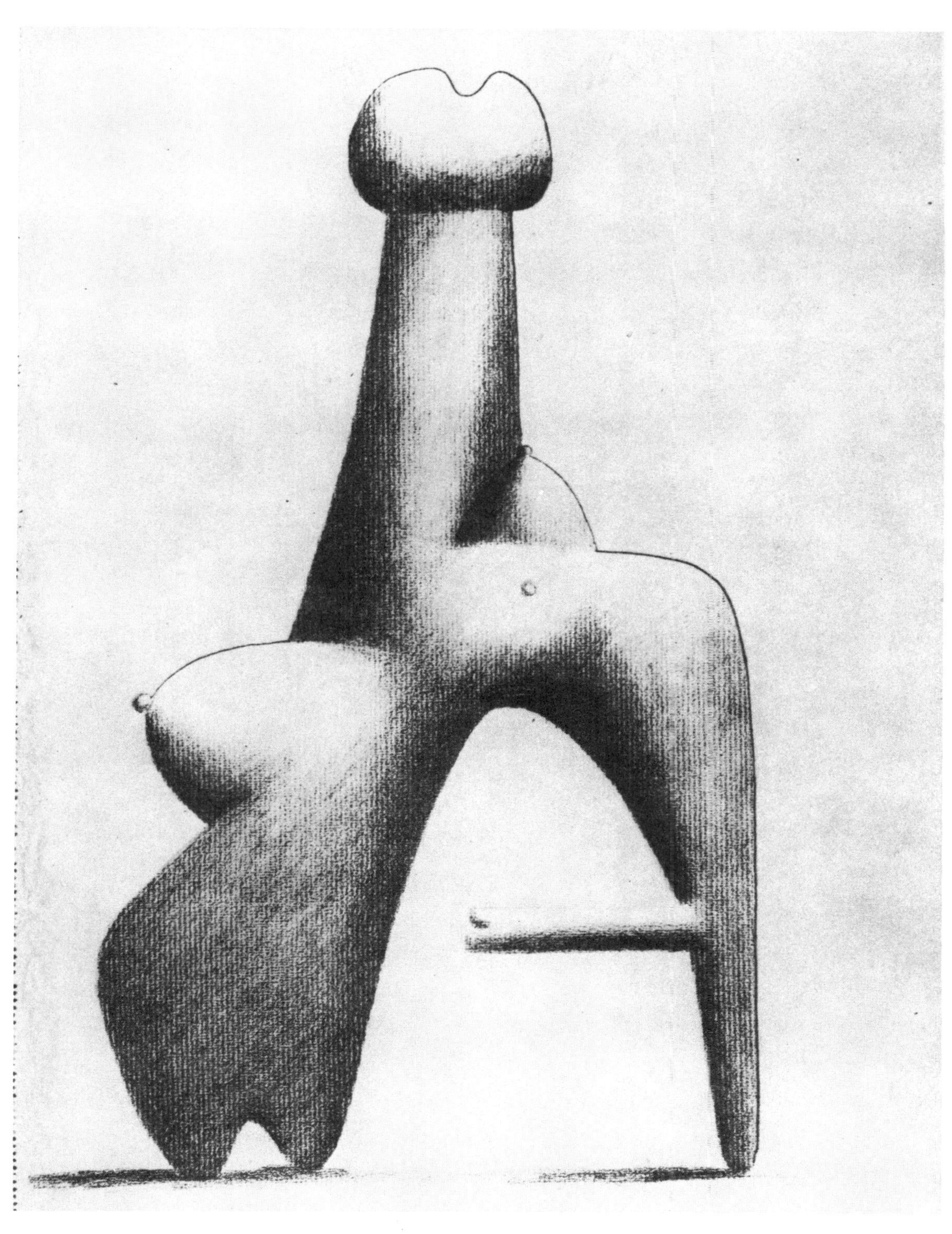

25
DRAWING
charcoal, sketchbook
summer 1927

And, as always, Picasso turned to sculpture to add spatial control to the validity of what he had proved on paper.

Picasso was encouraged in his boldness by the young group of Surrealists who were enraptured by the ballet *Mercure* and this new form of fluid and supple, curvilinear Cubism. This ballet, more than any other, was, visually at least, the work of Picasso (the music was by Eric Satie, the choreography by Massine).

Picasso, like André Breton, arrogated to himself the right to dream and, pursuing the dream, he celebrated revolution, love and woman, as the object and symbol of male desire and eroticism. This helps us towards an earlier acceptance of the fantastic figures of women that, from 1927 on, suffered all manner of distortion, deformation and sometimes impossible contortions under his pencil though without sacrificing their essential identity. This line of experimentation continued until 1932 and culminated in the large stone figures which were a homage to Marie-Thérèse.

Setting prejudice aside, one has to recognise the great presence and power of these figures. There they are before our eyes, flaunting their sexual attributes in all directions, and if a head raised towards the sky takes on a phallic look, is this not a result of our own obsessions? In deciphering the drawings, one is almost psychoanalysing oneself. This was the period when Picasso was closest to Breton, and when the Surrealists were avidly reading Freud.

Picasso, liberated once more, exploded volumes which, at first carnal, took on a marble coldness and finally appeared like bony masses, 'bones' which never existed in any human skeleton though were juxtaposed to suggest a woman's body. They materialised in the *Reclining Bather* and became almost systematic in the studies inspired by Matthias Grünewald's *Crucifixion* (one is included here), which resulted in that unique, mysterious masterpiece that is Picasso's

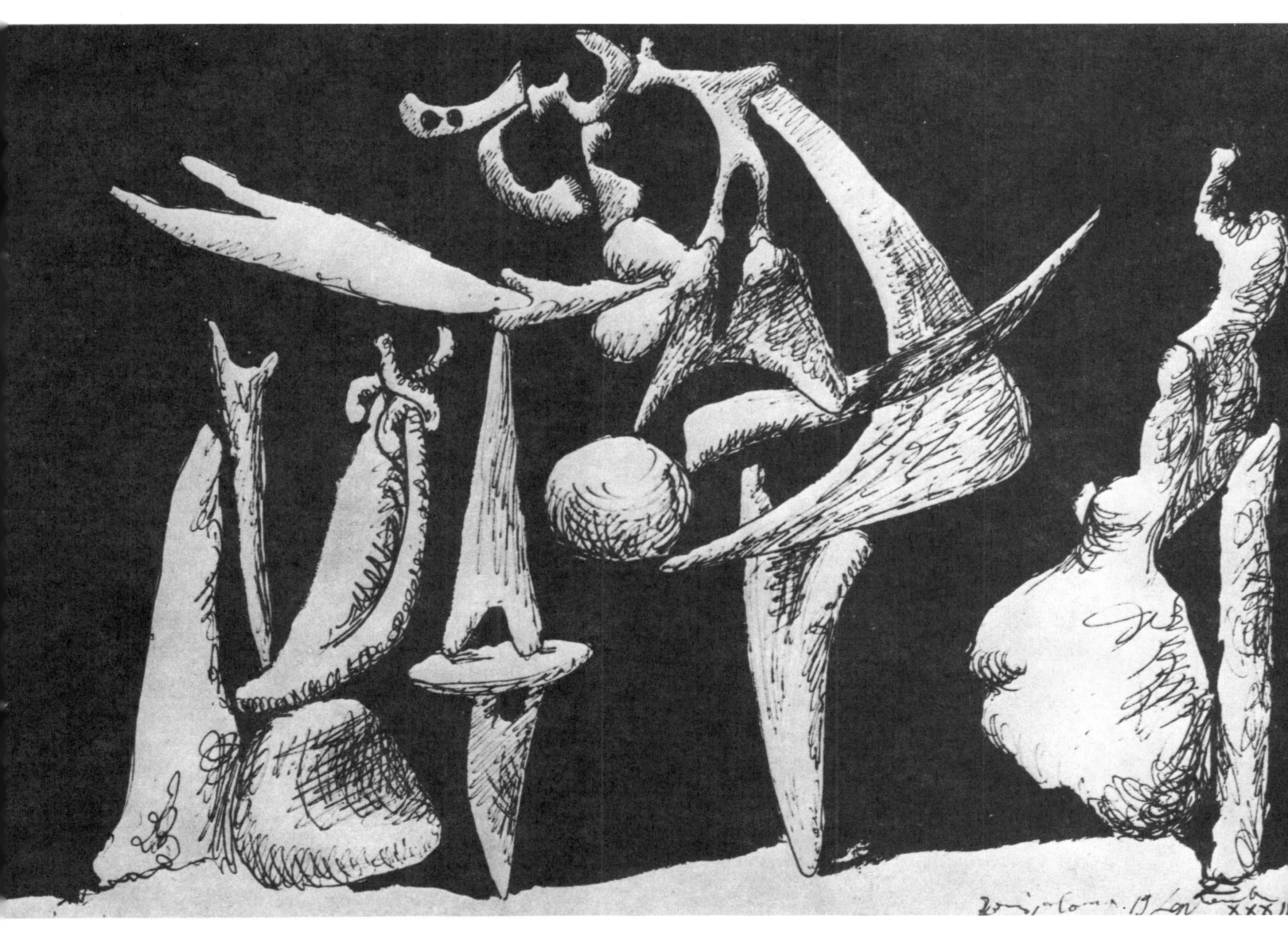

26
CRUCIFIXION
Indian ink drawing 34.5×50.5
Boisgeloup 19 September 1932
Picasso Museum, Paris

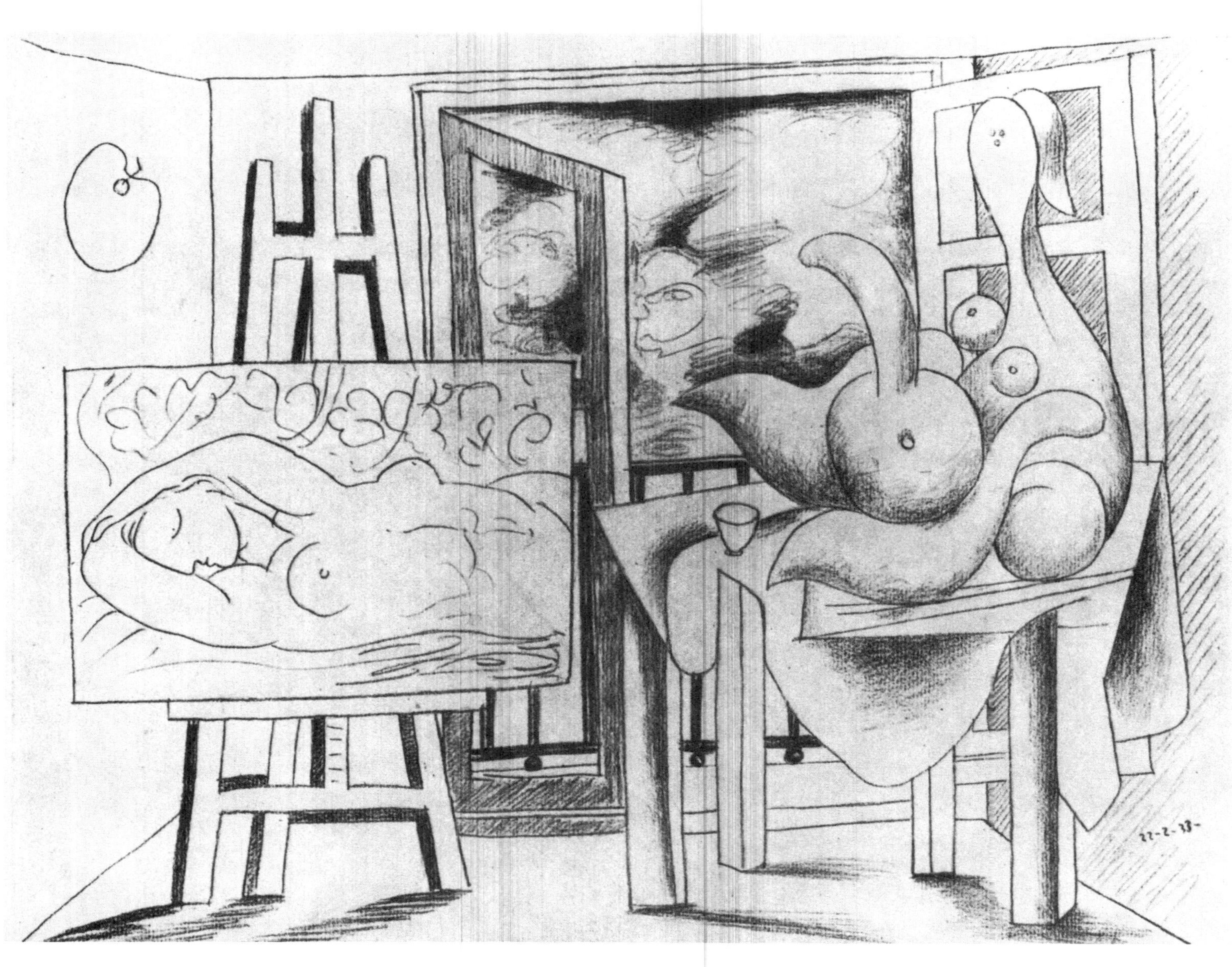

27
THE STUDIO
lead pencil 26×34.5
Paris 22 February 1933
P casso Museum, Paris

Crucifixion, now in the Picasso Museum in Paris. One can understand why he insisted that it stay in 'his' collection, because it is a unique and timeless work of art.

Picasso was so conscious of the duality in his work that he used it as the theme for many of his drawings and some paintings. *The Studio*, painted on 22 February 1933, juxtaposed the very sensual painting of a female nude and the no less sensual sculpture which probably inspired it. This work can be considered from various viewpoints and there is even a discernible touch of humour, as if Picasso were standing back to comment on his own work. There is also much to be read into the metamorphosis of line into volume. There were aspects of Surrealism that were less radical than these synthetic concepts: there was the Minotaur, Picasso's favourite monster! The Minotaur, mythological symbol of virility and sexual power, came like Hercules at Omphale's feet to roll on downy couches beside creatures that were all flesh and passion. Gone was the dry severity of line that sculpture demands. The line was there to seduce, to be as sensual as the subject, to coil itself into curves and arabesques, to multiply, ravel into a skein and disappear into the shadows of a poetic and mysterious chiaroscuro.

The theme of Man and Woman or Painter and Model had already appeared fleetingly in Picasso's work. Now it took on a new dimension, one that he was to return to, especially in the final period.

Picasso's themes constitute a permanent repertory into which he would dip according to his mood or his preoccupations, but this was one of his favourites. It disappears and resurfaces like a natural phenomenon, recurrent and familiar.

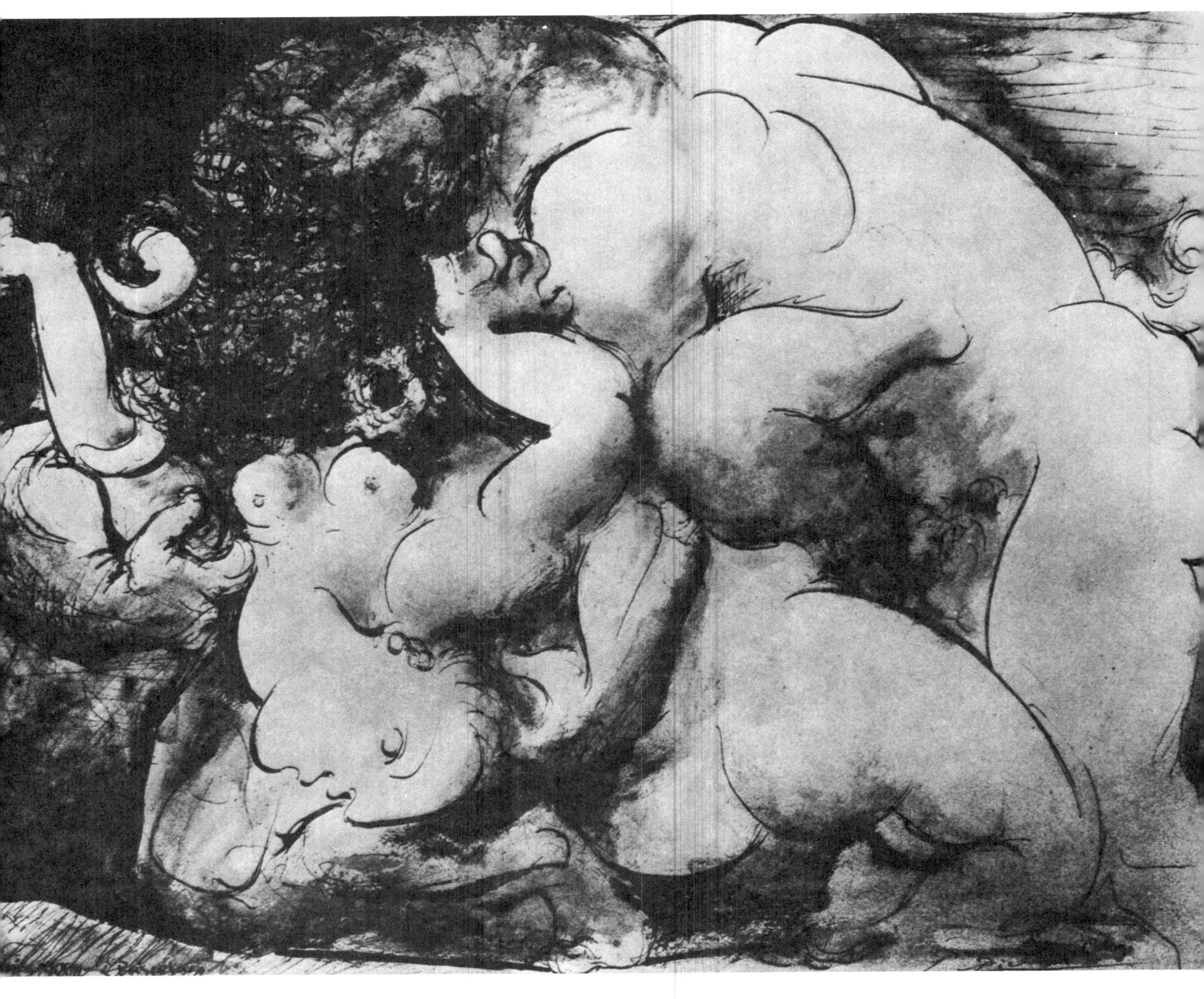

28
MINOTAUR
Indian ink 47×62
Boisgeloup 24 June 1933
private collection

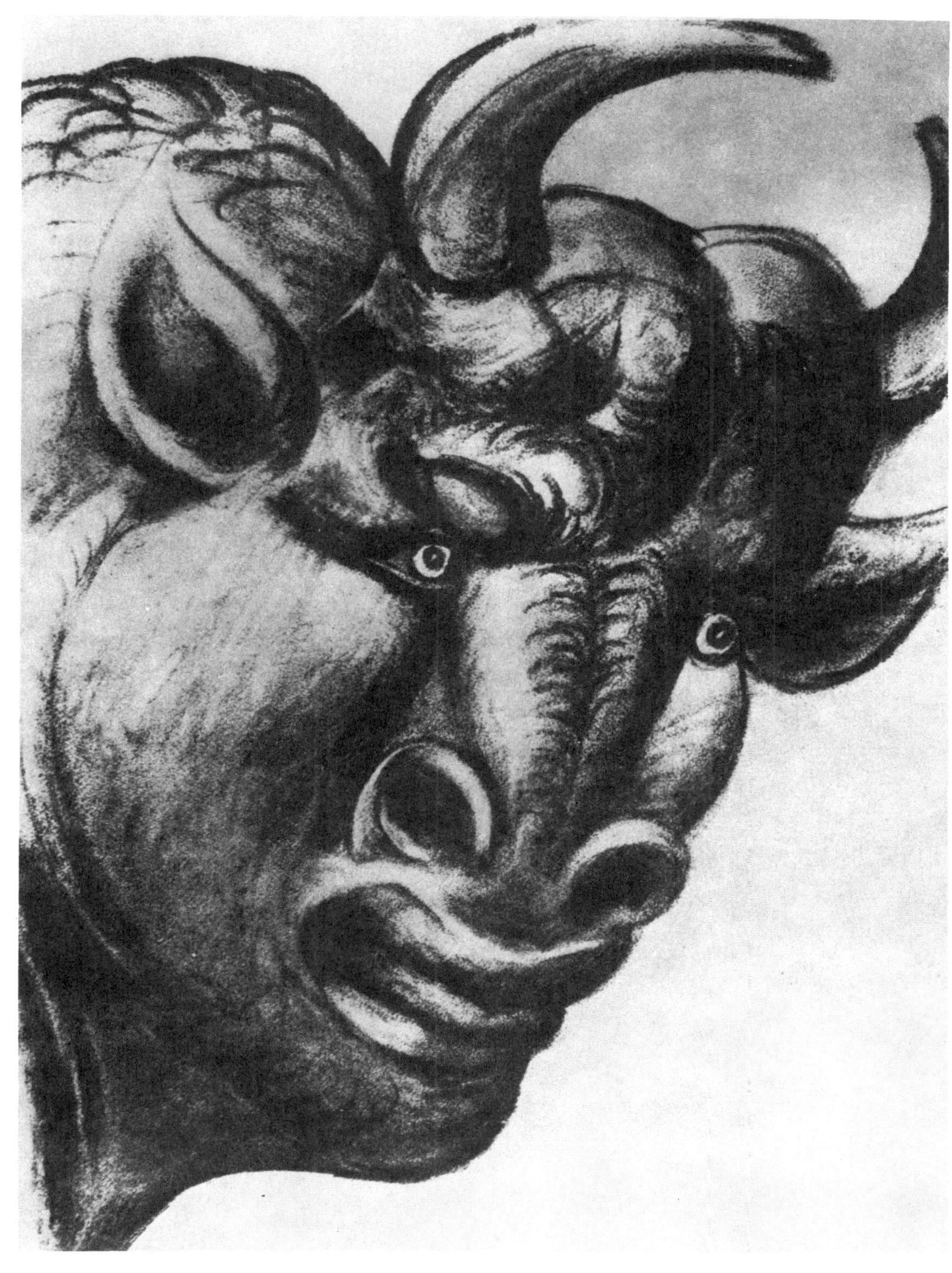

29
BULL'S HEAD
charcoal 50.5×34, 1933

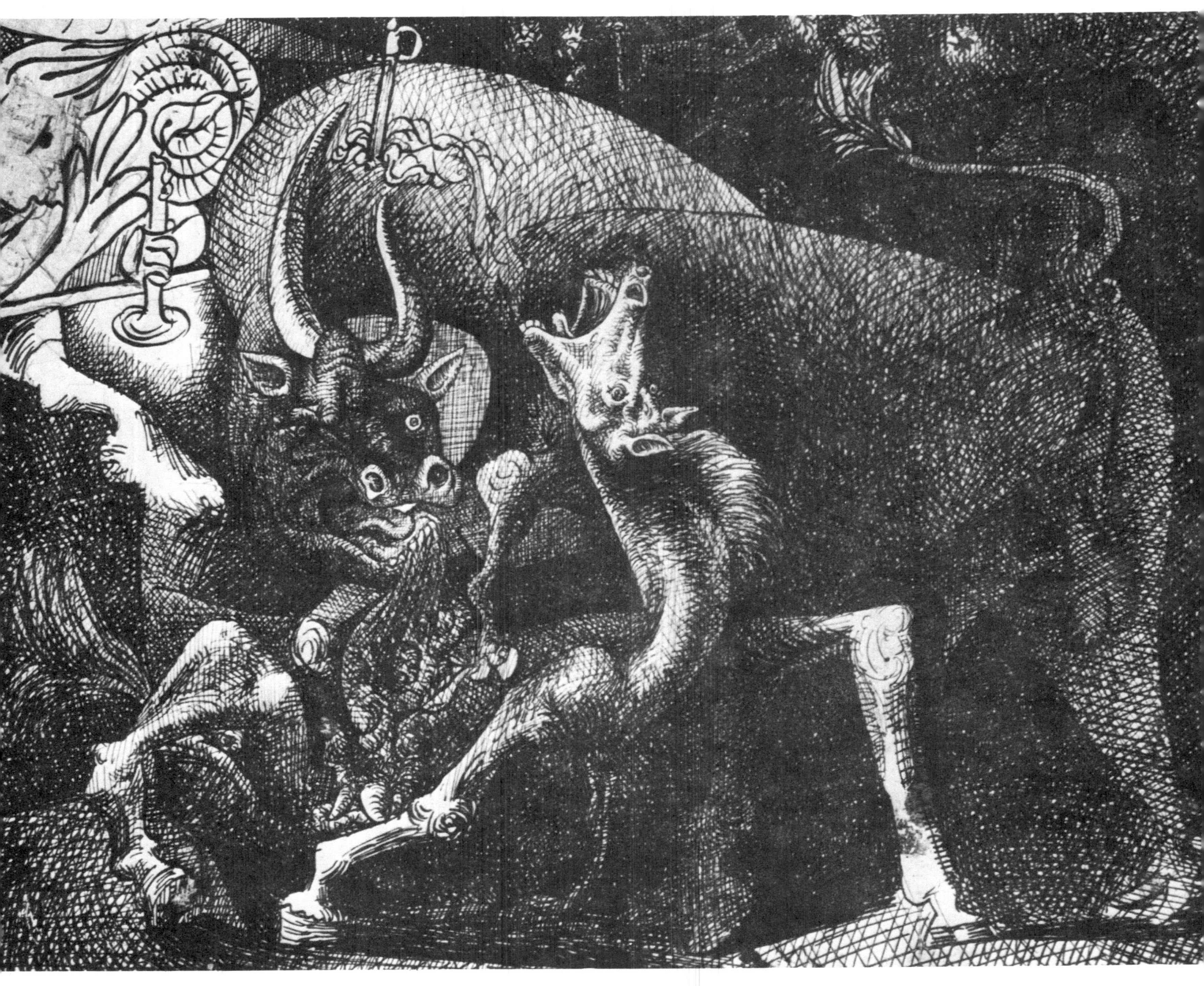

30
BULLFIGHT
Indian ink on wood panel 31.5×40.7
Eoisgeloup 24 July 1934

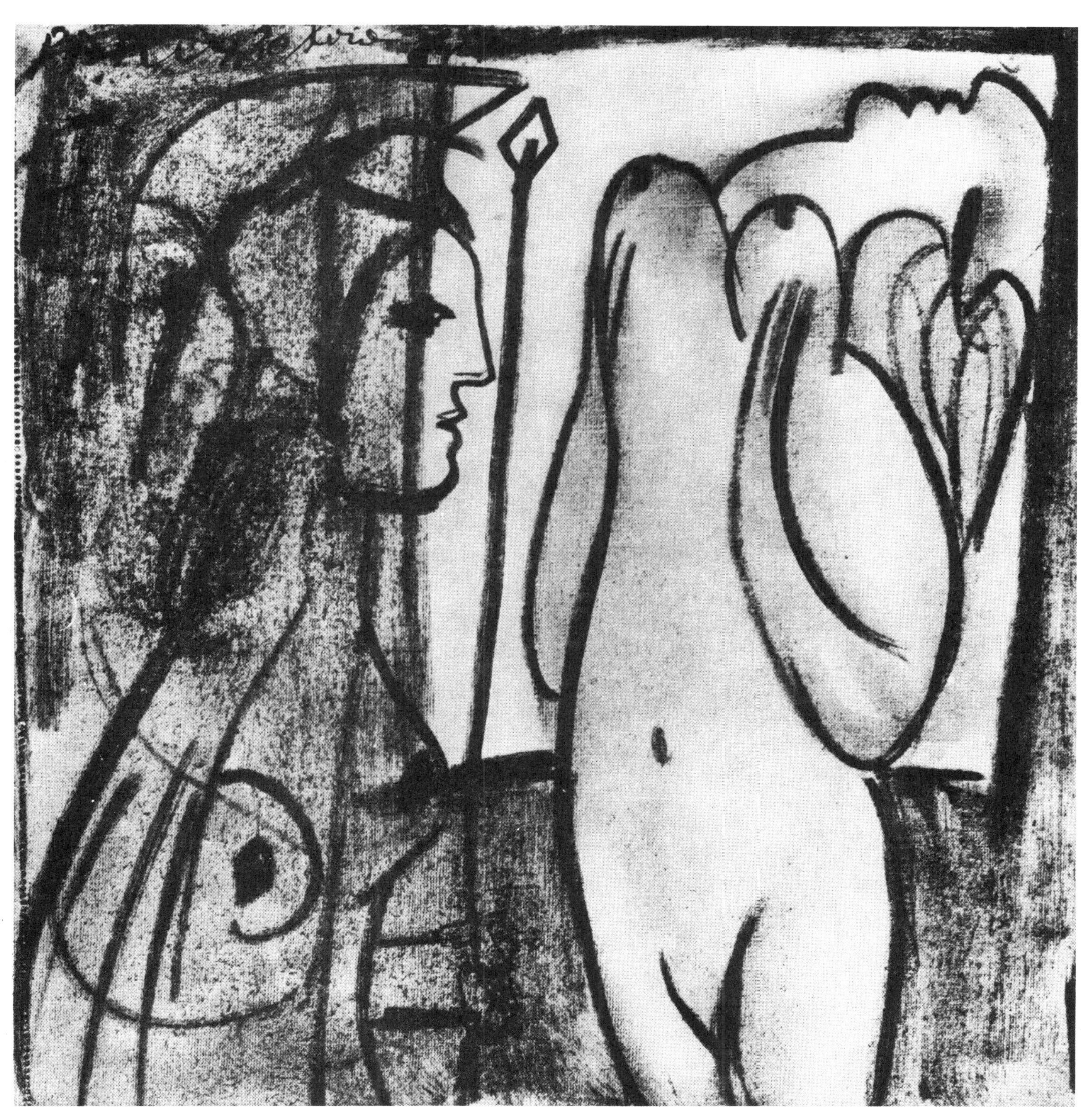

31
NUDES
charcoal 28×27
sketchbook, Paris 30 August 1934

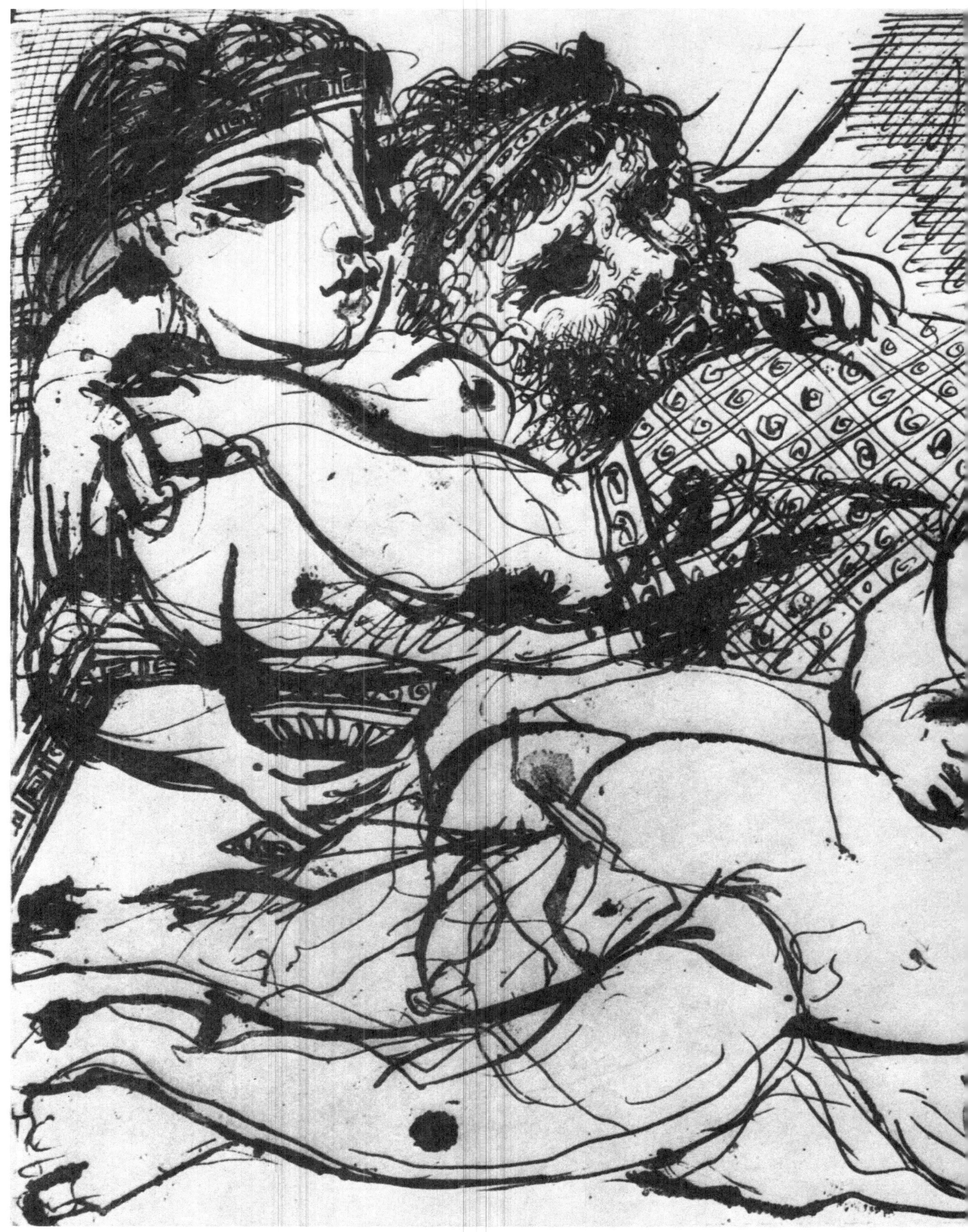

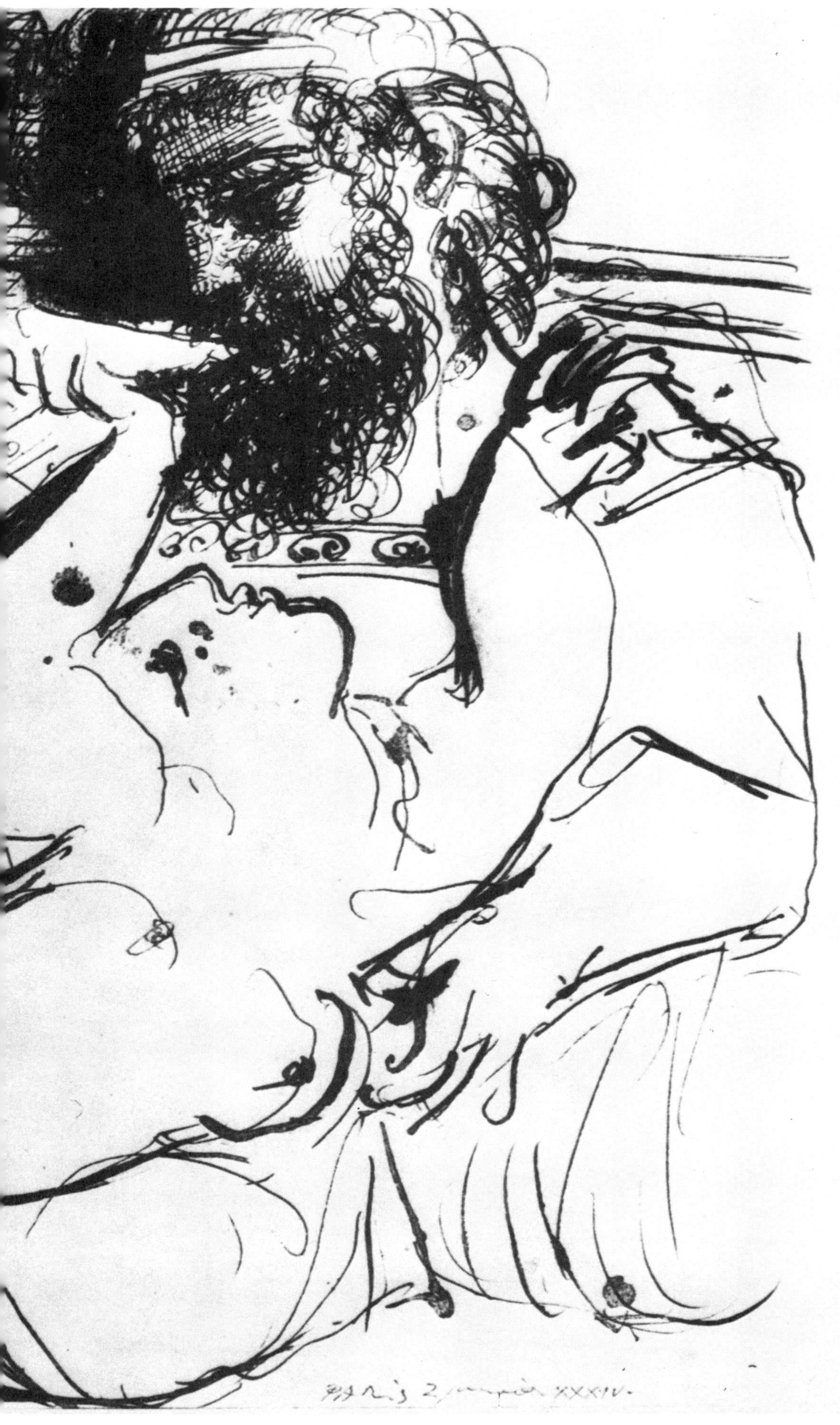

32
COMPOSITION
Indian ink 34.5×50.5
Paris 2 January 1934

VI

GUERNICA

This chapter could equally well be entitled 'The Tale of the Guernica Horse' or 'The Sad Story of the Weeping Lady'. We have noted that once Picasso's thematic repertory was firmly established he would draw from it periodically according to his current needs. The horse was another such theme. It appears very early, needless to say, in the setting of the corrida. As a Spaniard, Picasso adored bullfights and throughout his life produced any number of drawings, paintings and even ceramic plates and dishes (in the shape of an arena) on this theme.

In the corrida, the picador who pricks the bull with his lance is the villain. The horse, usually an old one, is the one who is gored and often disembowelled by the bull's horns. Its role of victim became a symbol to which Picasso returned again and again. In the pages that follow, we have chosen some of his horses which express despair, a cry of protest against injustice, war and barbarity. The earliest dates from 1917: the horse has just been wounded by the bull and its guts are spilling out. The realism of the subject is attenuated by the linear style and the stylisation of shapes, particularly those of the neck and head, which were often to recur. Here, Picasso escaped from all the conventions to create his own symbols, symbols that were to become classic.

In a 1934 *Corrida*, which is an Indian ink drawing on wood panel, the horse is in a similar position, raising itself up under the hooves of the beast that has fatally wounded it. It bears a striking resemblance to its counterpart in *Guernica* and the same is true of the bull, at least in the positioning of its head, which is turned towards the viewer.

There is one important difference: this bull is grimacing, it has long tapering horns; there is a sword planted in its withers from which springs an arabesque symbolising blood and fast-ebbing life; its eyes are round and staring. The *Guernica* bull is motionless, like an ancient god, its eyes too are motionless, but of human shape; it shoots out its tongue as if about to deliver a message. But enough . . . such interpretations are best left to poets. Reference to the first studies for *Guernica* will show the position of the bull as that of an involuntary witness taken by surprise by all this butchery and thus innocent and non-aggressive.

In the 1934 drawing, the battle is taking place before our eyes and unambiguously depicts the final scene of the corrida: the bull wreaking vengeance on the horse.

So, three years later, in *Guernica*, Picasso used the protagonists of the corrida again, but the script was different and so were their roles. Another similarity: in the top left-hand corner of the earlier work a face appears, not in a window as in *Guernica*, but in the stands, and this female figure is brandishing a lighted chandelier! If one follows the sweep of the stands, one sees what seem to be stars twinkling, but are probably other candles. There are similarities here and one can make out the elements of still earlier drawings that Picasso used in his masterpiece, whether consciously or unconsciously we will never know.

Picasso did once reveal the symbolic values of these figures, but only when pushed to do so in an interview with a particularly insistent historian. He explained that the horse represented the people; the bull was not Fascism, although it represented its brutality and blackness.

If John D. Russell has analysed *Guernica* with the prudence of the scientist, A. Oriol Anguera was less circumspect. He denounced the dictator in the bull. He wrote that 'this bull constitutes the best allegory of the *homo regens* of the 20th century. The bull in *Guernica* has its tail up to show enormous testicles. Hitler, Mussolini, Stalin . . . no matter!'

To see Picasso's constancy in his use of certain images and his desire to transcend the power of reality, one has only to look at the horses'

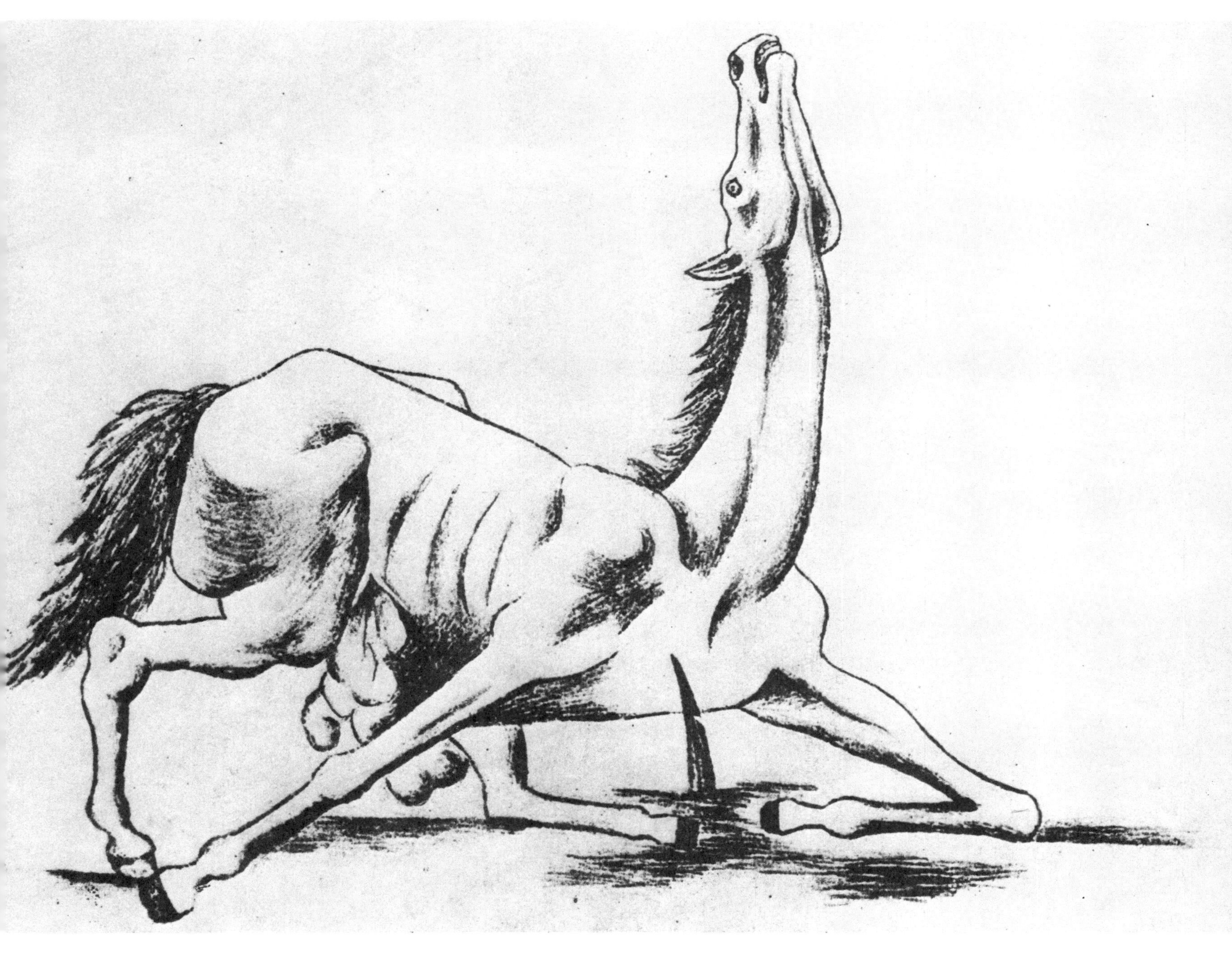

33
DISEMBOWELLED HORSE
pencil
Barcelona 1917

heads from a series of drawings of 1959, more than twenty years later, published in volume form under the title *Toros y toreros*. Each time that Picasso wanted to express the fear and suffering of the horse, he came back to the eloquent image of the head reared up to howl at the sky.

As is evident in his study of 8 May 1937, Picasso groped around for a long time before he reached the final stage of his most famous work. Dora Maar's photographs of the seven transitory stages reflect the doubts and uncertainties of the artist. The dying horse collapses, like the horse of the picador when it is gored by the bull, but first it lowers its head to the ground to cry out in pain, then raises it again to howl its indignation in the face of the world. Picasso made animals talk, or at any rate he knew how to exploit that idea in the power of ascending and descending lines and the collision of curves and straight lines.

This page from 8 May 1937 shows one of the first studies of the horse and a first glimpse of the woman with the dead child. Another one the next day is more detailed; in another (not reproduced here) the woman is holding on to a ladder, which allows the painter to pull her head further backwards. He abandoned this and returned to the first, inverted, position, which is totally improbable but much more dramatic.

Oddly enough, in a series of studies and some paintings from 1933 entitled *The Rescue*, there is a woman bent backwards holding her child aloft at the end of her arm. The series was probably inspired by an accident at sea that occurred while Picasso was staying in Dinard.

Leafing through the several volumes of Christian Zervos's catalogue of Picasso's work, one can find earlier forms of well-known themes, as if the characters of the gigantic fresco that Picasso's work represents, in the manner of Balzac's *La Comédie Humaine*, had no beginning and no end. Pure illusion, of course, but our knowledge of Picasso's work always allow us to find earlier references.

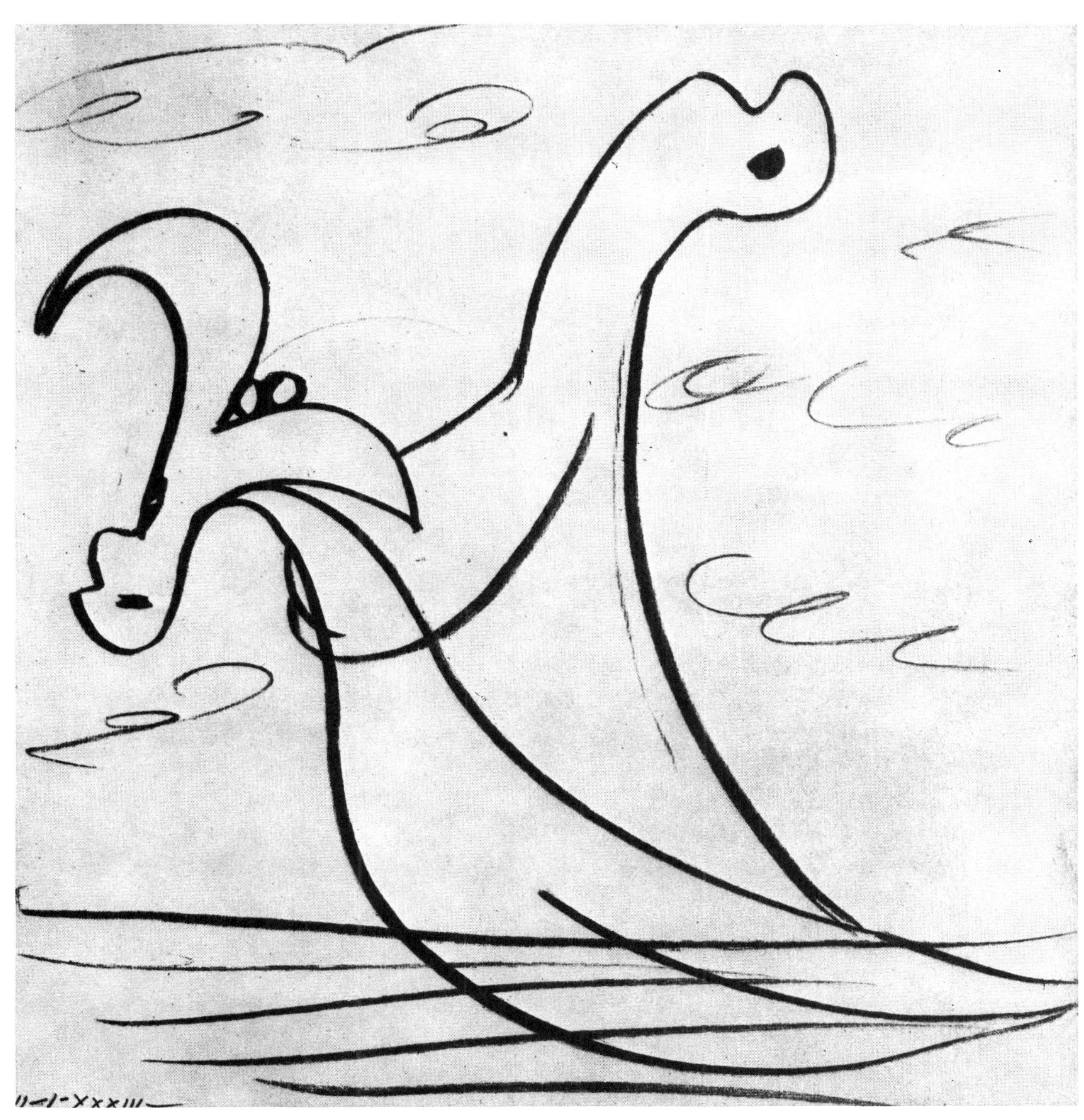

34
THE RESCUE
charcoal 28×27
sketchbook, Paris 11 January 1933

However, I do not believe this to be true of the *Woman Screaming*, a subject that appeared in Picasso's work with the outbreak of the Spanish Civil War in his first sketch for *Guernica* (which was commissioned by the republican government for the Spanish pavilion at the 1937 international exhibition in Paris). In Paris Picasso was to find himself in company with Julio Gonzalez, who was exhibiting his famous sculpture *Montserrat*, with Calder and his mercury fountain, with Salvador Dali and Joan Miró.

Picasso made the first studies of the *Crying Head* on 24 May and they proliferated in the following weeks, but eventually he did not use them. However, the subject obsessed him to such effect that he returned to it again and again until the end of October, well after he had completed *Guernica*.

A number of these studies, kept for many years at the Museum of Modern Art in New York, are now exhibited in the Casa del Buen Retiro at the Prado in Madrid, where they benefit by a special display. They are black lead drawings, brutally streaked and scratched with strokes of coloured pencil. An occasional touch of gouache imparts shadow. Picasso was drawing with such violence that he used tracing linen for his material!

The mouth is grimacing and twisted with pain, tears flow and, as in primitive Catalan sculpture, their tracks are etched into the face like the furrows and wrinkles left by suffering.

Picasso reworked this tear-ravaged face in various forms: as a painting in a sparer style, and as an aquatint etching in a more Baroque, nervous style hatched by the scores of blade and acid.

Picasso's model was a woman who had only recently arrived in his life, a painter and photographer of Yugoslav origin. What a cruel fate for Dora Maar to make her appearance in Picasso's painting during such a tragic period. After the full-blown and sensual women of previous

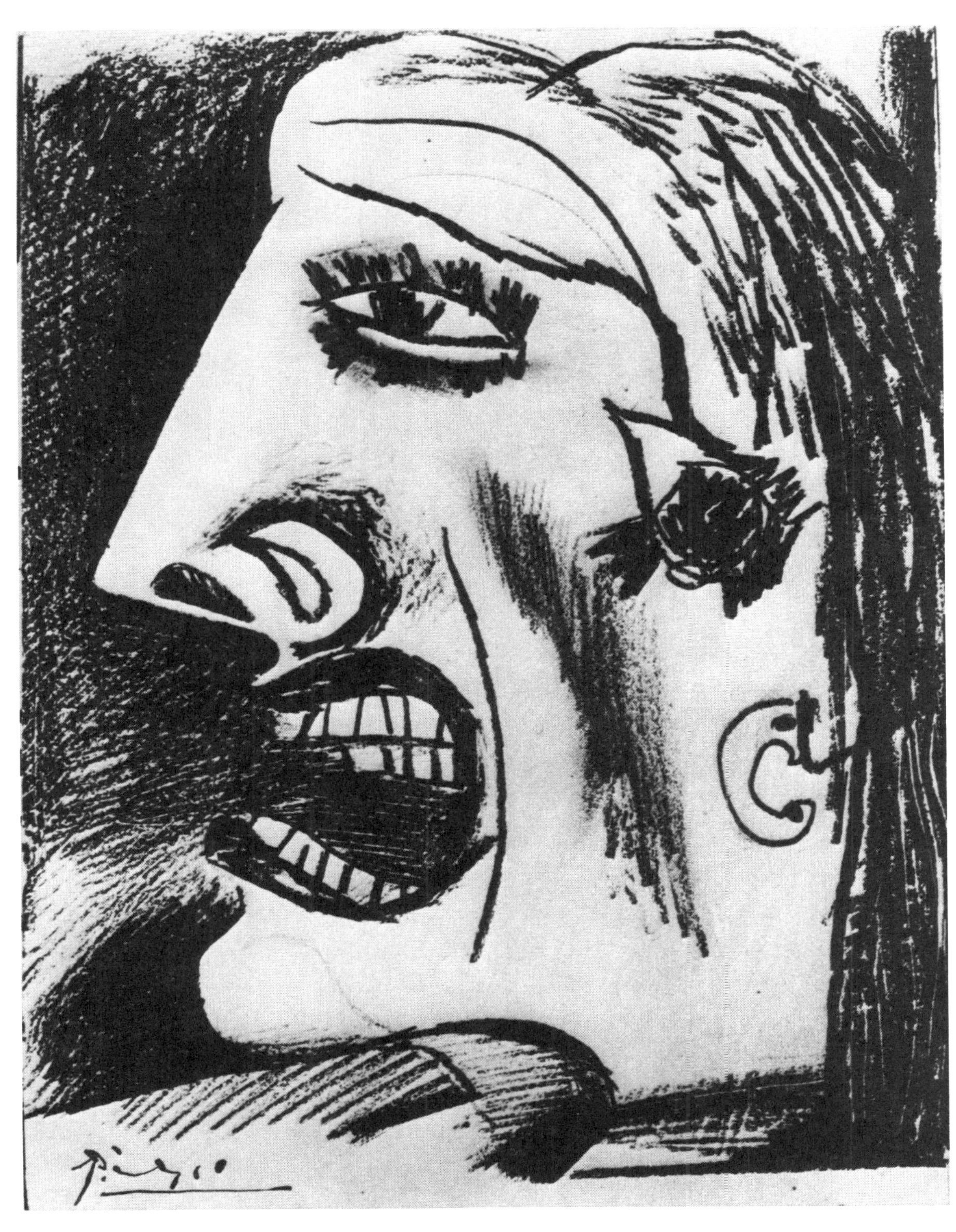

35
WOMAN HOWLING IN PAIN
pencil 29.3×21.2
private collection, Lucerne

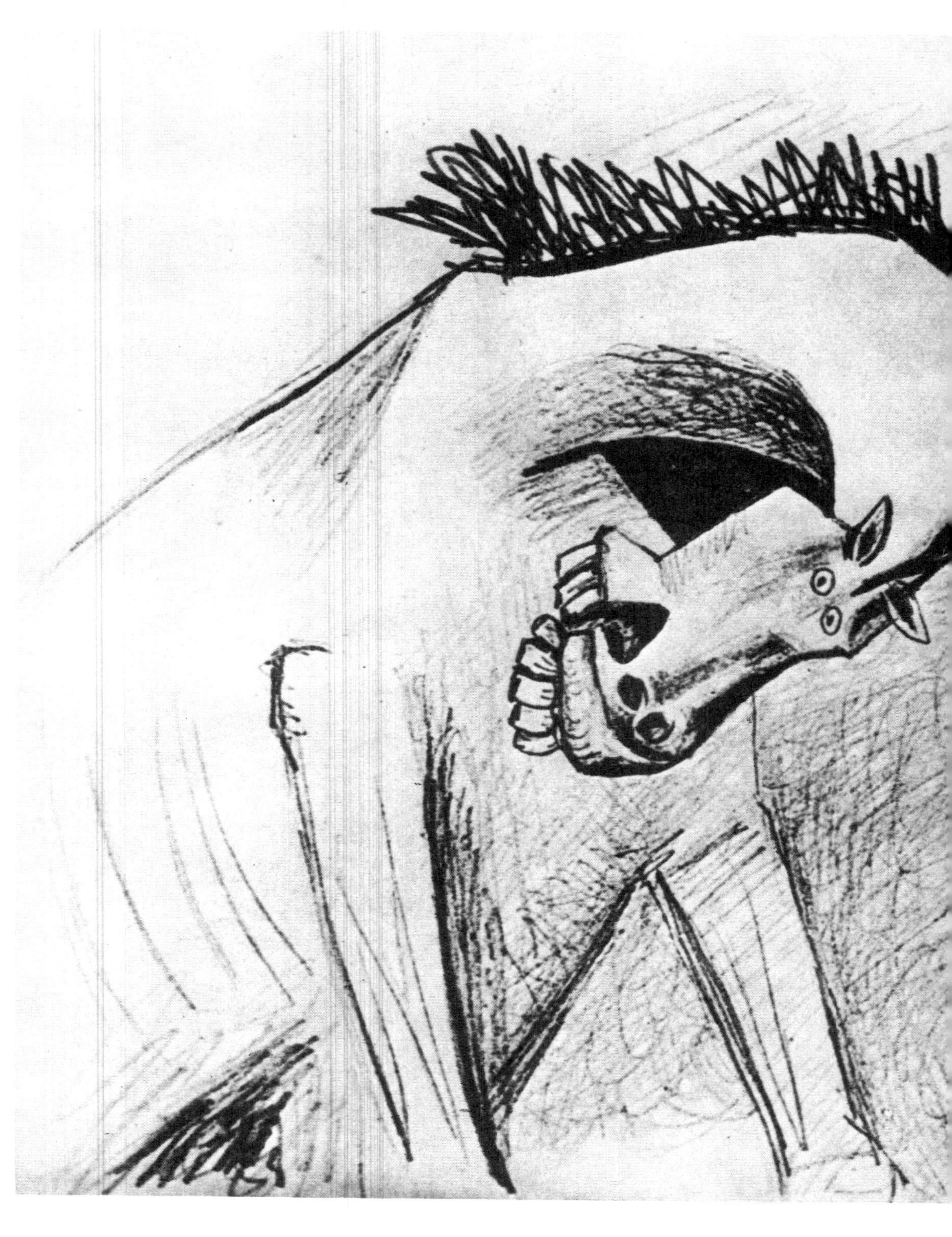

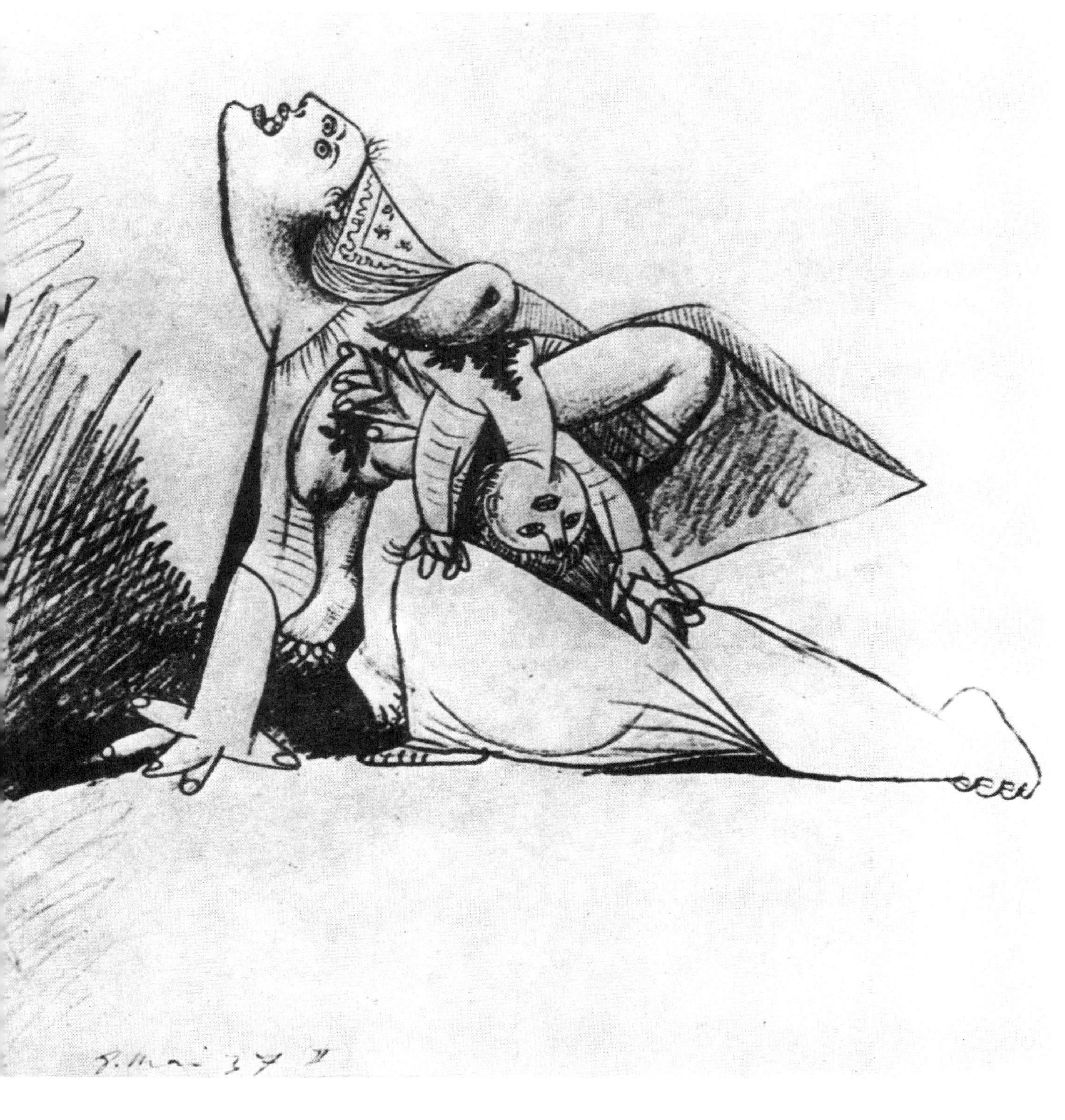

36
STUDY FOR GUERNICA
pencil 24×45
Paris 8 May 1937

years, Dora Maar would be remembered in the history of art chiefly for her tears, though also for a few tender images that Picasso left of her.

In this brief study of the drawings that denounced the horrors of the civil war, its violence and the suffering of its victims, the subject itself has so dominated the discussion that the aesthetic aspects of the work have been all but forgotten. That is a measure of the power of Picasso's style.

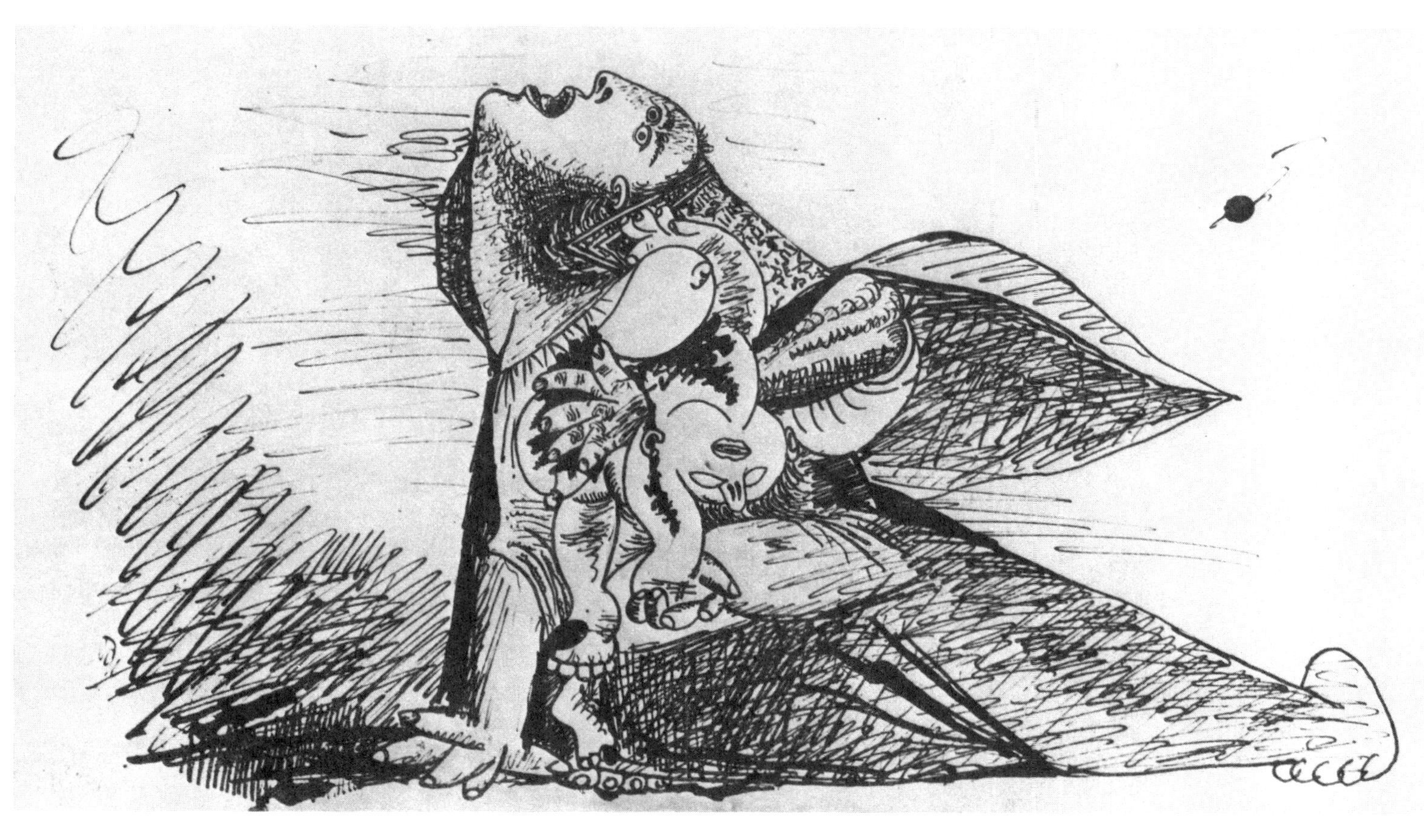

37
STUDY FOR GUERNICA
Indian ink 24×45
Paris 9 May 1937

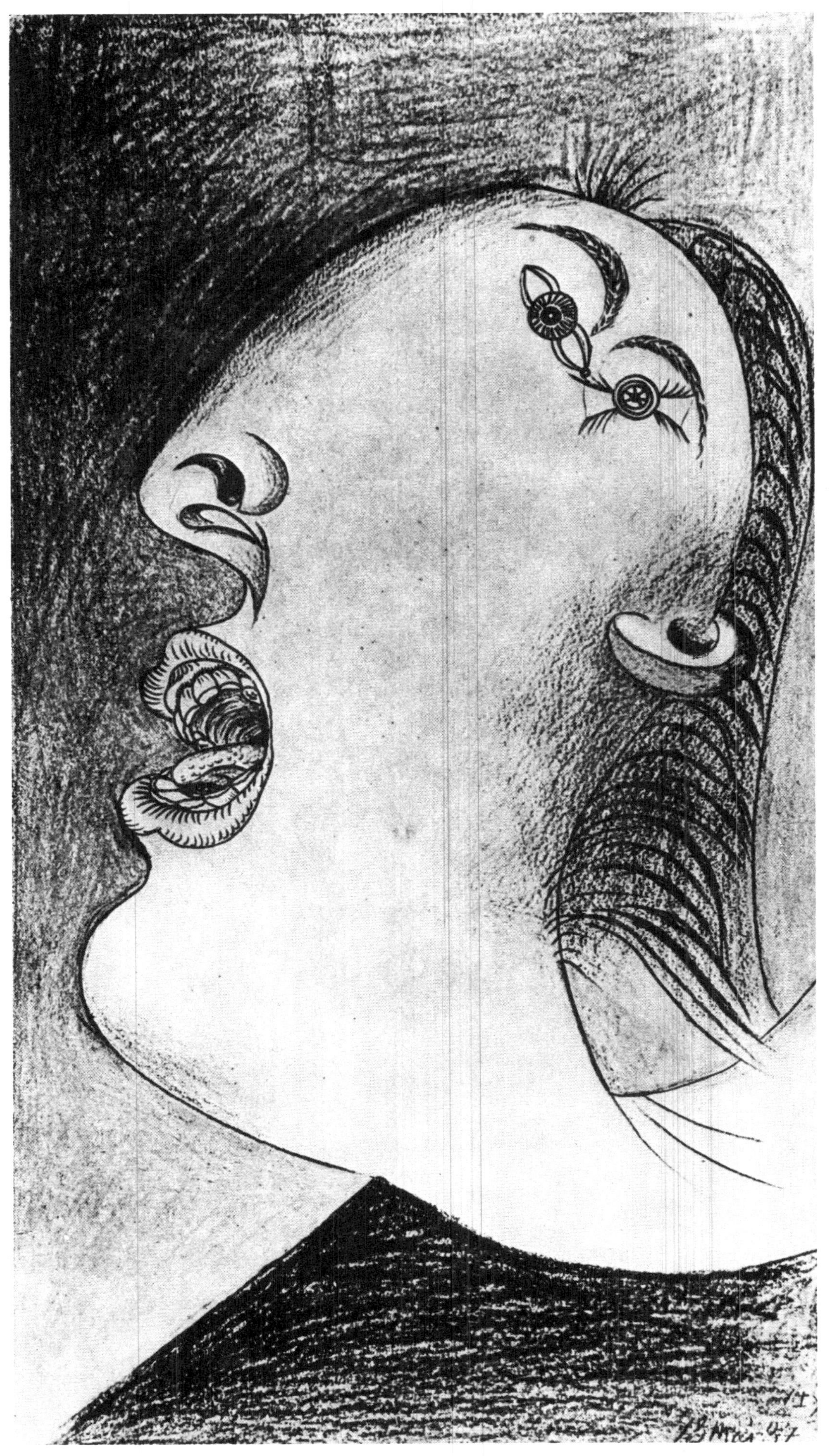

38
STUDY FOR GUERNICA
black and coloured pencil
45×24
Paris 13 May 1937

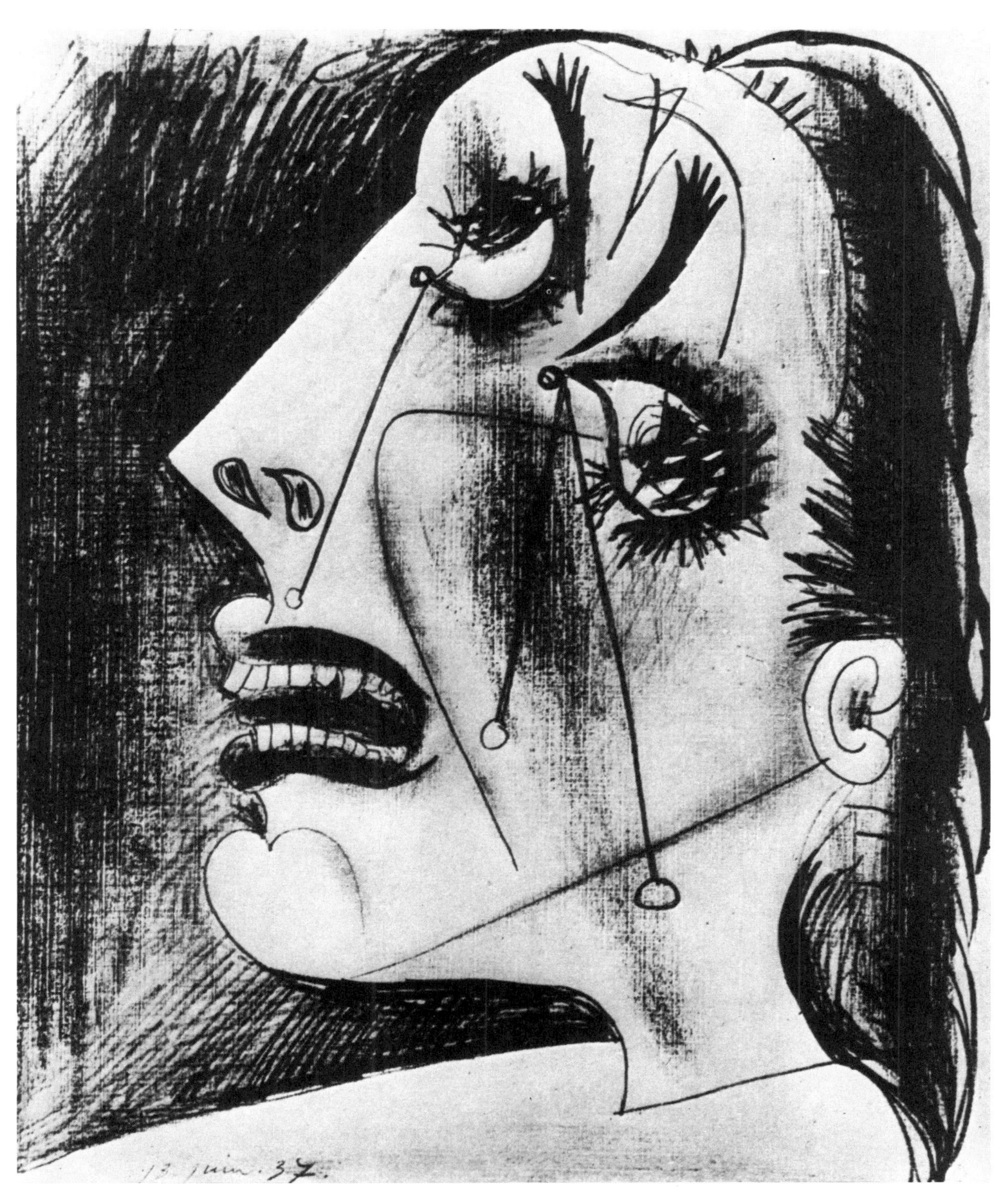

39
STUDY FOR GUERNICA
black and coloured pencil and gouache on tracing linen
Paris 13 June 1937
Prado Museum, Madrid

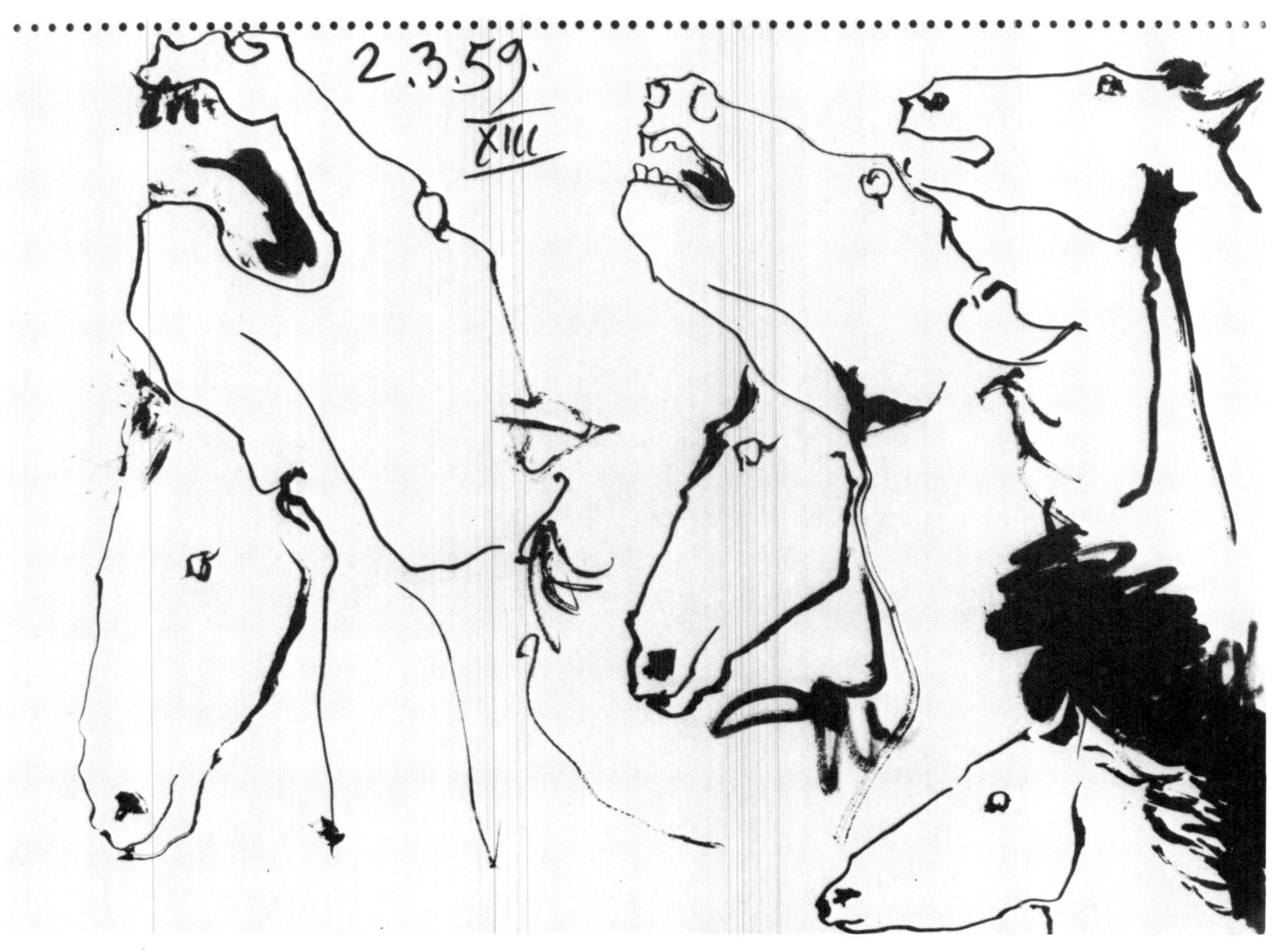

40
STUDIES, TOROS Y TOREROS
2 March 1959

VII

AFTER THE CIVIL WAR

Scientists are undoubtedly notorious for their habit of cutting time up into thinner and thinner slices. Their only rivals in this respect are historians with their mania for compartmentalising events in periods, reigns, centuries, dynasties, and so on.

Art historians are no exception in their steadfast belief that in order to understand, you must have chronological compartments and categories. Otherwise the problem becomes unmanageable.

But what *is* the problem? What is the problem with Picasso? All one needs to do is just look at his work, to follow one's own pleasure and fantasy, especially where the drawings of the last important creative period are concerned. Out with Blue and Rose, out with strict Cubism, out with neo-classicism! It is impossible to hem Picasso in with classifications of style: he had them all, he forgot them and he used them without even thinking about it.

Far more important than a division into periods is the fact that the painter lives in continuous time and for him at least all that matter are the preoccupations of the moment. It could as well be the joys of fatherhood, when he painted Claude and Paloma, the horrors of war or, happily, lighter subjects such as women and love, and over and over again the corrida!

Unfortunately, like all of us, Picasso often had cause to worry about the future of mankind. The Antibes period, of the *Joie de vivre,* of fauns and satyrs dancing with nymphs in a Mediterranean light recalling that Antibes was once the Hellenic city of Antipolis, was well and truly over. But the *Flower-Woman* would linger yet a while surrounded by children to brighten the gardens of Antibes.

Picasso told Claude Roy that an artist's work is like a thermometer and it is true that even when he did not expressly show the object of his horror in his painting, Picasso could not hide his distress. Every time a cat makes an appearance, it is pretty easy to guess that something serious was going on in the world at the time, especially if the cat had a fish in its mouth!

Thus, not only his drawings, but the whole of his work is to a certain extent like an illustrated diary.

His dream of peace: an allegory. *The Man Carrying a Sheep* was conceived far earlier than the actual sculpture which has made the town hall square in Vallauris famous. As early as August 1942, with a world war raging, he had made a sketch of it, a very pure drawing in pen and Indian ink. And those bearded shepherds' faces were to recur often later, incarnating the peace of a simple natural life.

It is in the light of this inspiration that his contribution to the chapel in Vallauris should be seen. It follows in the line of *Guernica* (1937), the *Charnel House* (1945), *Night Fishing at Antibes* (1951), *Homage to the Spaniards who Died for France* (1946), *Massacre in Korea* (1951). There is also *The Fall of Icarus* (1958) which is in the hall of the conference chamber of the UNESCO building in Paris.

Picasso did not like monuments; for his grandeur was not a matter of dimensions. But under the pressure of events he would undertake anything, including the transformation of a deconsecrated chapel into a Temple of Peace. He owed a debt of thanks to the town of Vallauris where he had worked for many years and become an honorary citizen. He ensured the prosperity of all its little ceramic workshops by attracting a great influx of tourists. But perhaps he was also thinking about his friends and contemporaries who already had 'their' church, like Fernand Léger at Assy, or Matisse with the chapel of the Dominican convent at Vence. He was not moved by envy or rivalry, but probably by a desire to put himself to the test.

41
MAN CARRYING A SHEEP
Indian ink 68×44
20 August 1942

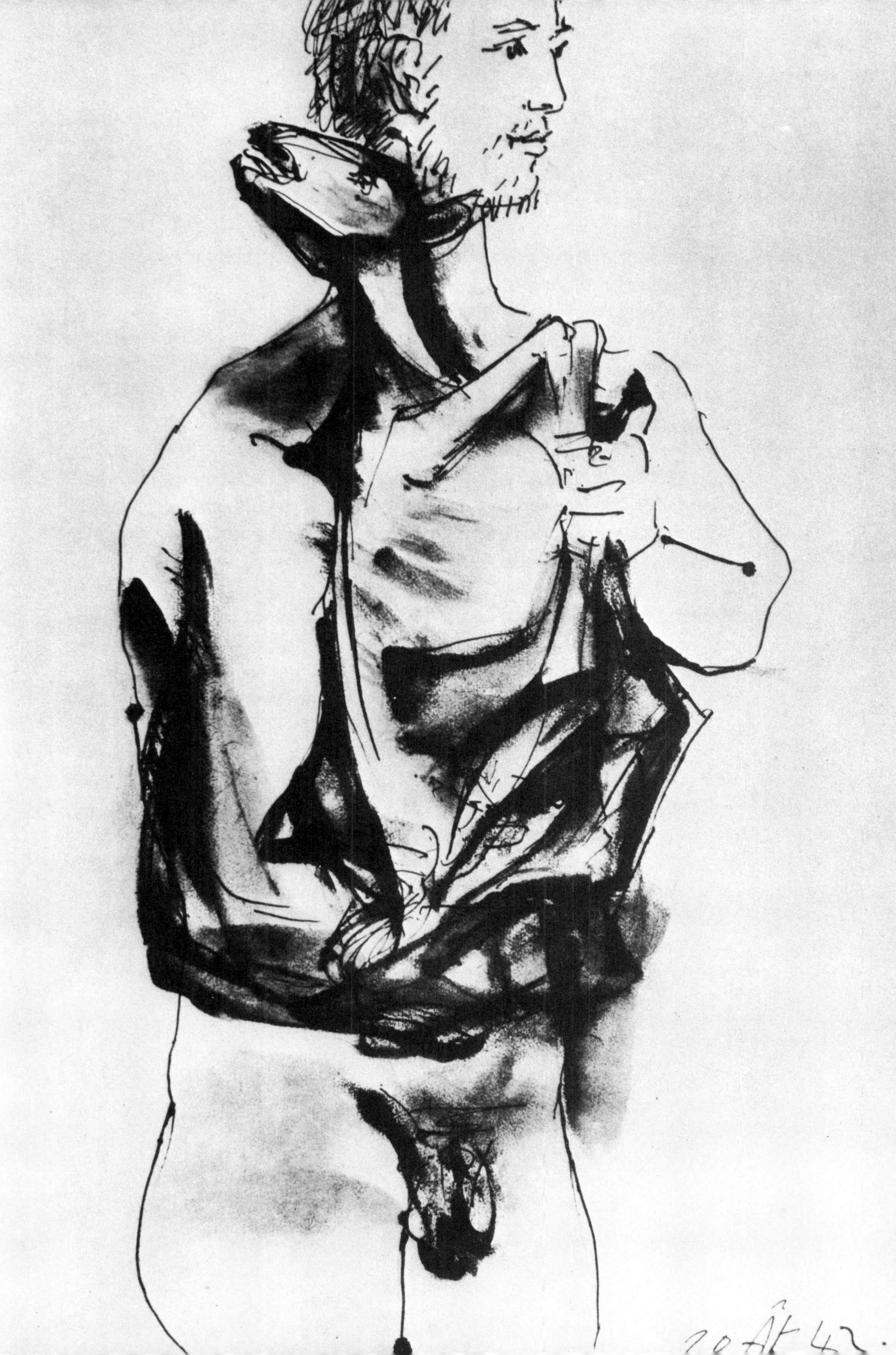

The Temple of Peace was to be a long hard labour which was to take up virtually all his time for a period of several months, as his preparatory drawings bear witness. The body of the chapel was long and vaulted. Picasso decided that there would be on the one side peace, and on the other war.

He began his work on the theme of war. Of course, war is a more obvious subject. After all, no one talks about peace except under threat of war! The imagery of war is imprinted on our minds: fallen bodies, blood, engines of destruction, brandished weapons. Picasso opposed war and the forces of evil with the pacifist who represents the forces of good. He imagined a terrible engine of war, half tank, half monster, spitting fire. Opposite, a bearded shepherd protects a dove behind a shield which has a woman's face, the face of peace, and holds a sword above his head.

Many studies testify to Picasso's interest in that tank, though it was finally replaced by a hearse.

For Picasso, the quiet space at the bottom of a courtyard was to become a kind of moral testament. He raged against anyone who disturbed him and said that it brought him close to despair: 'It is not true that the most beautiful songs are songs of despair. And anyway, even if it were true, the people who sing them need to be calm and not desperate while they are writing desperate songs. The Greek tragedians were surely peaceful men in their calm and comfortable offices with neon lighting . . . '

The creative artist's need of solitude leads to irritability at times of creative intensity.

It was not by any manner of means a question of reassembling old figures into a new order so as to fit the available space, but of making something completely new, of calling up once again all the innovative power of his youth. *War and Peace* was to be, for Picasso, as important

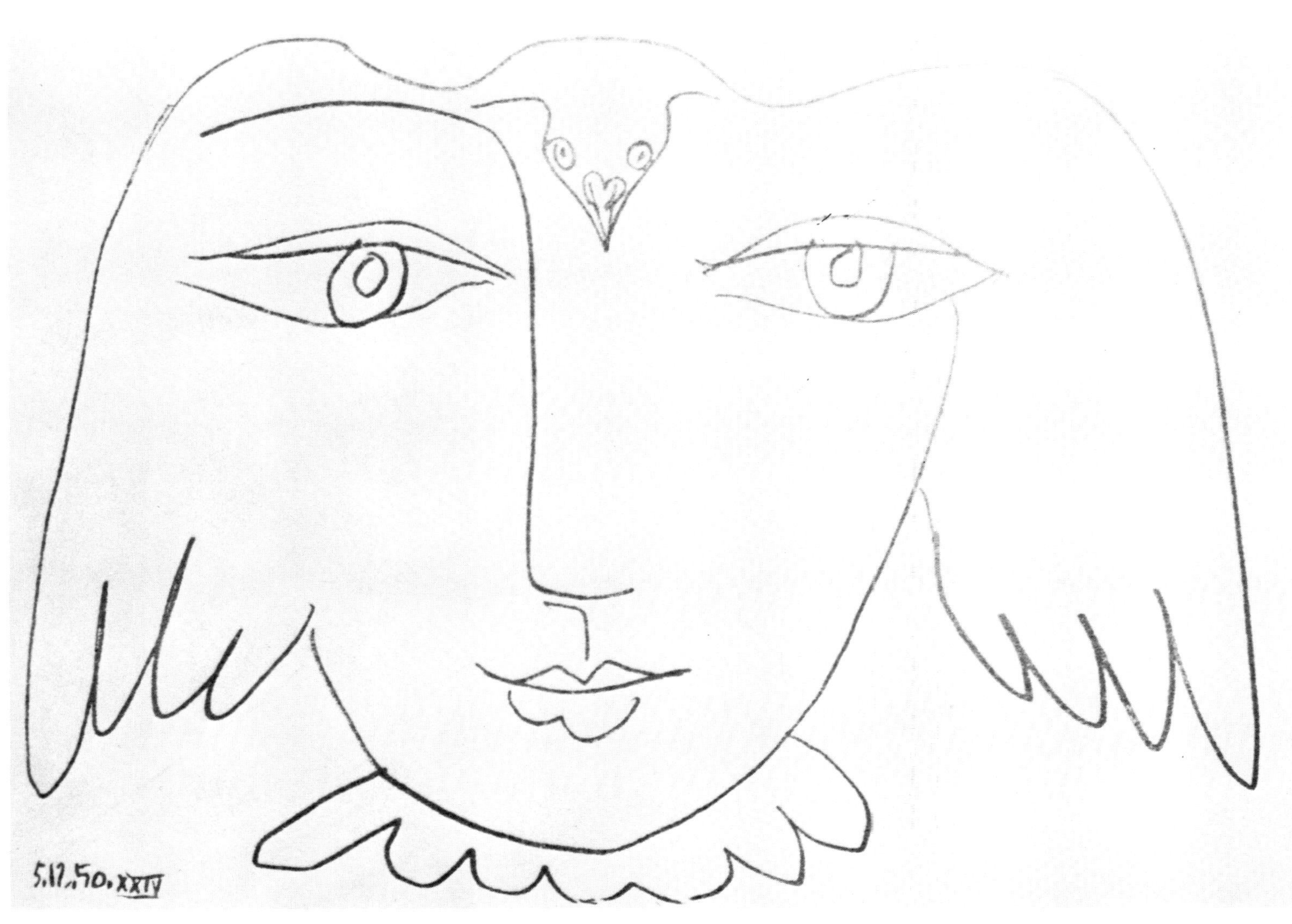

42
THE FACE OF PEACE
Indian ink on Ingres paper 51×66
5.12.50 XXIV

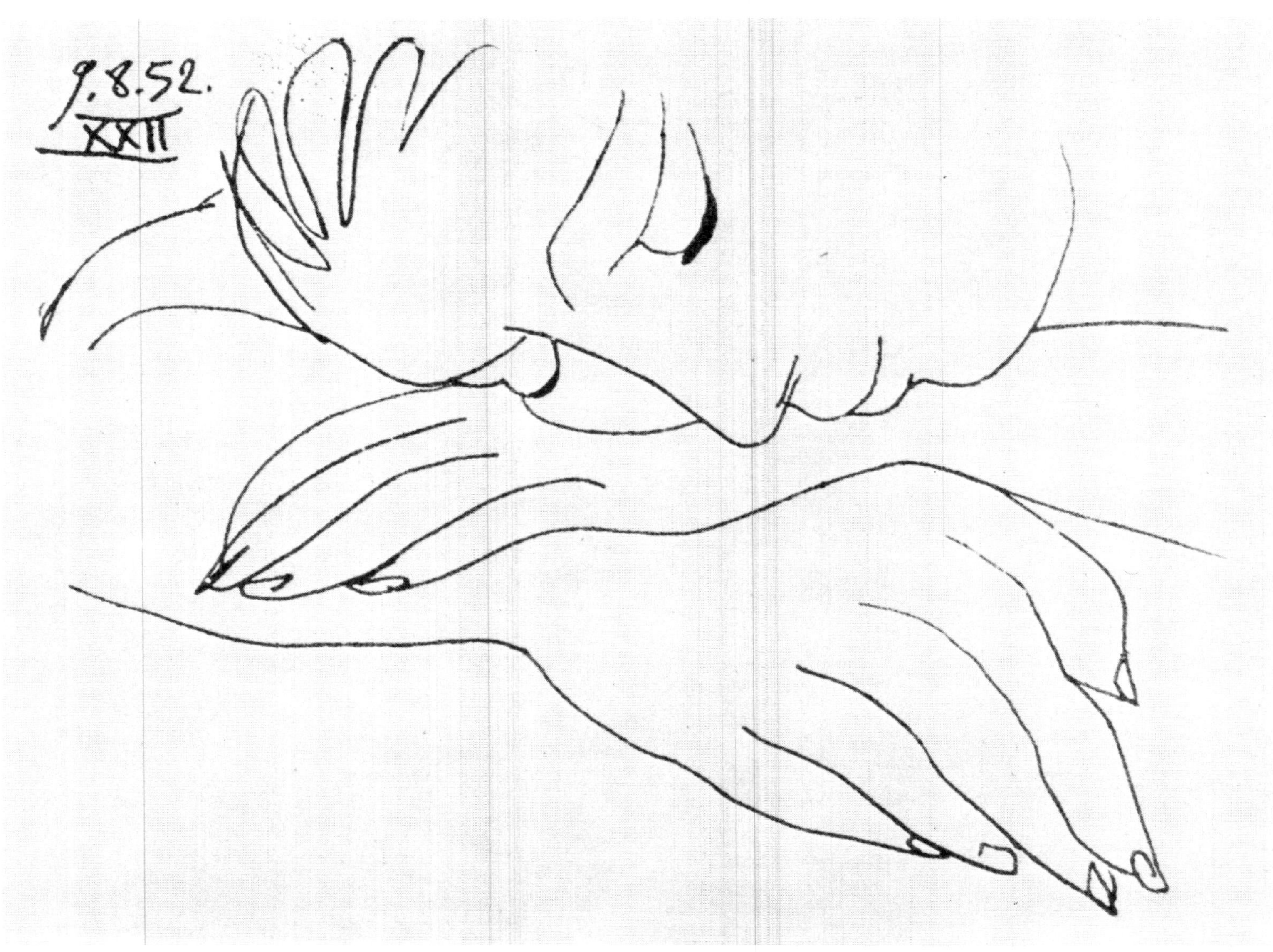

43
WAR AND PEACE
Indian ink on Ingres paper 51×66
9.8.52 XXII

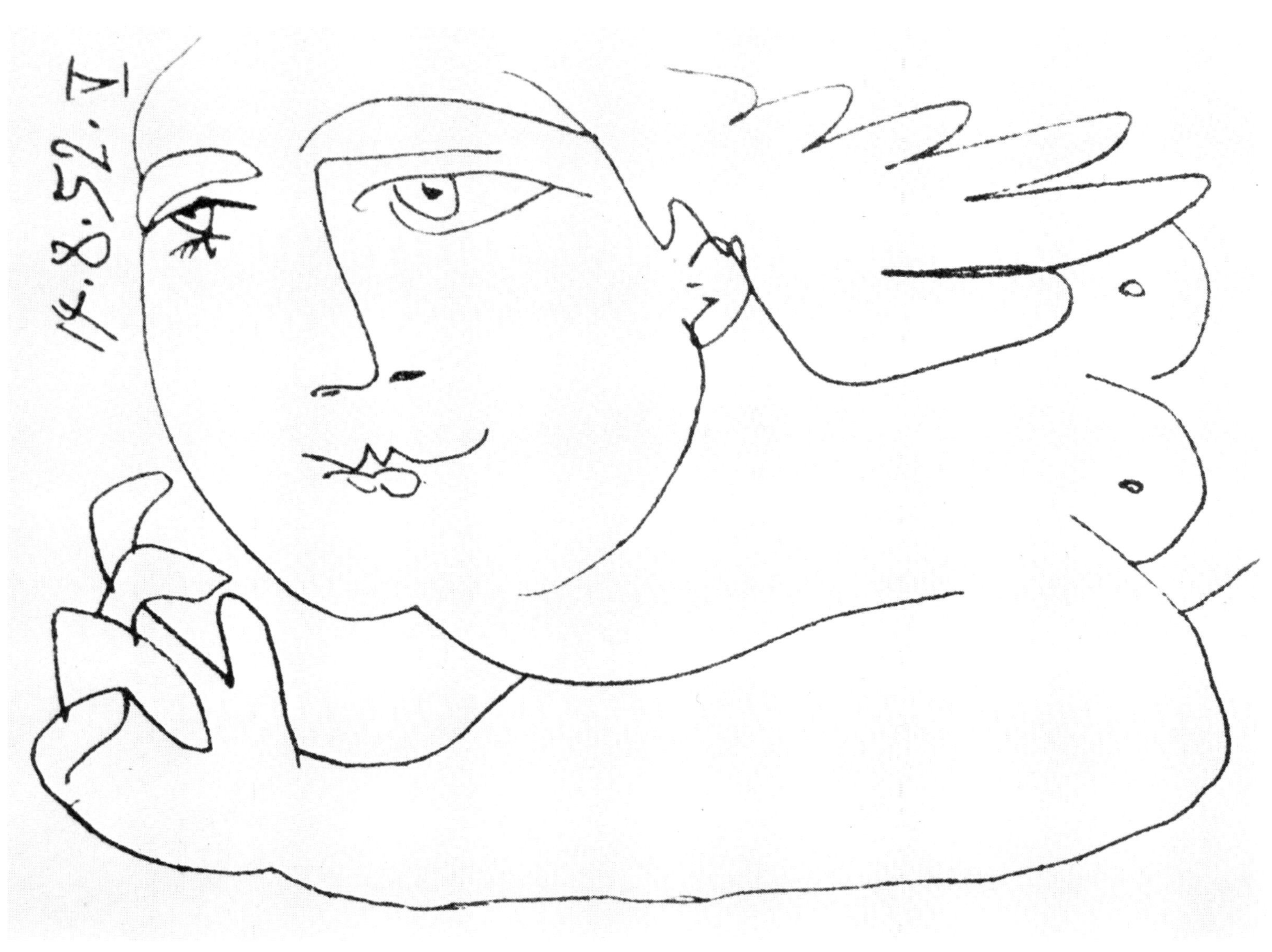

44
WAR AND PEACE
Indian ink on Ingres paper 51×66
14.8.52 V

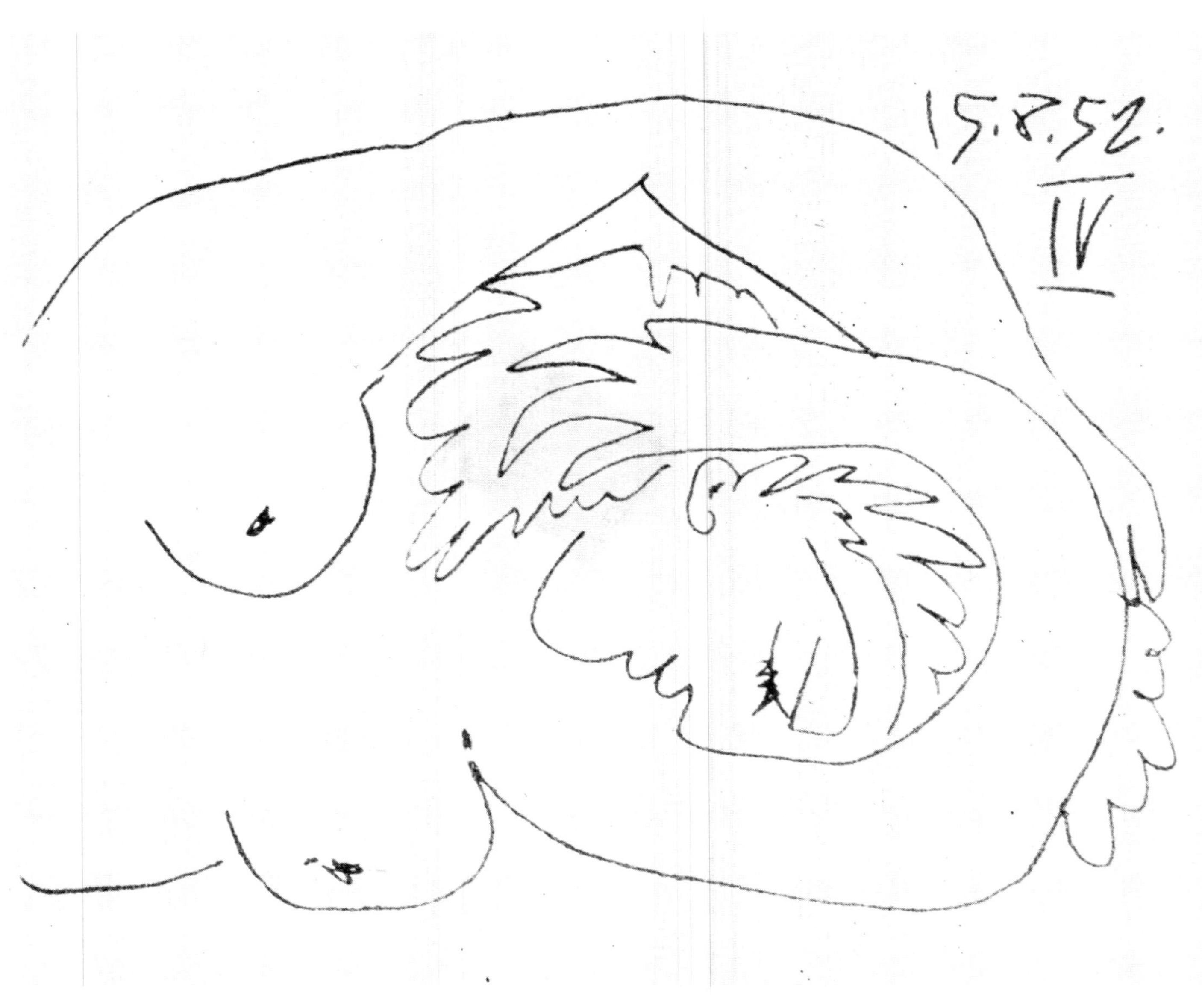

45
WAR AND PEACE
Indian ink on Ingres paper 51×66
15.8.52 IV

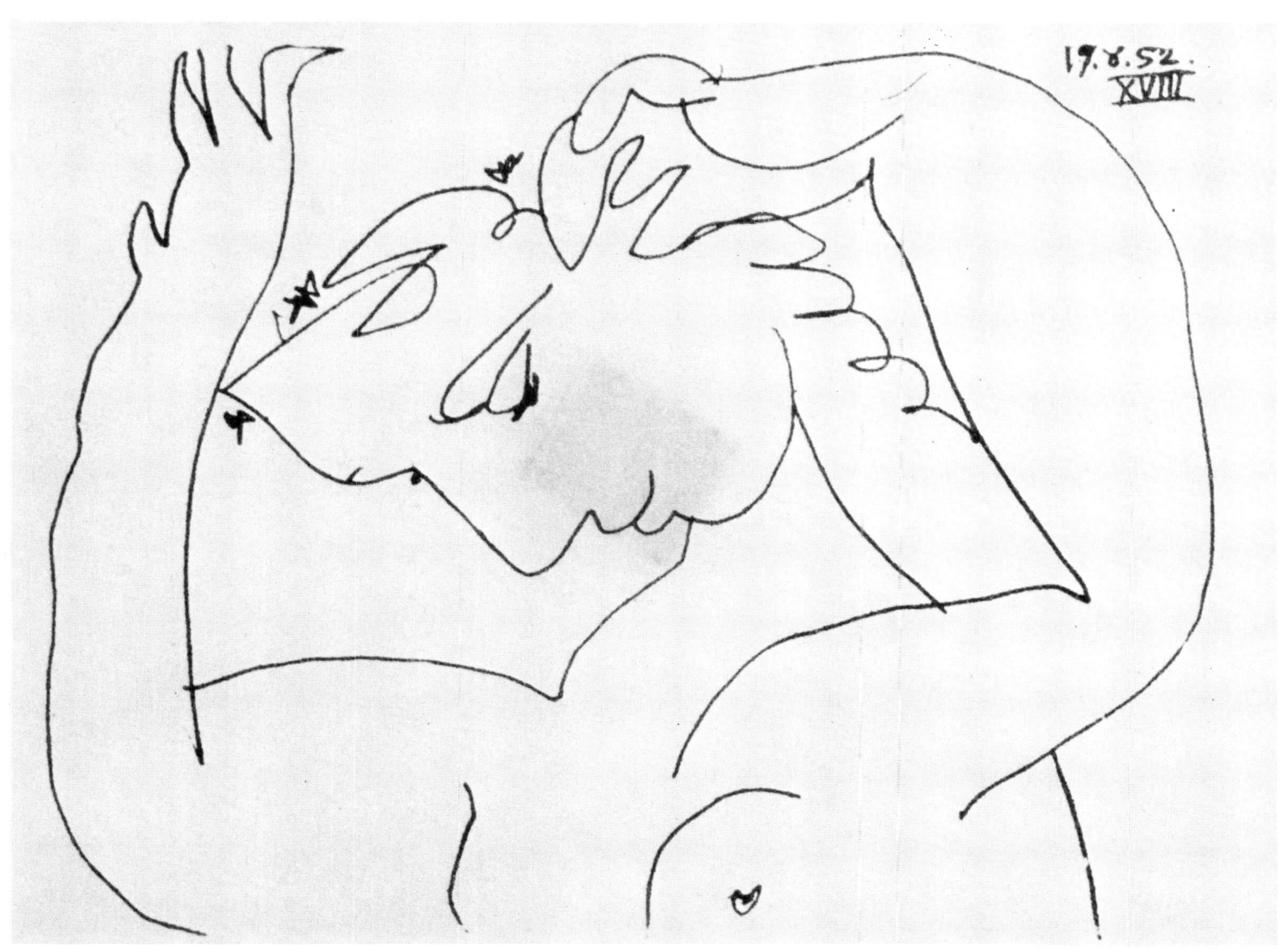

46
WAR AND PEACE
Indian ink on Ingres paper 51×66
19.8.52 XVIII

a commitment as *Guernica* and Claude Roy, who followed him through this period of his life, noted that *Guernica* and *War and Peace* are explosions detonated by the (apparent) means of painting . . . It is naive to say: the reality of our time, the bombings, napalm, the atom bomb, is hideously dislocated, so Picasso painted hideously dislocated figures.

'Neither *Guernica* nor *War and Peace* is a description of a battlefield, a town in ruins, an atom-bombed house . . . They are creations that are more eloquent than the best photos of the most daring reporters. This is the prestige of art and its privilege, to say more with less and to create a scandal.'

Peace is a dream constantly sought after, never attained. It is an earthly paradise that Picasso imagined. So he abandoned the half-panzer, half-humanoid tank that he had drawn so often and drew on the wall a sort of rustic hearse surmounted by a horned devil holding a bloodstained sword, not the owl or the bird of prey for which he had done many studies. The hearse is drawn by three black horses, ready to take you all the way to hell. Behind the hearse are the black silhouettes of warriors brandishing white weapons, halberds, axes and others. The horses are trampling burning books.

Everything here is symbol and allegory. Picasso did not show us war but what it signifies, and above all the stupidity of the use of force, the foolishness of those who use it.

In the face of this surging hatred, a naked man stands alone. He is not holding a threatening sword, as in previous studies, but a lance and scales, the symbol of justice. The dove that he was protecting behind his shield has become its ornament.

Thus, quiet strength seems capable of putting an end to violence and ignorance.

The man who embodies the forces of good was initially portrayed

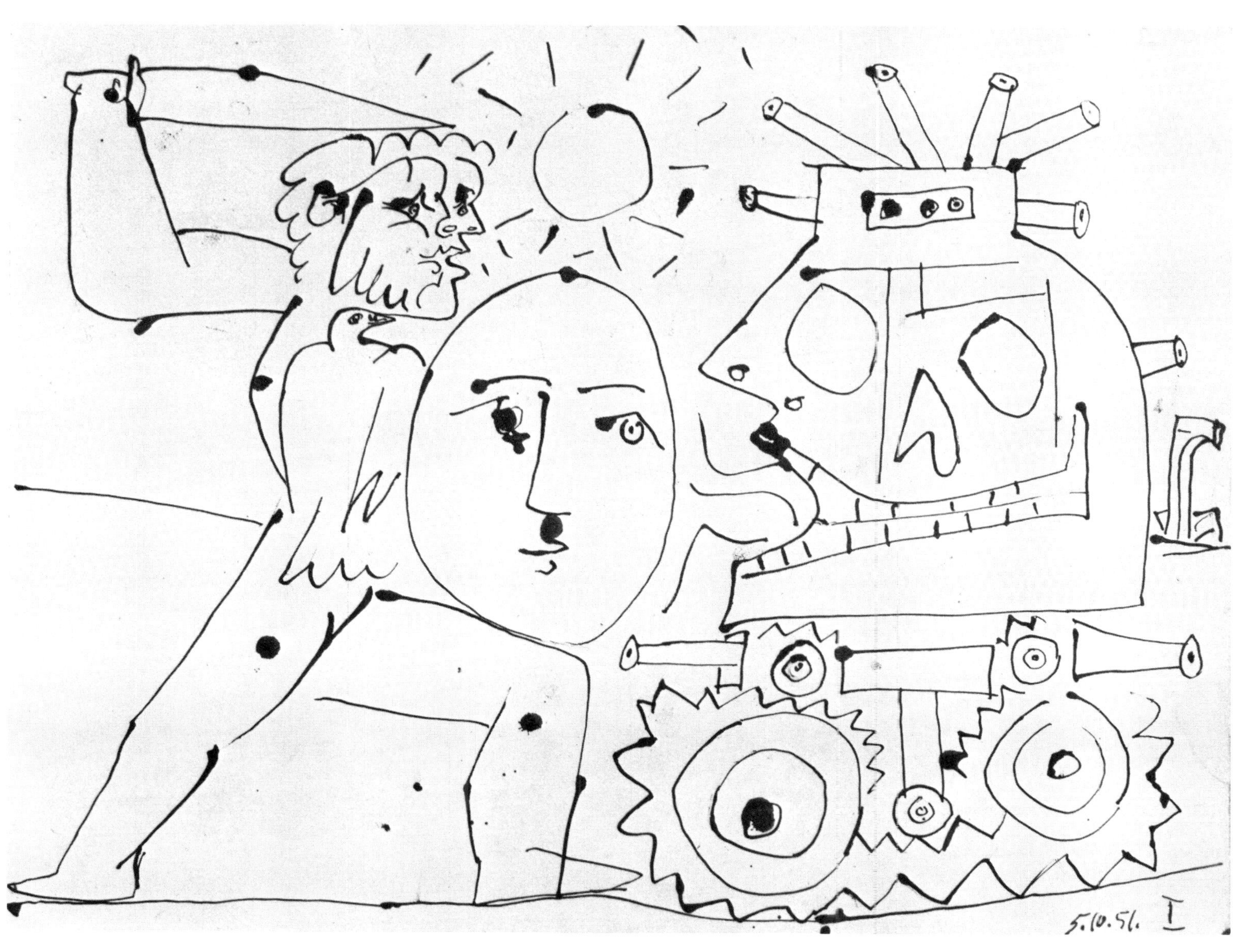

47
WAR AND PEACE
Indian ink on Ingres paper 51×66
5.10.51 I

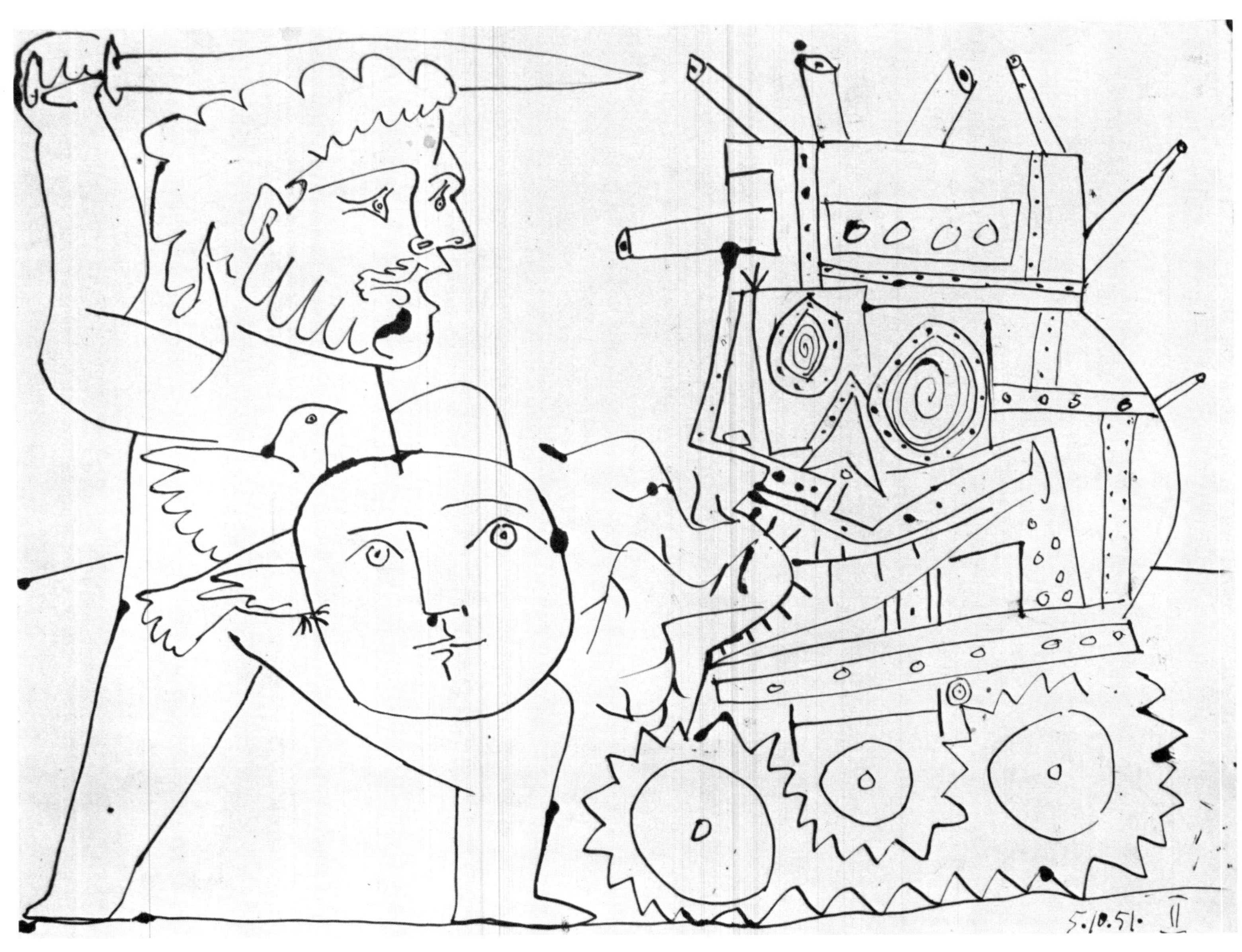

48
WAR AND PEACE
Indian ink on Ingres paper 51×66
5.10.51 II

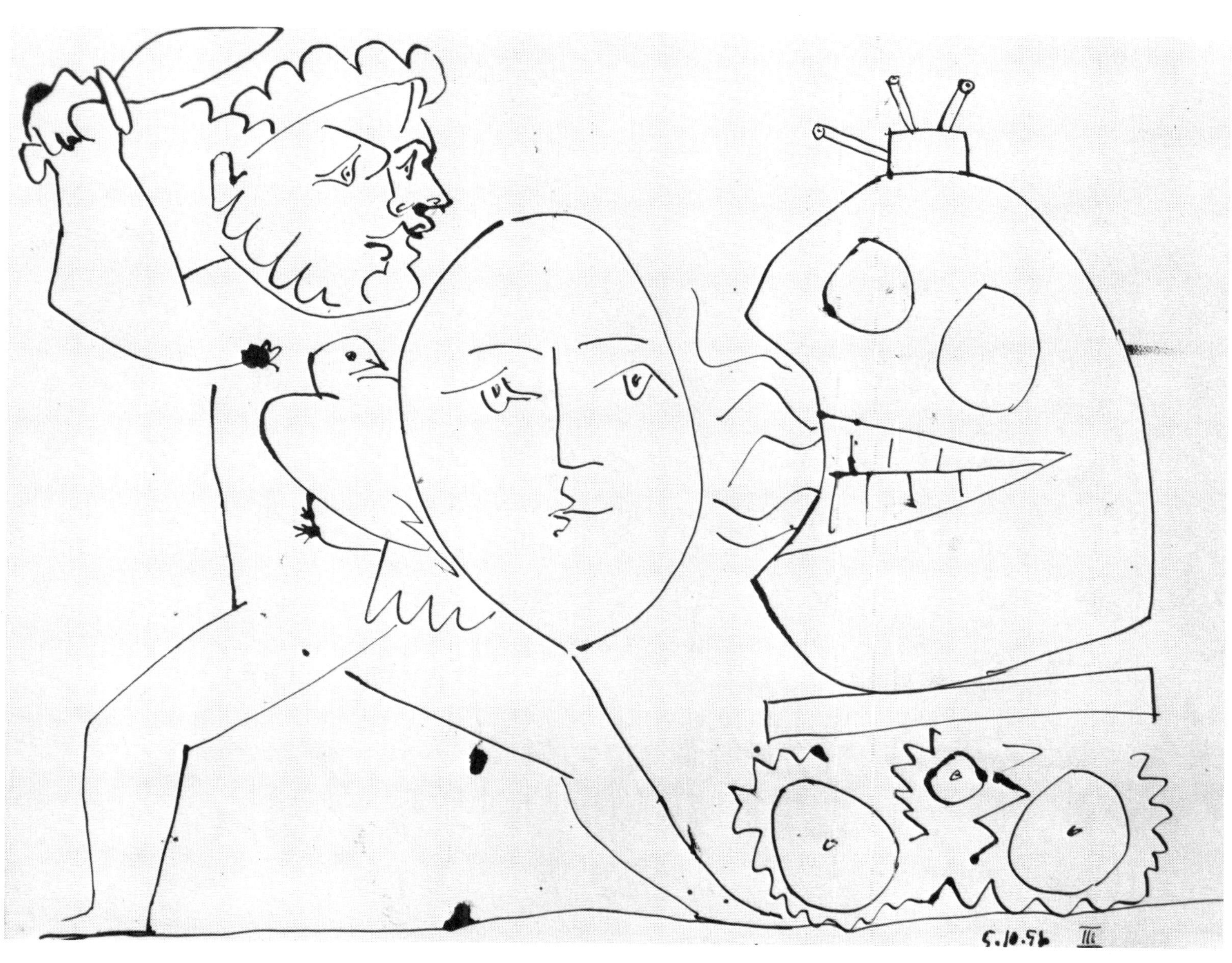

49
WAR AND PEACE
Indian ink on Ingres paper 51×66
5.10.51 III

with the face of the bearded shepherd, as we show here. Picasso eventually stripped him of all his clothes and accoutrements, even his beard.

While he was deep in these studies, Picasso occasionally relaxed by covering the pages of a sketchbook with silhouette profiles in Indian ink which one can guess to be of Françoise Gilot, alone or hugging a very young child. Extreme simplicity together with sincere emotion make this silhouette a poignant testimony and a counterpoint to the more ambitious humanitarian work.

All these sketches are dated 4 September 1952. A month earlier, towards the middle of August, Picasso was already painting pictures of happiness in the form of a young woman, lightly sleeping, brushing her hair, and with her hair turning into wings, another image for peace and one that he would make use of in engravings and lithographs, though it was not to be included in the final version of *Peace* either. Picasso preferred a Pegasus as ploughman, led by a child and women dancing, as in the 1946 *Antibes Bacchanal*, to the sound of a flute played by a faun. At the extreme right are three figures. One is reading, one is suckling a baby, the third is cooking, all activities pursued by people happy and at peace, under a multicoloured sun like a flag with no nationality.

The chapel of Vallauris in its great generosity preserves the peaceful gentleness of the first sketches and one is led to ask whether there is not as much emotion in each of the drawings, which only prefigure a *part* of the total work, as in the whole. *Peace* here is perhaps even more confident of its lasting existence, motherhood more confident in the future of generations to come, while the lone man standing against the forces of evil knows that he will triumph because he has right and all men of good will on his side. This interpretation is undoubtedly a simplistic one but it is nevertheless credible, and the emotional

I
SMOKER
pencil and coloured chalk
16.5.64 IV

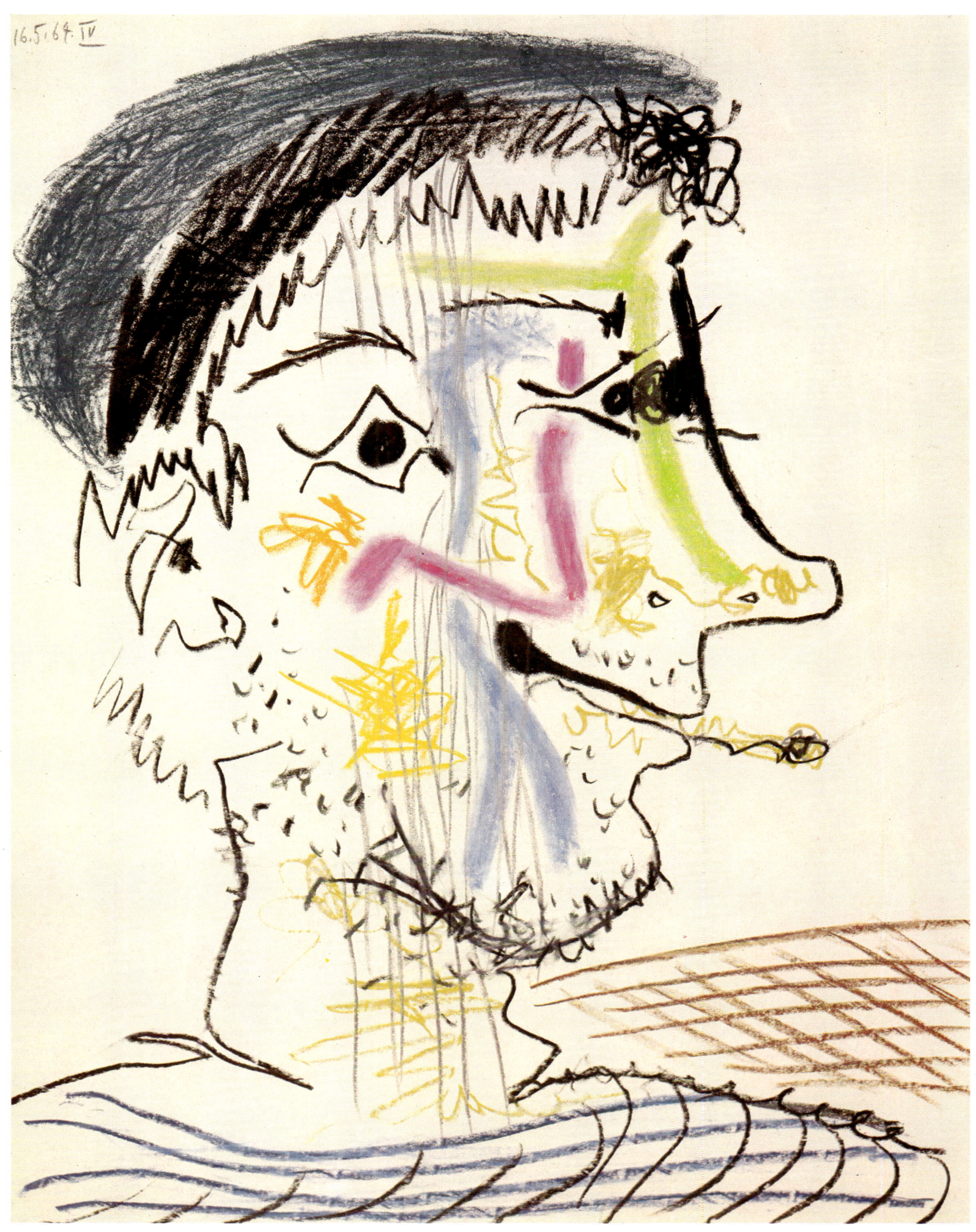
16.5.64. IV

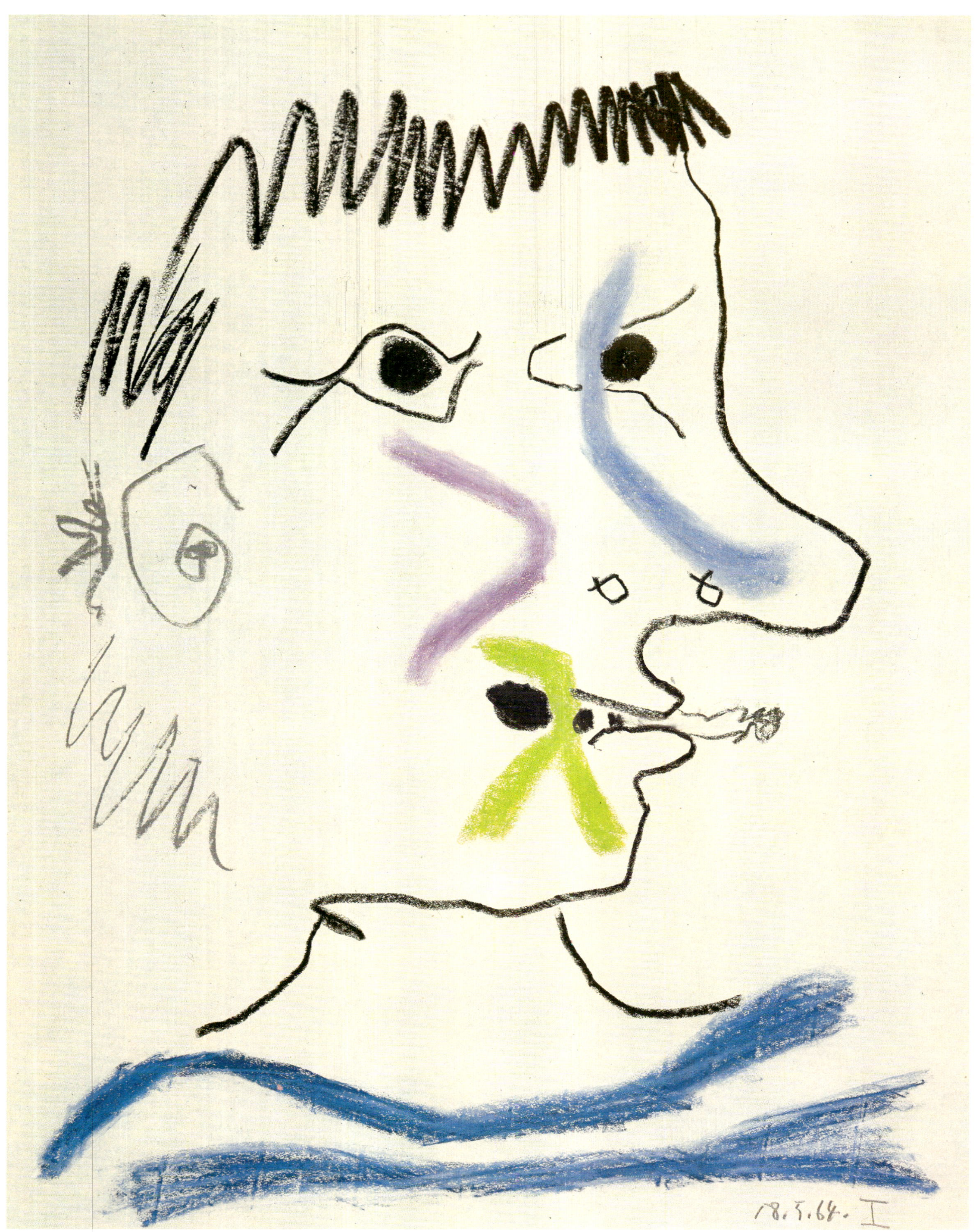
18.5.64. I

reaction to viewing these studies is less powerful but no less deep than that inspired by the life-sized brightly coloured figures in the Temple of Peace.

Its message speaks to everyone. Claude Roy relates that a child was asked: 'What is Picasso talking about?' 'About war,' the child replied. 'And what does he say about it?' 'He's against it!'

II
SMOKER
pencil and coloured chalk
18.5.64 I

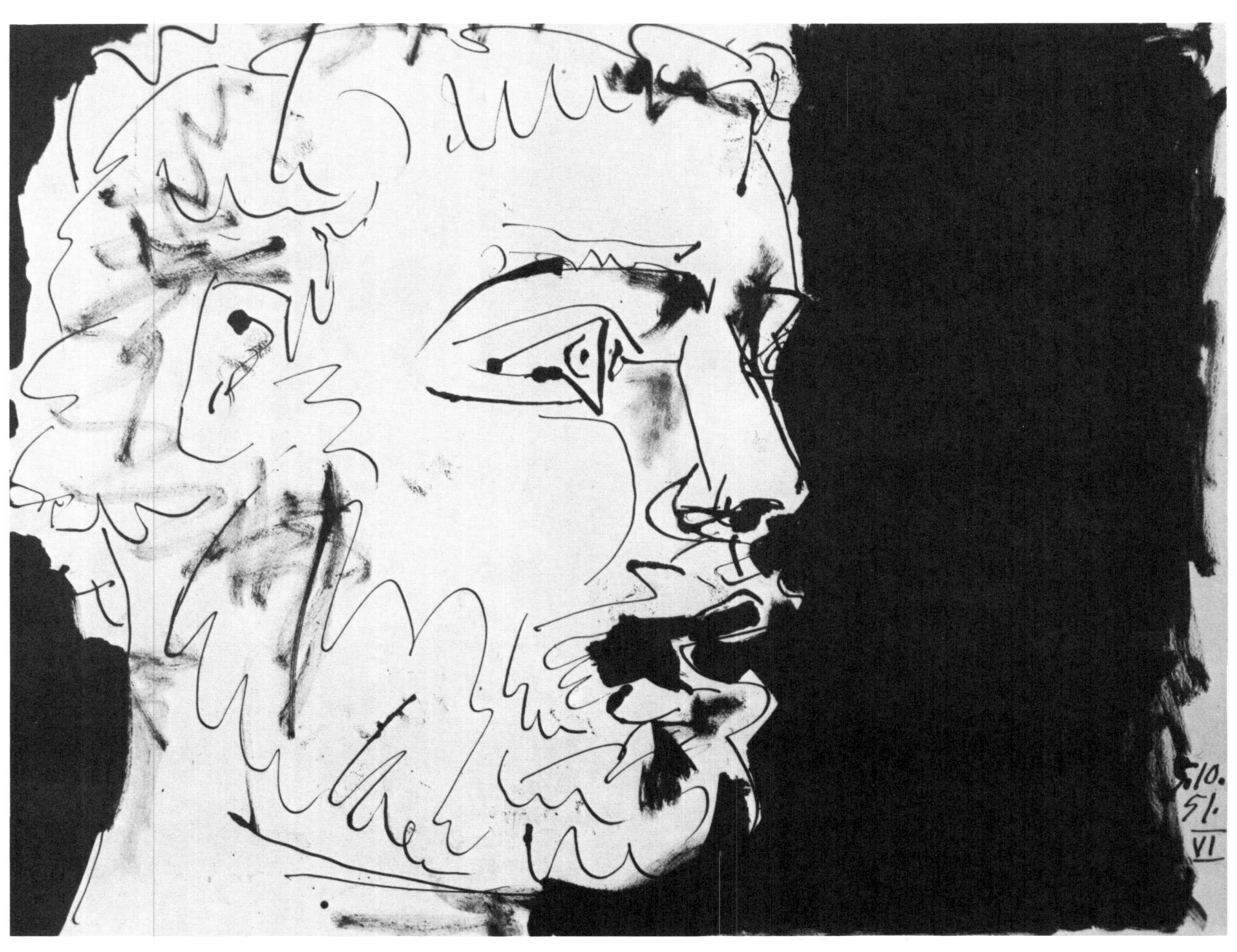

50
WAR AND PEACE
Indian ink on Ingres paper 51×66
5.10.51 VI

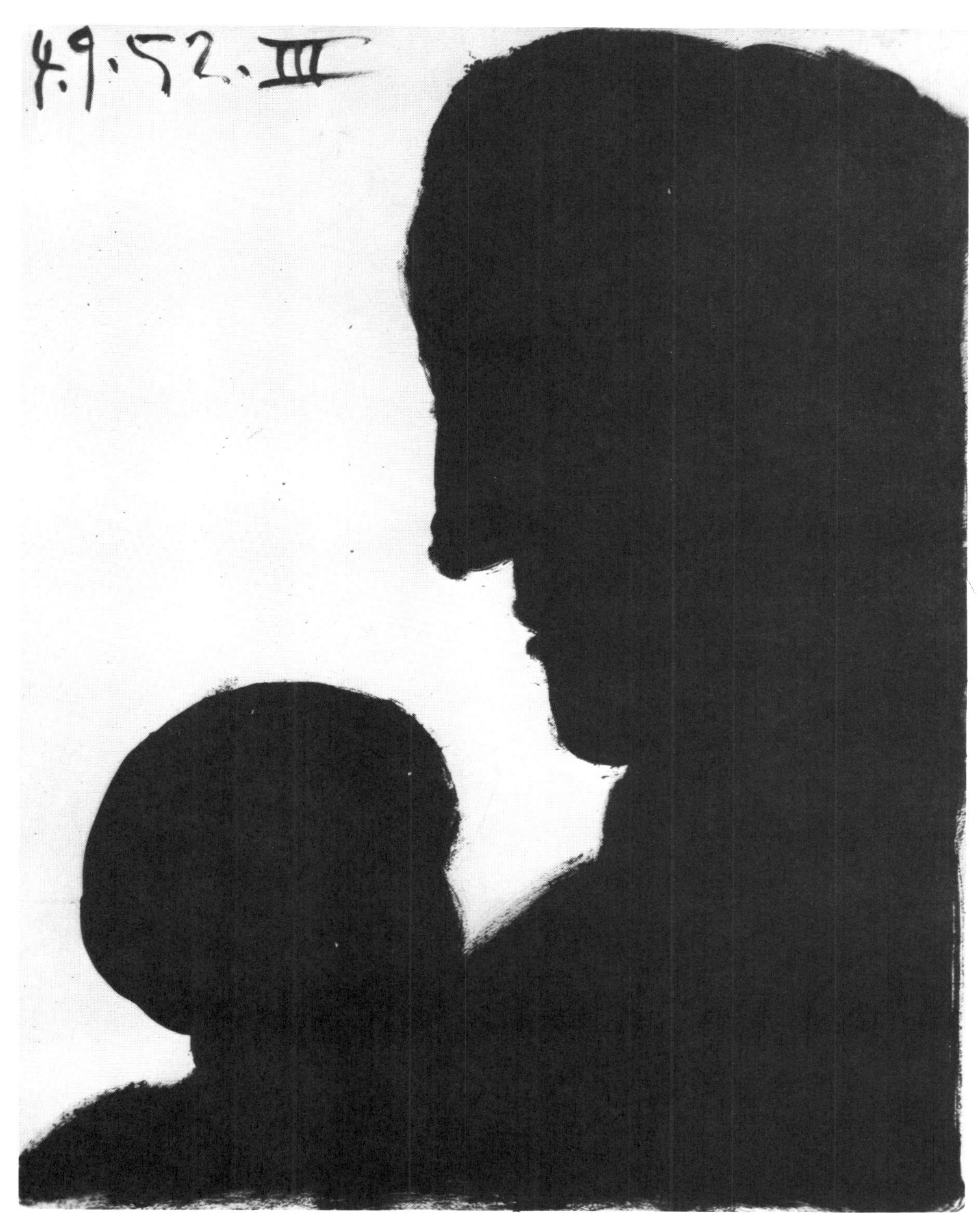

51
MOTHERHOOD
study on Ingres paper 51×66
4.9.52 III

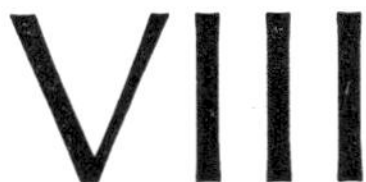

VIII

THE LAST PERIOD

During the last ten years of his life, Picasso continued to work with as much passion and perhaps even more tenacity than ever. He practised every technique — painting, etching and, of course, drawing. This last period presents a relative unity, but it is not distinguished from previous periods by a new style nor by original themes. It represents greater depth, more variations and some unexpected daring.

A study of this period is greatly facilitated by three particularly important celebrations of Picasso's work: the two exhibitions at the Palais des Papes in Avignon in 1970 and in 1973 (after the painter's death) organised by Jean Vilar, and the more recent one 'The Last Years, 1963–1973', at the Guggenheim Museum, conceived and mounted by Gert Schiff for the Grey Art Gallery and Study Center, which is part of New York University. We shall refer to them often since we are indebted to them on many counts.

The works recently received by the French state in settlement of inheritance tax, presented to the Grand Palais in 1979 and on display at the Picasso Museum since 1985, contained some revelations. They numbered two hundred drawings, twelve sketchbooks ranging from 1905 to 1963, one of which contains the first studies inspired by Manet's *Le Déjeuner sur l'herbe*, and in addition sixty-nine engravings or etchings which are now on view and complete our knowledge of his graphic work.

There are also fond memories of the annual exhibitions at the Galerie Louise Leiris where the latest arrivals from La Californie or Notre-Dame-de-Vie were unveiled.

There, with his old friend and art-dealer Daniel Kahnweiler, one would meet all the old faithfuls, art lovers and dealers from England,

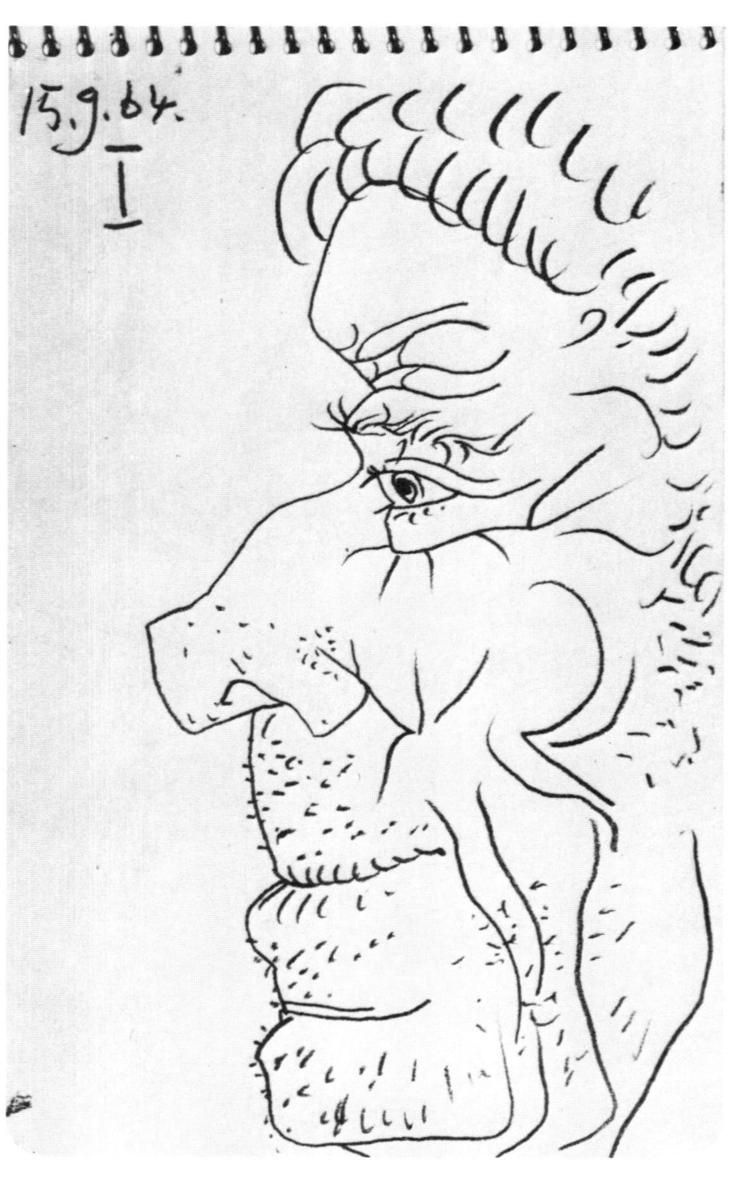

52
HEAD
15.9.64 I

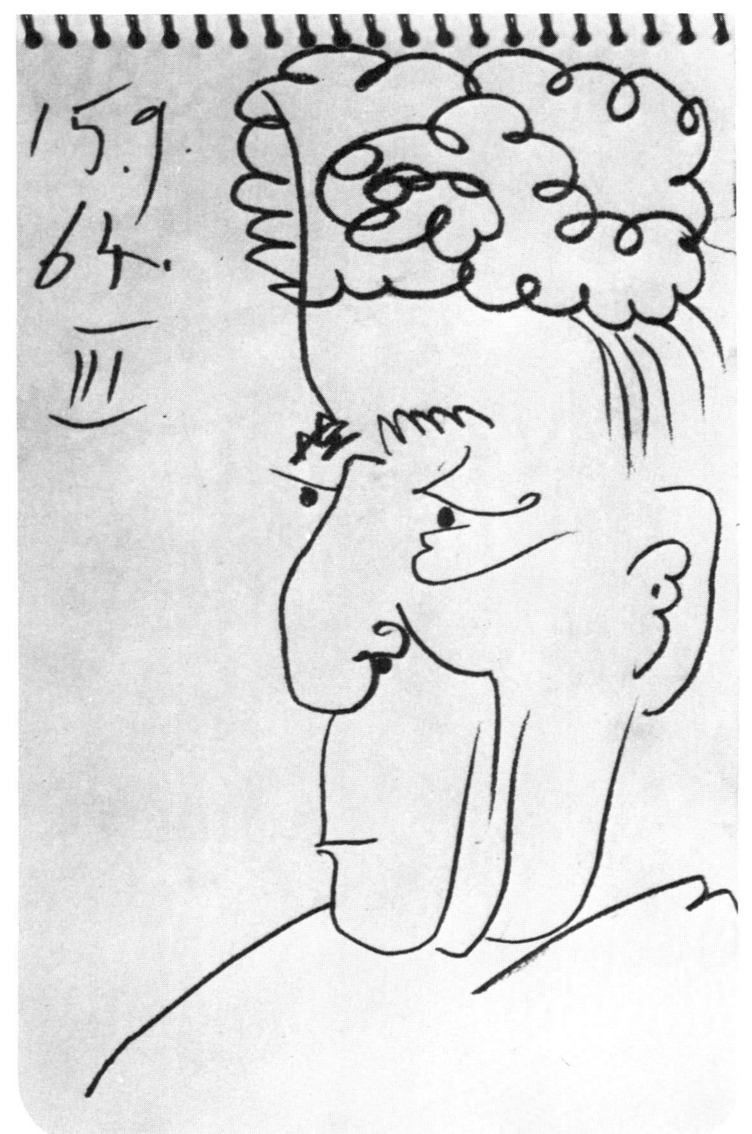

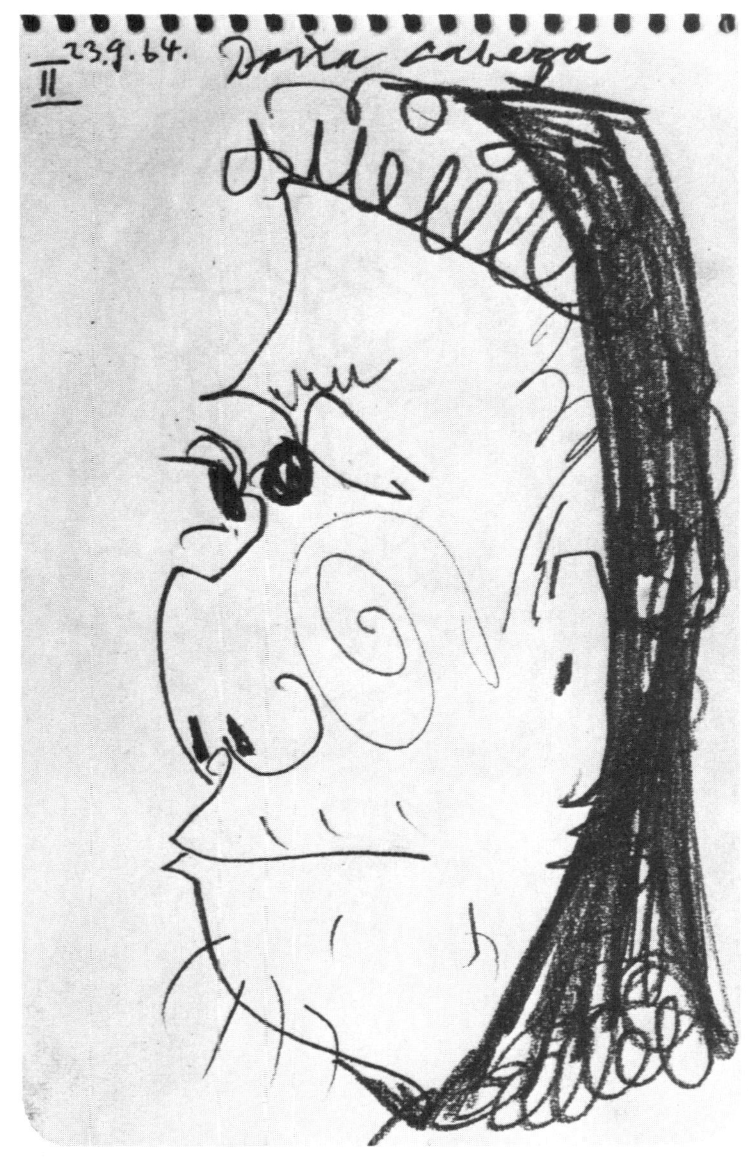

53
HEAD
15.9.64 III

54
DONA CABEZA
23.9.64 II

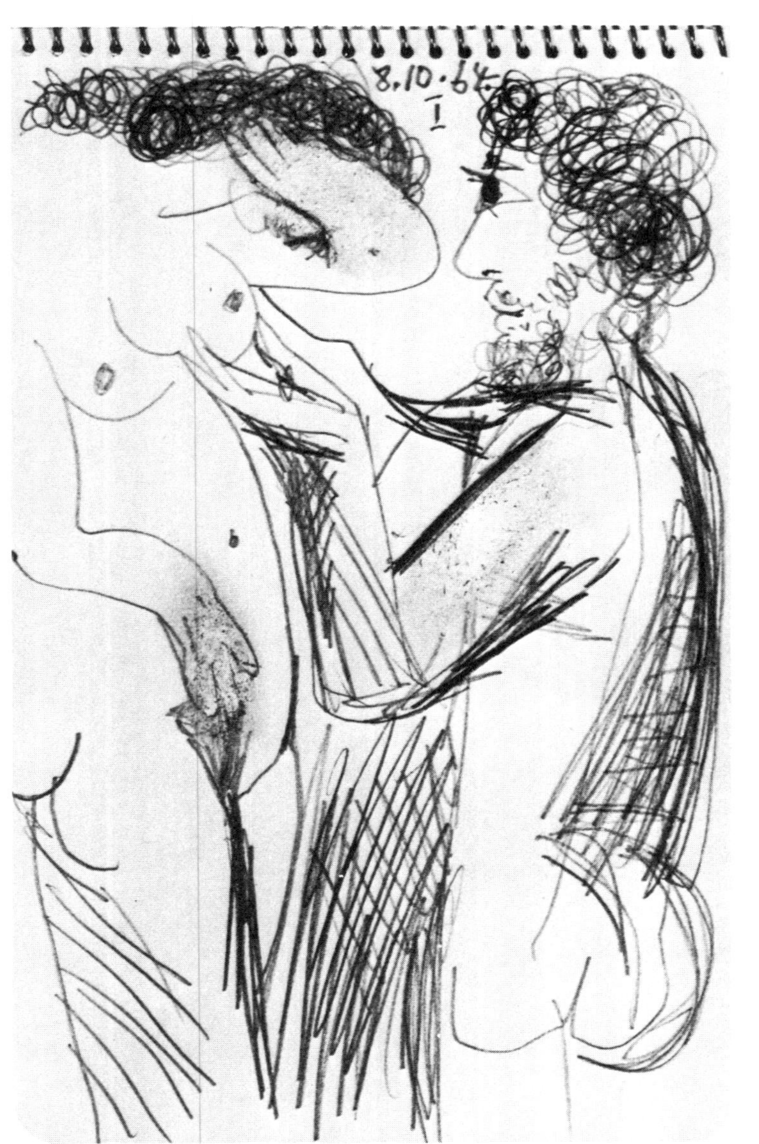

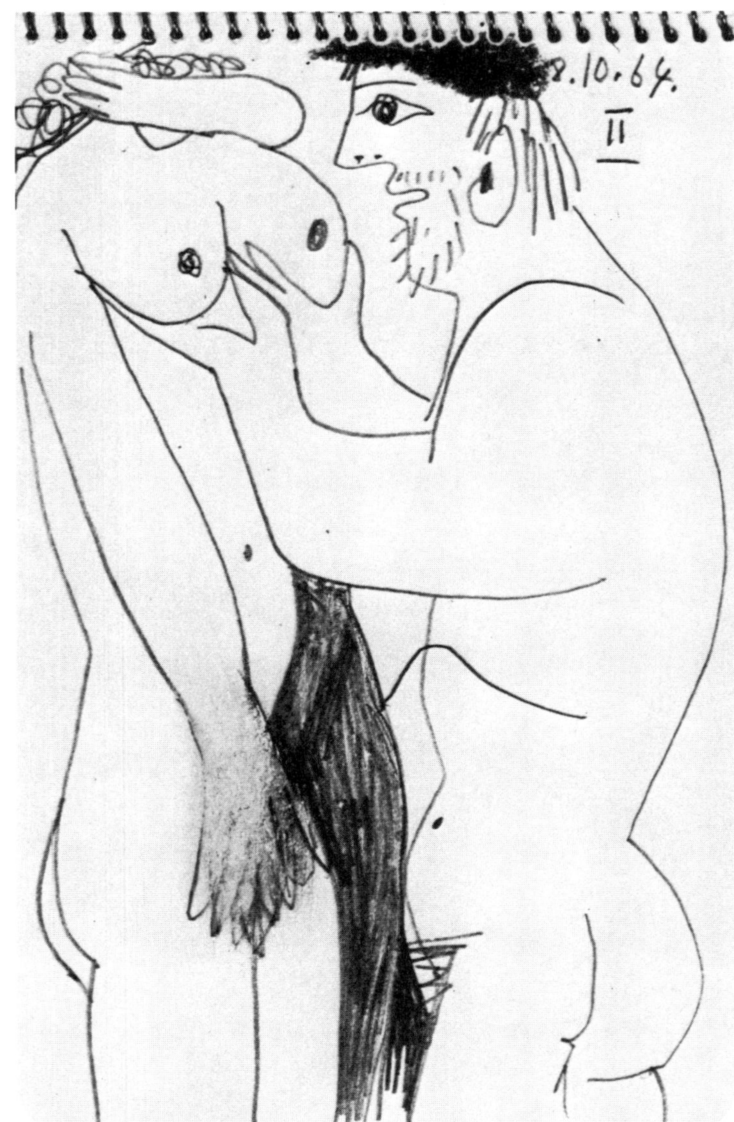

55
MAN AND WOMAN
8.10.64 I

56
MAN AND WOMAN
8.10.64 II

America and elsewhere. Some of those exhibitions became historic occasions, like that of the sensational 347 erotic etchings, for instance. The Grommelynck brothers, Piero and Aldo, engraving specialists, had installed themselves at Picasso's with a copperplate press. The results exceeded all expectations.

January 1973 was another important date: the last etchings, 156 in number, were exhibited just a few months before the painter's death.

We must also mention the 1966–67 drawings, about which Michel Leiris wrote in his introduction to the catalogue: 'By setting us face to face with a person, or a couple or a group of people whom fate seems to have set face to face with each other, Picasso, as usual, leaves the commentator at the foot of a wall in front of which he has no option but to hold his tongue: how could commentary, any commentary (this one for example) add anything at all to that which is fascinating at first sight?'

But we shall not follow his advice and shall continue our commentary, from a historical standpoint at least.

The exhibition of drawings from late 1969 to early 1971 was unusual in that it included many works in coloured pencil and black and white chalk on paper or grey- or brown-coloured card.

Finally, at the end of 1972, the Galerie Louise Leiris exhibited 172 fantastically varied drawings, a great wave of eroticism and musketeers' heads with, at its centre, a disturbing self-portrait, the last one with a story.

Picasso's work has often been misunderstood, which is the risk run by an artist who is always ahead of his time. But, with the years, that must change: problems shift, and often the fascination of his work, its immediate effect on anyone who looks at it, makes us forget Picasso's age and context. In 1946, when he was celebrating the return of peace, the joy of life and refound love, the flower-woman and soon the joys of fatherhood, this natural phenomenon was sixty-nine years old and he was to carry on for more than another quarter-century. At this stage, he was painting a great deal and drawing less. Some themes were treated exclusively on canvas, such as *The Rape of the Sabines*, the *Déjeuners sur l'herbe* and *Las Meninas* which is why they are missing from this book. By contrast, the couples, the various Painter and Models, the circus and brothel scenes, the Turkish baths proliferate in all possible forms. The historian is led to ask himself – and to enquire of Picasso's work – about old age and its effects. They can be so cunning that one has difficulty discerning their content. Even the obsessional nature of certain themes can hardly alert one to it.

One thing that never changed was Picasso's passion for portraits, which were as close as possible, of people who caught his attention for their physical characteristics and which he enjoyed putting down on paper, either immediately or from memory, since his visual memory remained undiminished.

As illustration, one has only to look at the clowns' heads (is that really their title?) from September 1964, because their veracity is evident in spite of the humorous sting that is slipped in. There are a hundred others, but these three conjure up the man so well that they suffice to illustrate the genius of Picasso.

What had changed, not fundamentally but in its form, was the image, or rather the images, that he presented of woman. Whether she was alone or with a man, whatever the relationship between her and the man, painter's model, conversation, an embrace, be it kiss or copulation, she was always at the heart of the work, and the centre of the subject herself was her genitals. As Gert Schiff pointed out, Picasso 'who was never a master of understatement . . . never hesitated to say or show what he felt like saying or showing [and] confident in his years and his fame, granted himself total liberty'.

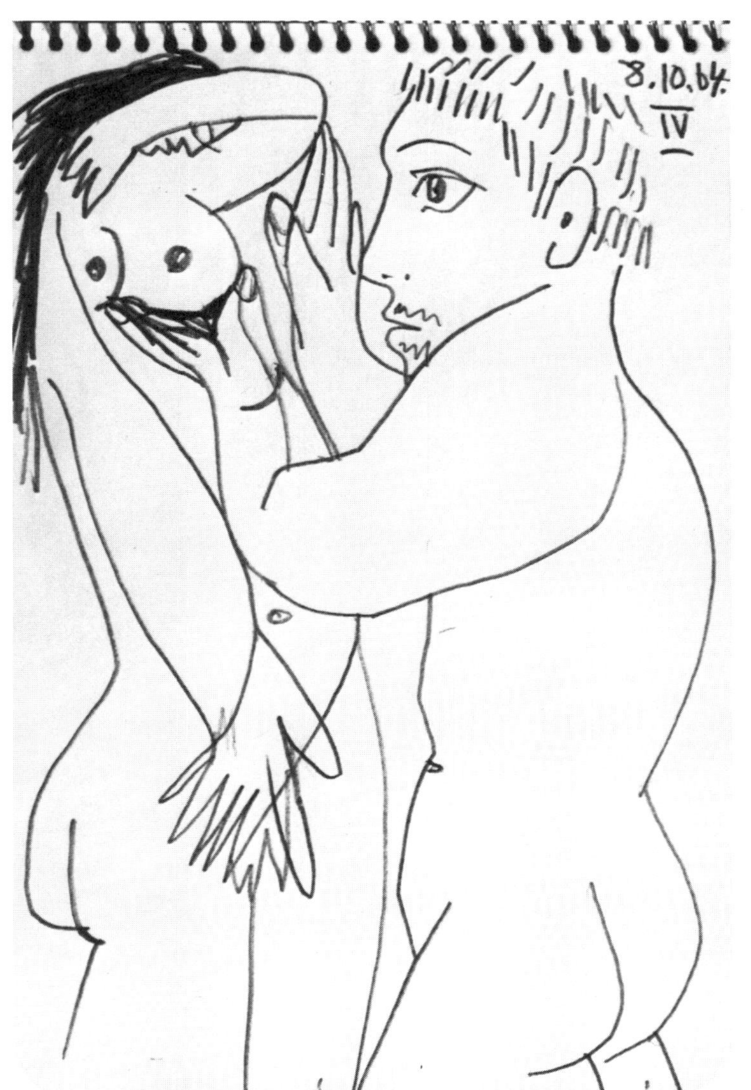

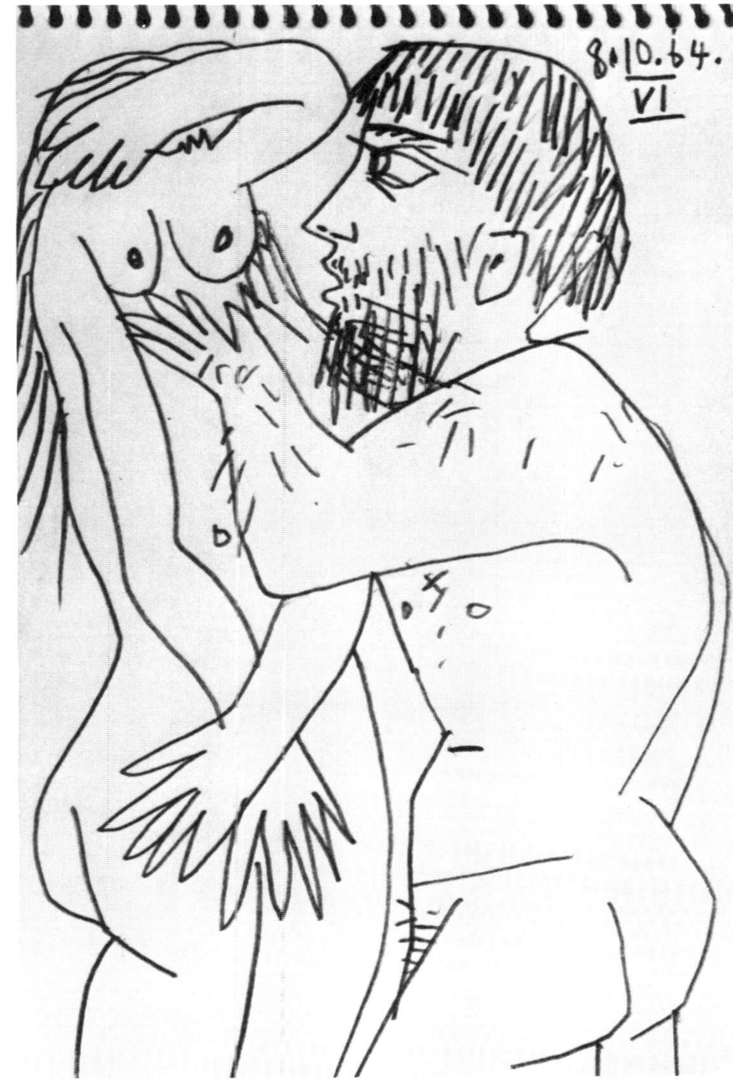

57
MAN AND WOMAN
8.10.64 IV

58
MAN AND WOMAN
8.10.64 VI

From a formal point of view, one could go into raptures over the infinite variations in the graphical transcription of a woman's genitals. One might think: they are all different, but Picasso can somehow show us the same ones in a thousand different ways.

It is interesting to note that while female genitalia were unrestrainedly flowering, blossoming and expanding, male genitals were discreet, small, soft, shy, mere symbols.

So exhibitionism followed modesty, discretion was succeeded by provocation. Still Picasso's images of physical love were for the most part so natural, so spontaneous that they should be acceptable to the widest possible audience.

Indeed, the phrase from the cinema is pertinent, since many of the series can be read like a cartoon strip or a plan in drawings for a film.

Picasso in his seventies and eighties developed what one might call 'interior vision'. He saw into the depths of woman, he penetrated her with his eyes, he developed as far as possible the principle according to which all women are exhibitionists and all men voyeurs. And Picasso's voyeurism knew no bounds!

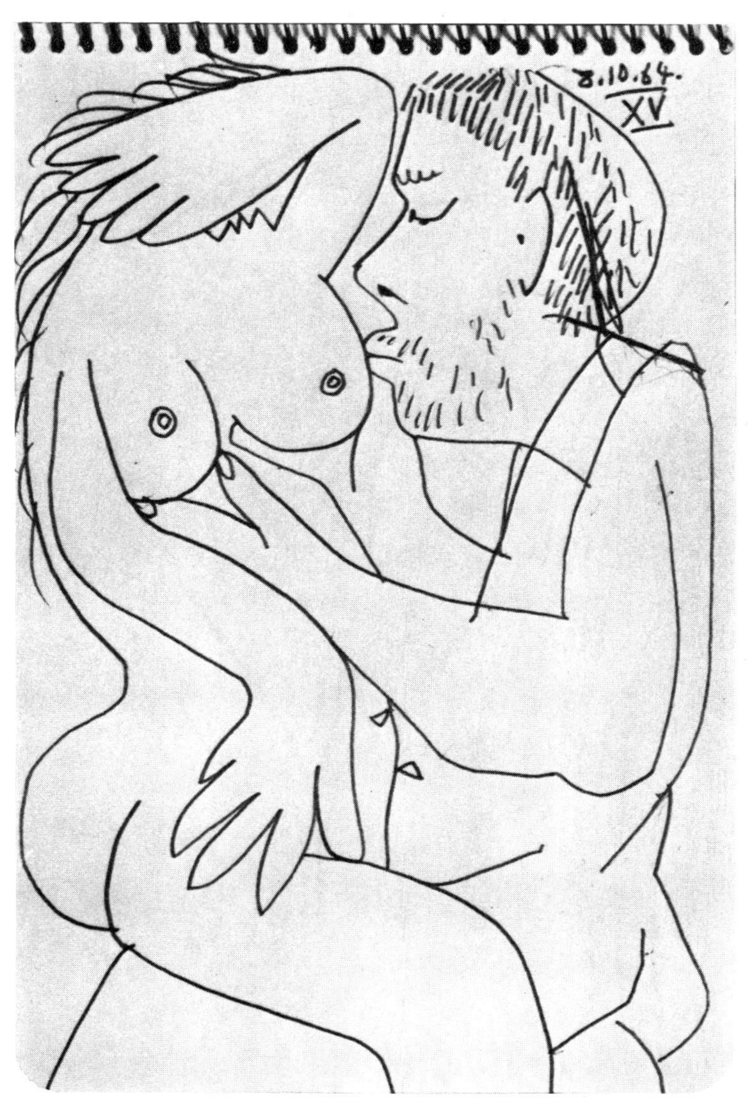

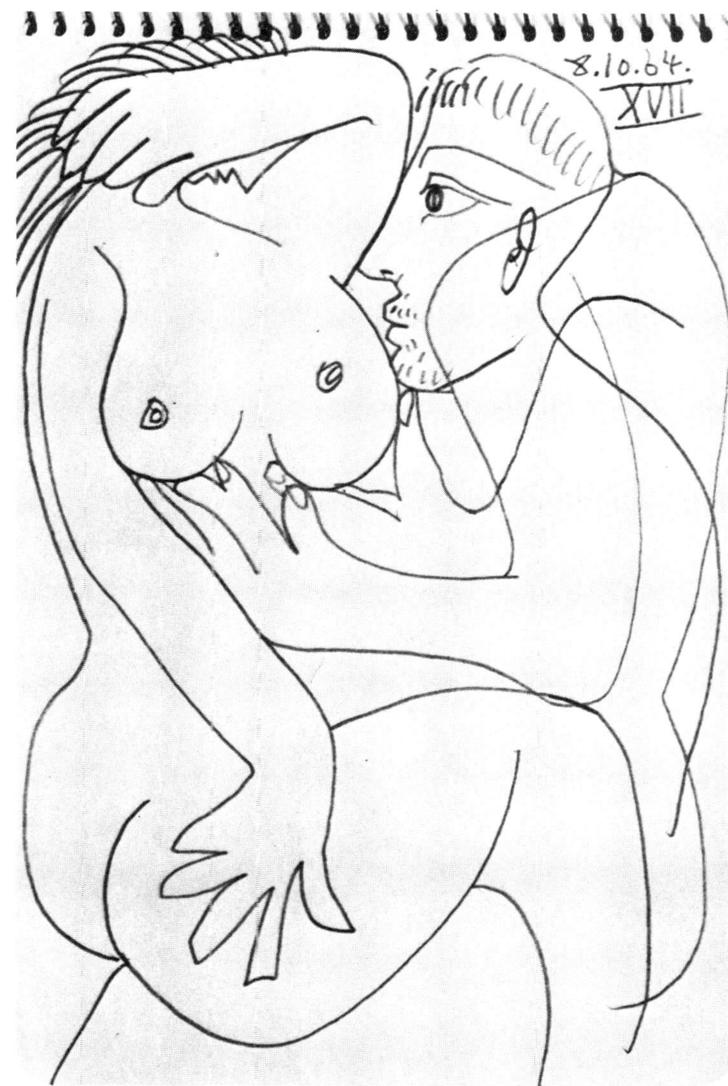

59
MAN AND WOMAN
8.10.64 XV

60
MAN AND WOMAN
8.10.64 XVII

IX

THE SMOKERS

The Smokers are a case apart in Picasso's work from the 1960s. They are not mythical figures, they are not friends, they were not inspired by some historical masterpiece, they are not taking part in any action or scene, they live for themselves, they exist in themselves. In the event, one can guess, and we shall show, that they are merely a pretext for research and experiments in plasticity.

But what event, incident or accident moved Picasso to choose this particular subject from thousands of possibilities? Friends say that the Smokers originated in the gardener, who was always walking around 'with a fag hanging out of his mouth'. Picasso always chose his subjects close to home, as he did when the gardener's wife had a baby. But there was more to it than that. Picasso, according to those close to him, tried several times to give up smoking, and it seems that he was making such an attempt in the spring of 1964. To be constantly confronted with an otherwise very pleasant young man with a cigarette hanging from his lips must have either weakened his resolve or simply exasperated him. Whichever it was, Picasso fixed the features of the gardener and his fag on paper for all time (though there are also portraits of him without the cigarette!).

Moreover, when one looks at the sixteen examples shown here from among several dozen, there are obvious constants. The outline, often blurred, soft and indistinct, at least until 19 May, suggests an ill-kempt man, badly shaved, with stubble on his chin. Another constant is the application of thick, heavy strokes of colour to the face, which cannot be taken for a tattoo and which therefore has a plastic value. The closeness of the lines in the faces drawn on the 18 May 1964 suggests a code to signify relief, the modelling of the face, like the contour lines on a map. In fact, if one turns back to the preceding faces, it becomes evident that those coloured chalk marks signify both the modelling of the face itself and the play of light on a rather flat surface. At times, the cigarette disappears but the innocent, rather stupid expression remains: there is no doubt that it is the same person, known as 'the smoker'.

The portrait evolved. In June, the character grew a beard and found new vigour with it. His features were firmer. It was no longer just a head, but a bust in centre frame, as they say in the cinema. The blue-striped sailor top was effective and Picasso made good use of it.

The series was a revelation to his friends. Hélène Parmelin relates: '. . . in 1964, one night at midnight, at Notre-Dame-de-Vie, Picasso said, "There are still hundreds of drawings that you haven't seen. I'll show you. They are great fun. They are of men with a cigarette. They are holding it, raising it to their lips. Or taking a drag (or haven't got one). They are heads with sometimes just a hand or an arm" . . . He explained that all he wanted was that we should feel ourselves to be *in their presence* – not in front of drawings but in front of gentlemen smoking a cigarette.

'What he hoped that he had achieved or would achieve was such a degree of truth that the human presence in these drawings would exist as people and not as lines of ink or colour.

'So they are heads of men like the men you see in the cafés. This one is happy. That one is worried. That one is thinking about nothing.' (Hélène Parmelin, *Notre-Dame-de-Vie*, Editions Cercle d'Art, 1966).

Thus, where we see plastic effect, Picasso wanted us to see life and presence.

III
SMOKER
pencil and coloured chalk
18.5.64 II

IV
SMOKER
pencil and coloured chalk
18.5.64 VI

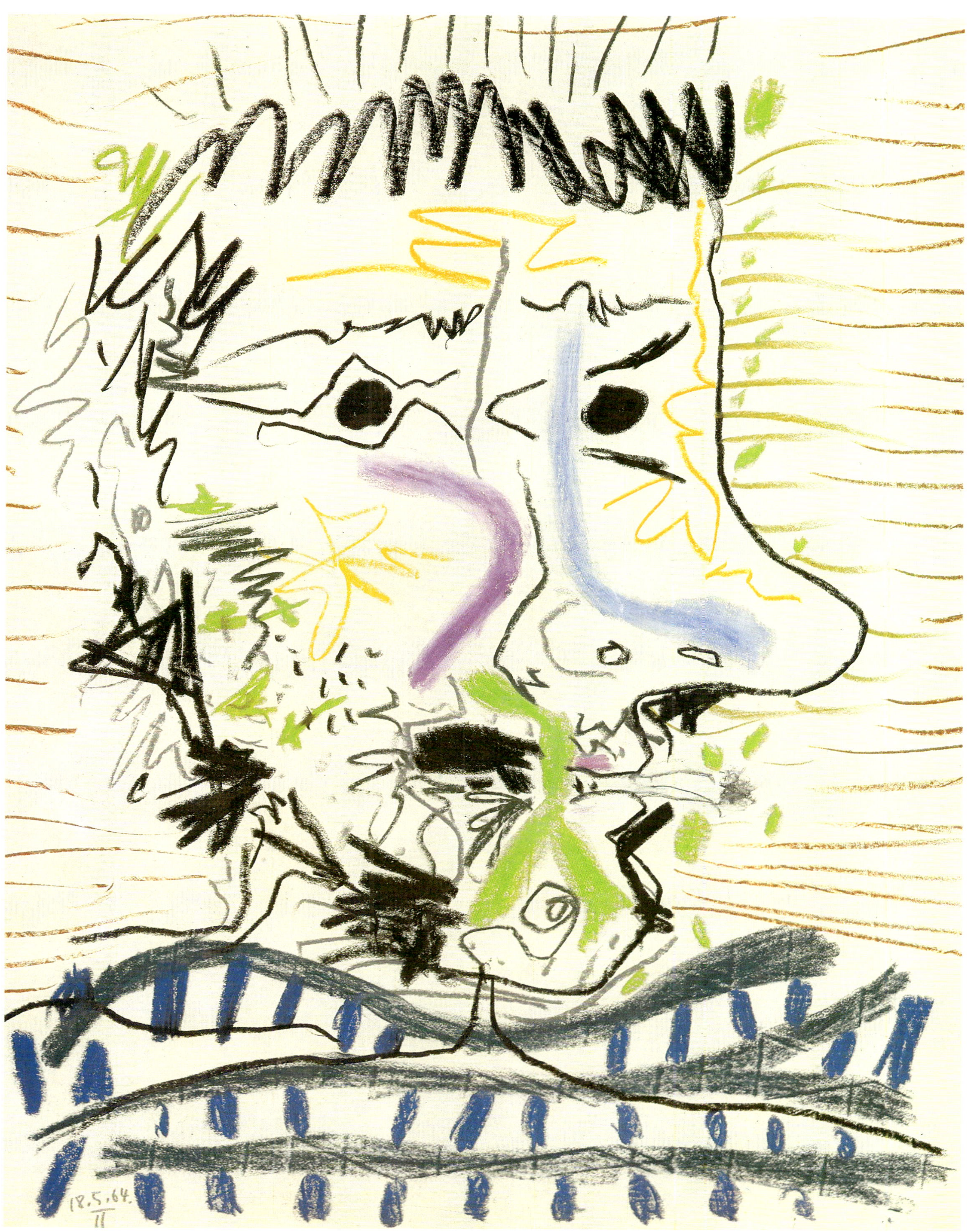
18.5.64.
II

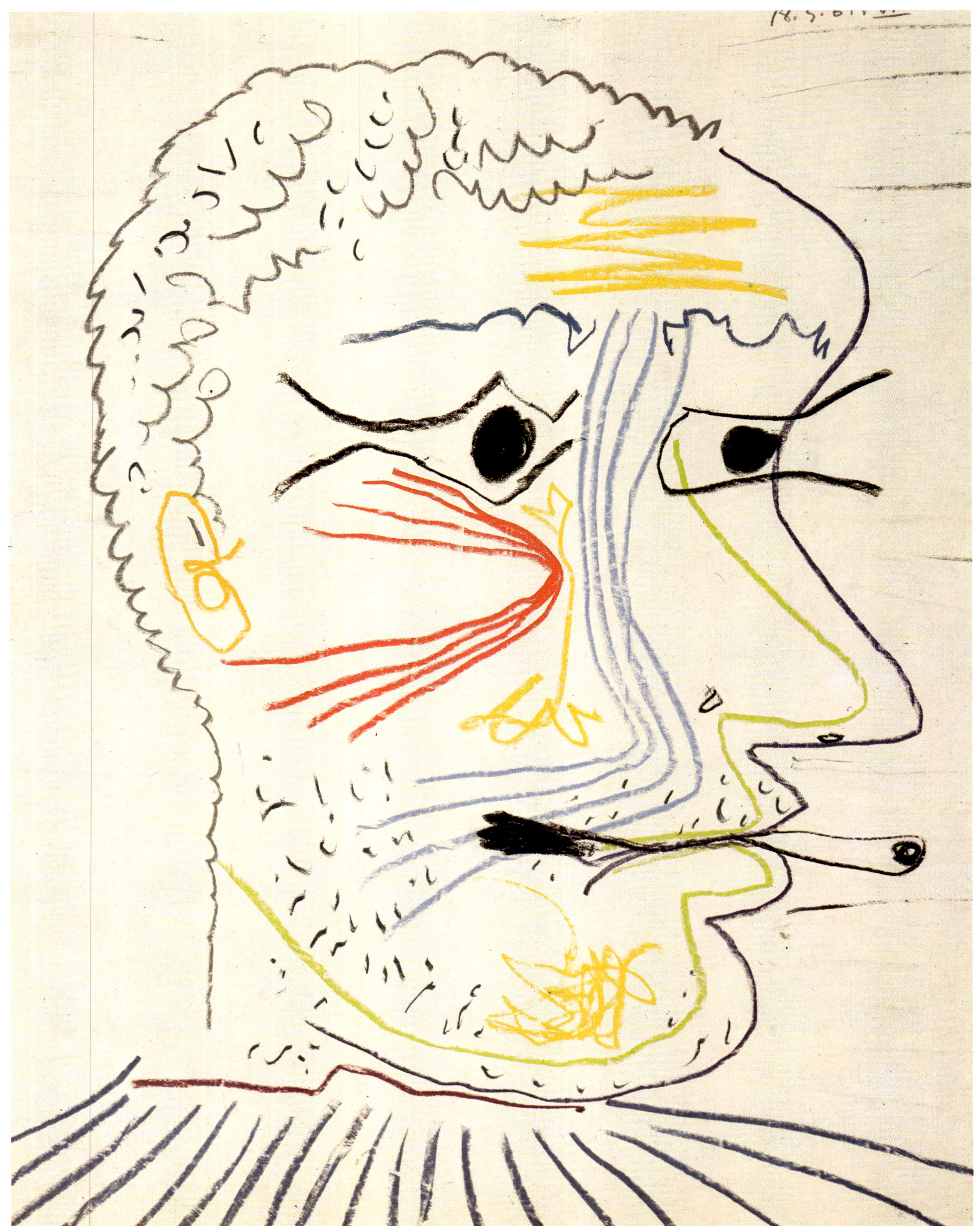

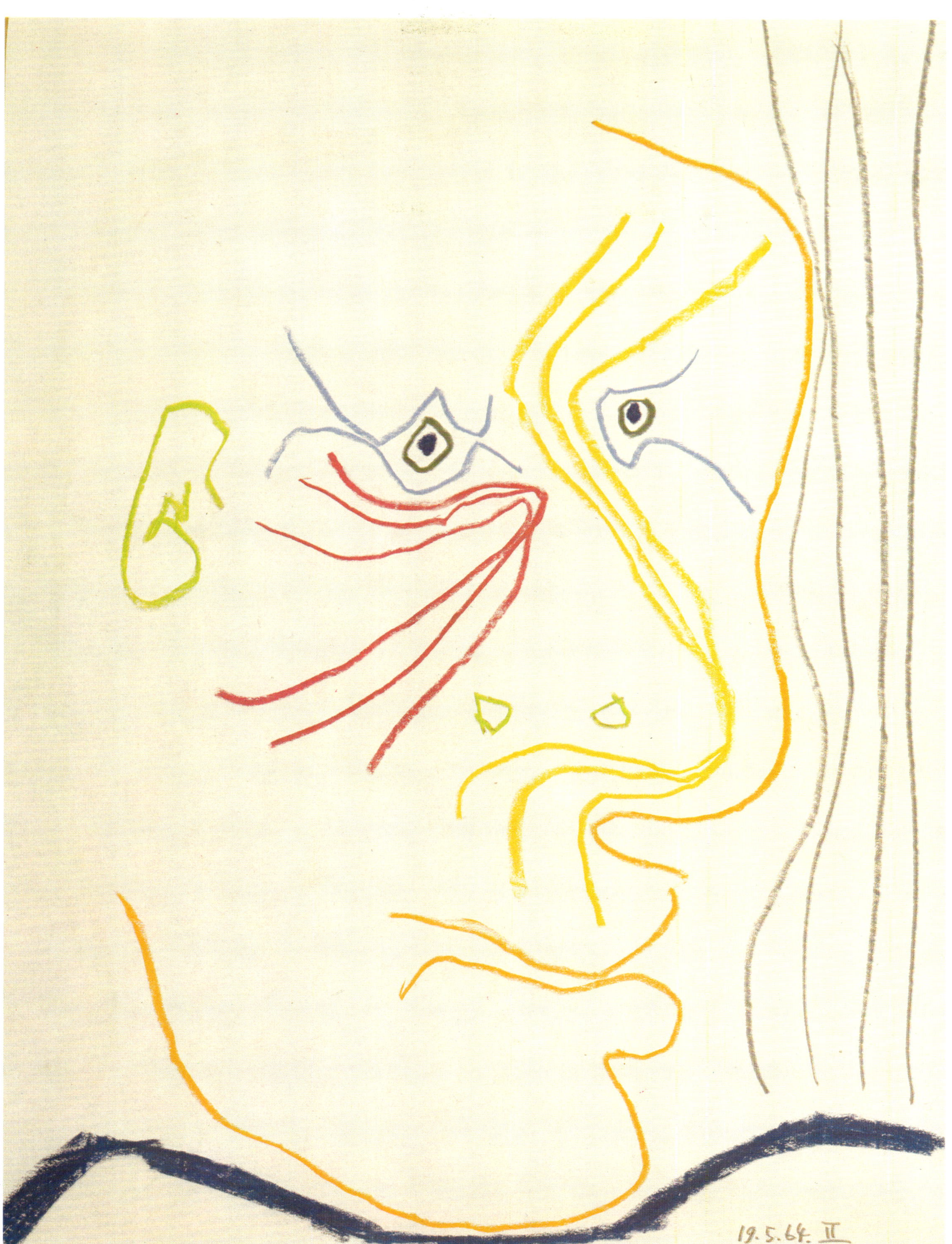
19.5.64. II

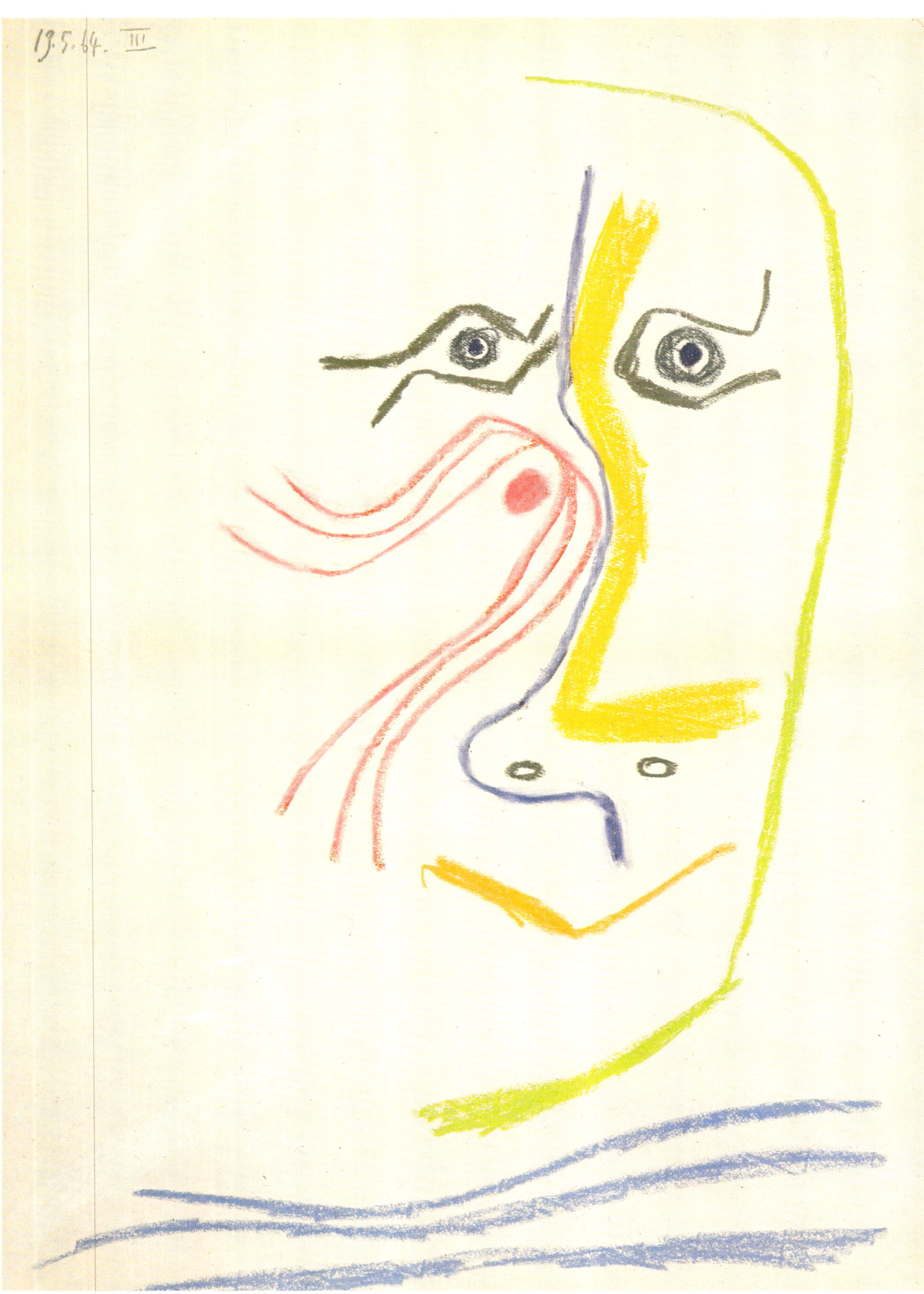
19.5.64. III

X

THE MUSKETEERS

The Musketeers hold an important place in the last period of Picasso's work. Where did they come from, what are they, where are they going?

First and foremost, the Musketeers are explosions of forms and colours. They are faces that look at you, that are alive, that smoke (that old obsession again) a pipe, that have long hair; occasionally they have a sword, a distinctive mark of their rank. But that is of no historical significance; it is just for the painting – or the drawing. André Malraux asked Jacqueline about them: 'Picasso had discovered these musketeers during his last illness, in a book about Rembrandt, Jacqueline said. Encounters which are renewed over a period of five years are no chance encounters. One of his men with a moustache at the last Exhibition was called *Rembrandtesque Figure*. There is no more rivalry between these figures and those of *The Night Watch*, despite the hats, than between the *Bathsheba* in the Louvre and those at Mougins. An odd dialogue indeed: in Picasso's colour drawing, Bathsheba has become Jacqueline and the serving woman, a man's face more or less that of the poor painter in the *Painter and Model*. Picasso himself? What does he have in common with Rembrandt, in his art or in his life? Unless . . . ' (André Malraux, *Le Miroir des Limbes*, II *La Corde et les Souris*, Ed. Gallimard).

Unless . . . It is all there, in that 'unless' which is a great deal, which is everything.

Of course, the thought of Rembrandt was there at the root, as it was in the case of the couple drawn on 10 June 1967, inspired by the *Self-portrait with Saskia*. But if Picasso painted so many of these beribboned, behatted, moustachioed, vociferous, and bragging military men, it was because they crystallized for him a number of important

V
SMOKER
pencil and coloured chalk
19.5.64 II

VI
SMOKER
pencil and coloured chalk
19.5.64 III

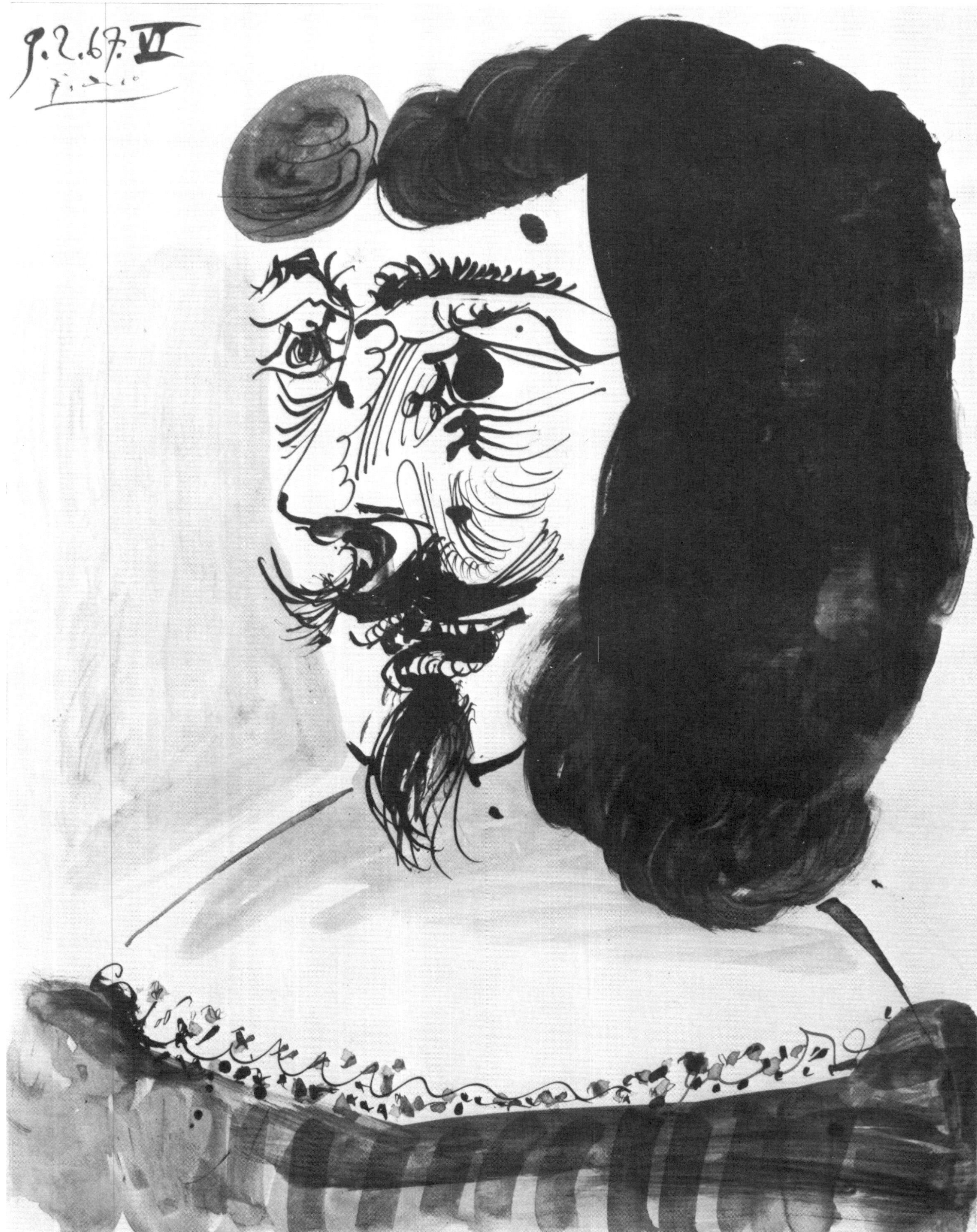
9.2.67. VI

psychological as well as pictorial references.

As early as 1894, at the age of twelve, he had been to see the plays of Lope de Vega and had sketched them. He had read not only Edmond Rostand, but Alexandre Dumas and the adventures of his musketeers. He had seen not only Rembrandt, but also Meissonier's military scenes, each uniform correct down to the last button.

But all this is no more than the surface of the subject, and one has to look deeper into childhood memories, the Mardi Gras, the masquerades, in which all little boys dreamed of taking part, dressed in a gold-spangled suit and a feathered hat. Looked at objectively, there is a great deal of youth in the faces of these musketeers. Picasso himself had fun with them, as witness once again Hélène Parmelin: 'On the little terrace or in the studio, the eyes of the canvases, by the way they had of staring into ours from deep inside those painted heads . . ., never ceased asking us questions.

'We would look at the canvases straight in the eyes. We played at giving our opinions of the man in front of us who was watching us all the time.

'I wouldn't like to meet that one. That one is making fun of us. That one is enormously self-satisfied. That one is a boring intellectual. And that one, Picasso would say, look how sad he is, poor thing! He must be some sort of a painter . . .

'Gradually we started to sort the canvases into human categories. One day, the heads represented the apostles: we named them, from Thomas to Judas. We laughed about it and couldn't get over the fact that we had got them all absolutely right. We found the good, the bad and the painters . . .

'By means of this power in the eyes, Picasso was looking for the key to an enhancement of the human quality of painting and he had the impression that he was getting close.' (Hélène Parmelin, *Voyage en*

61
MUSKETEER
wash 65×50
9.2.67 VI

Picasso, Ed. Robert Laffont, Paris, 1980).

It could be argued that this obsession with realism was in Hélène Parmelin's mind more than in Picasso's. What is more to the point here is how the Musketeers became 17th-century Dutch painters. The faces that you see here, that 'look at you' according to Hélène Parmelin, are not, with the exception of the one from 5 June 1967, the faces of warriors, but of peaceful observers, philosophers, painters perhaps. They do indeed look at us, because they are looking at the world as a whole and we are part of it. This is not true of the face – no, the mask – of 5 June, which wears a tragic sneer and has empty eye sockets. Picasso probably didn't like it, because he drew more human profiles in the margins and in the blank spaces of the paper.

One further question: How strong an influence did his attraction for Rembrandt exercise here? One moment, it is an exercise in style, a pastiche, a caricature, a challenge to himself; a moment later, Picasso has forgotten the Dutchman and found again, in the tracing of the same conventional mask, the hand of Velasquez, of El Greco or, at worst, Murillo.

What comes most naturally always assumes the upper hand, and his Spanishness reappears just when one is least expecting it.

Technically, it is Indian ink, pen and brush, thinned down to pale grey wash, a technique he used with complete mastery.

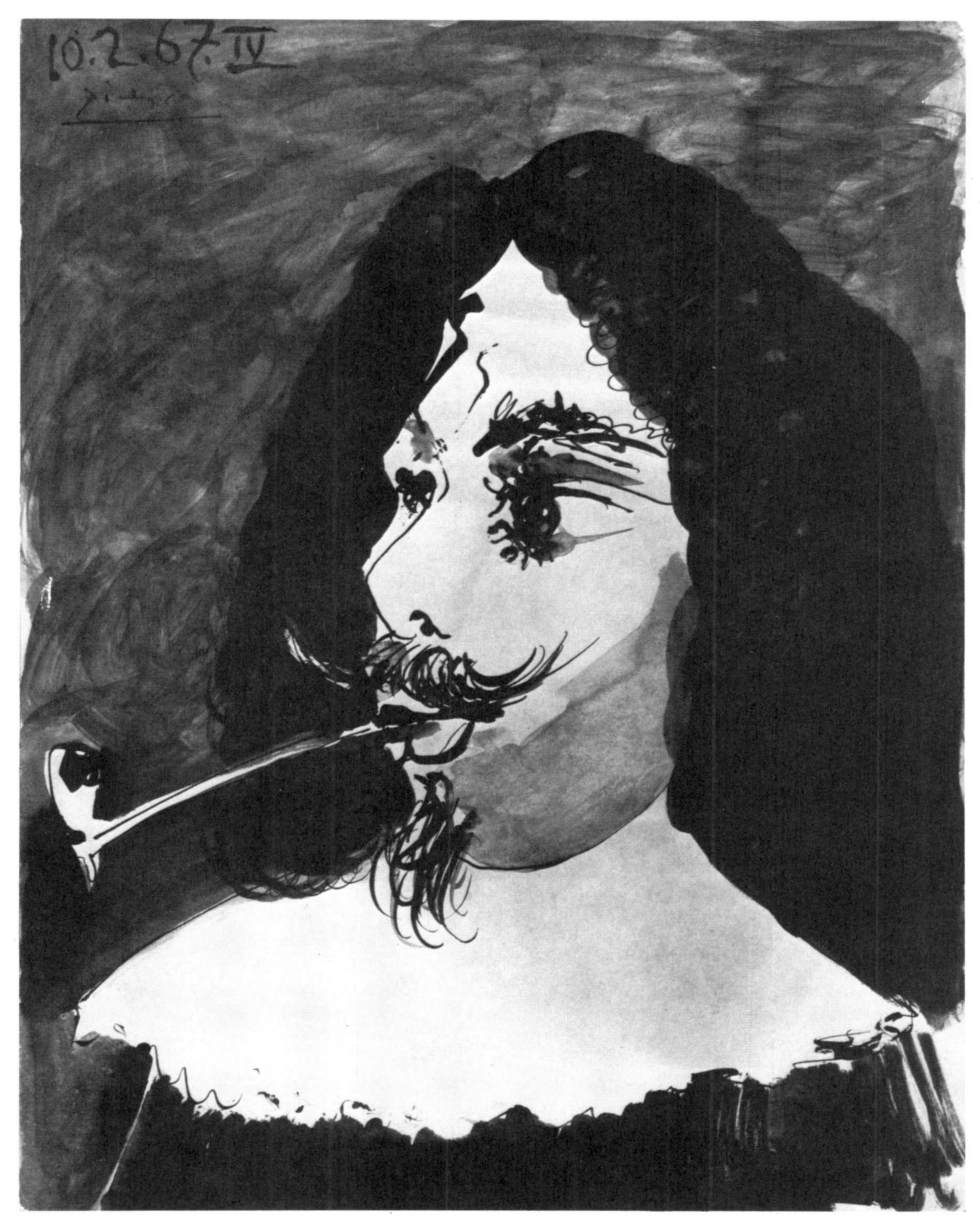

62
MUSKETEER WITH PIPE
wash 65×50
10.2.67 IV

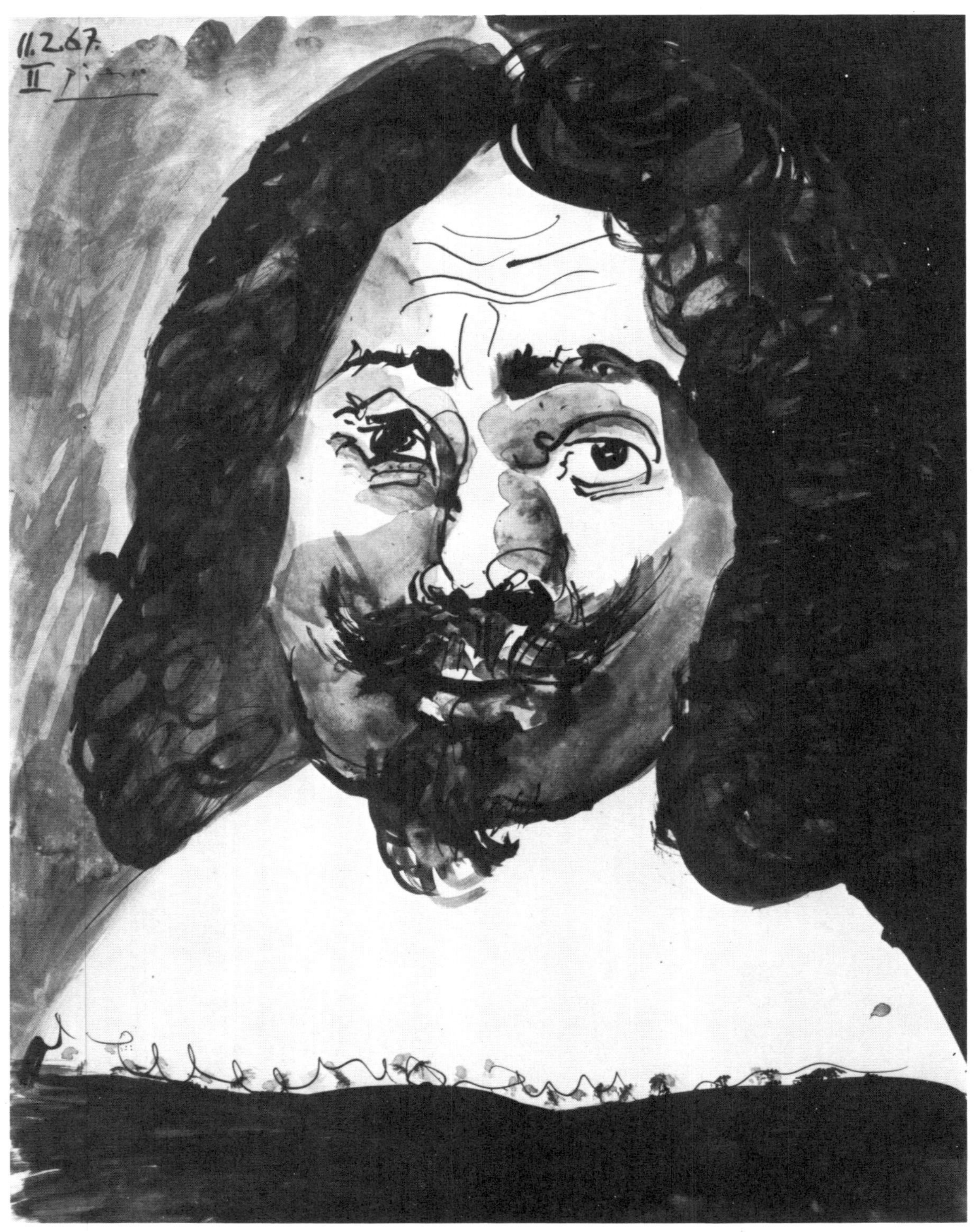

63
MUSKETEER
wash 65×50
11.2.67 II

64
MUSKETEER
wash 60.5×49.5
5.6.67 II and 8.6.67
(the small heads in the margins)

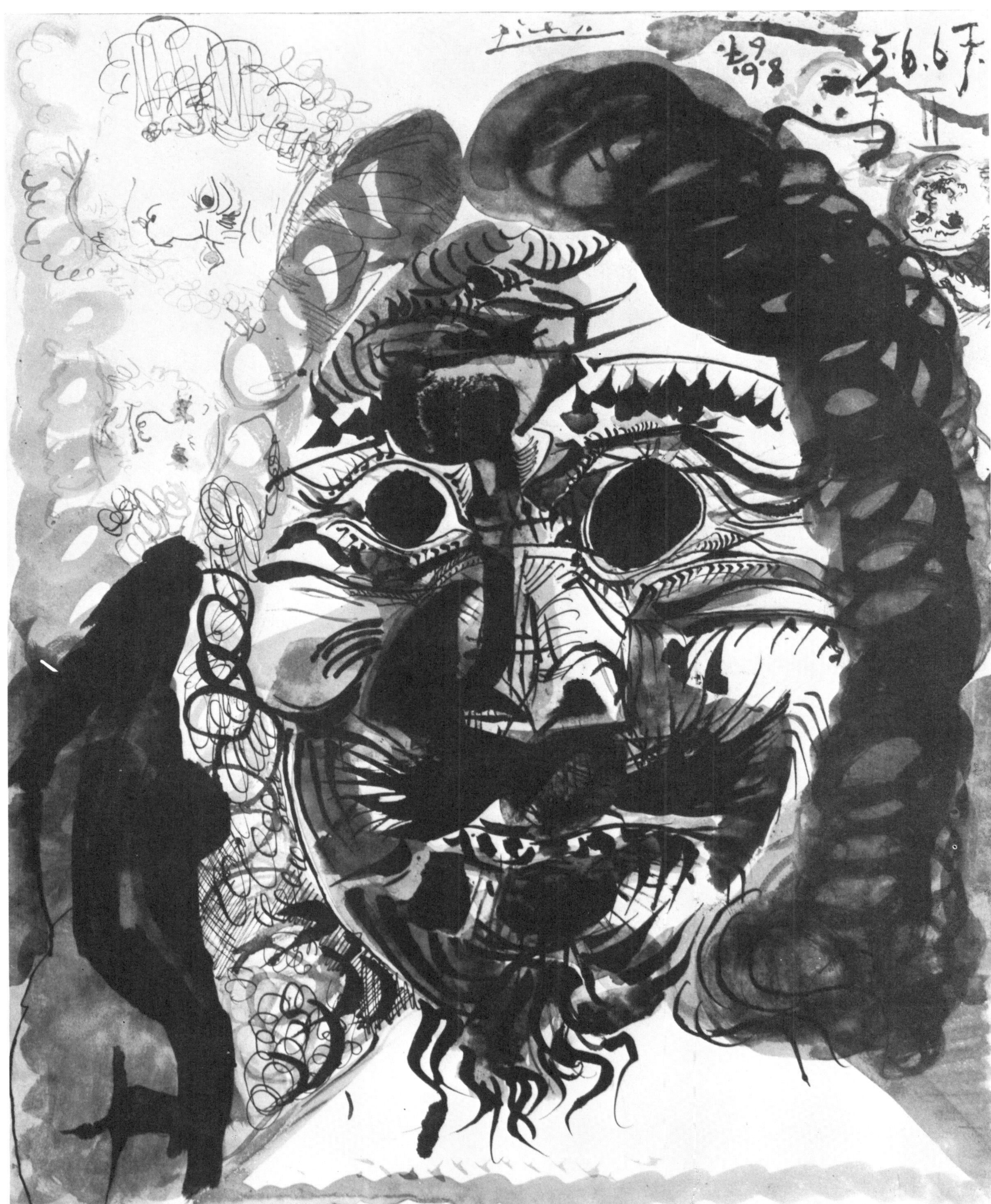
5.6.67.

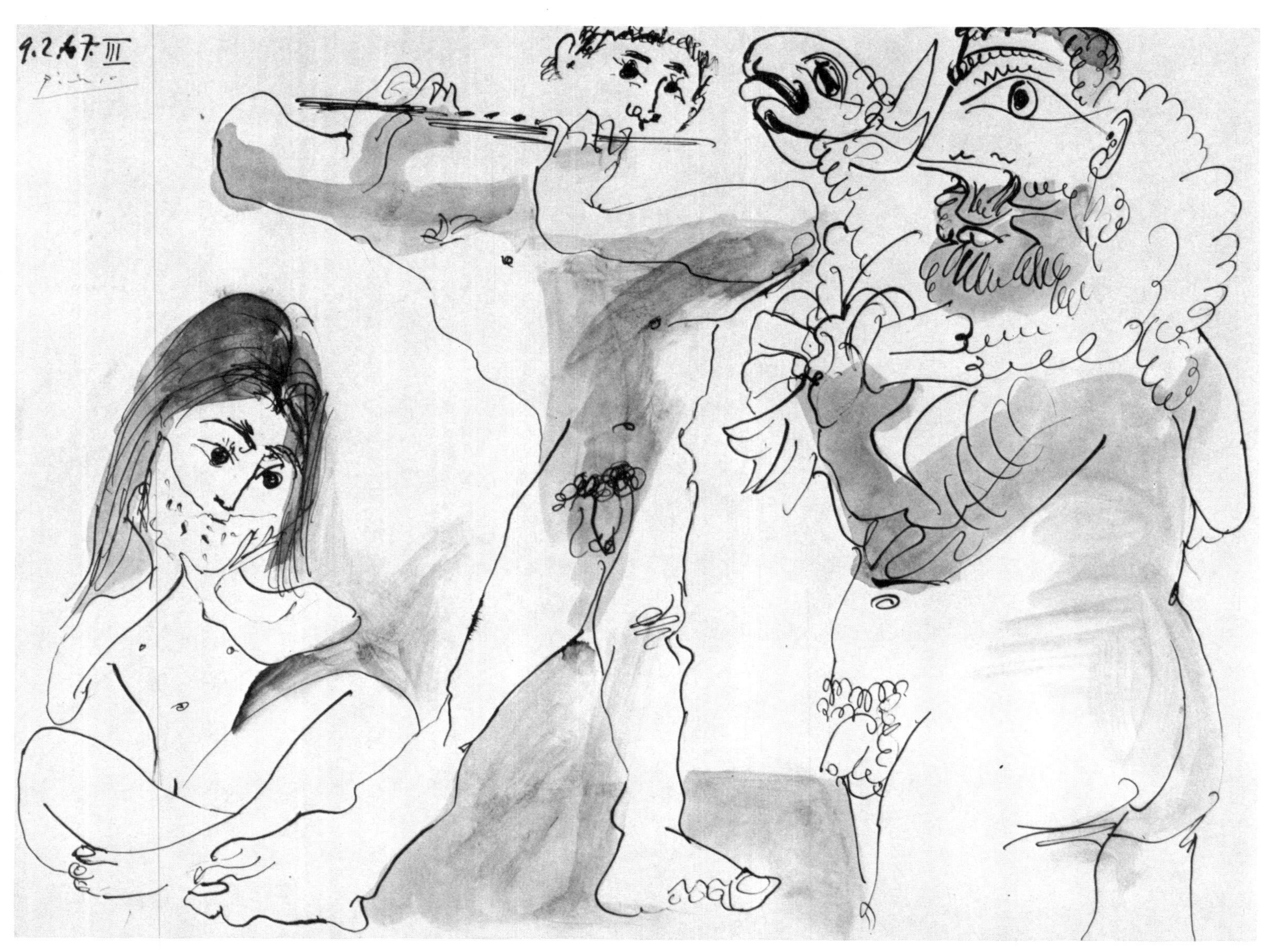

65
MAN WITH LAMB AND WATERMELON EATER
wash 50×65
9.2.67 III

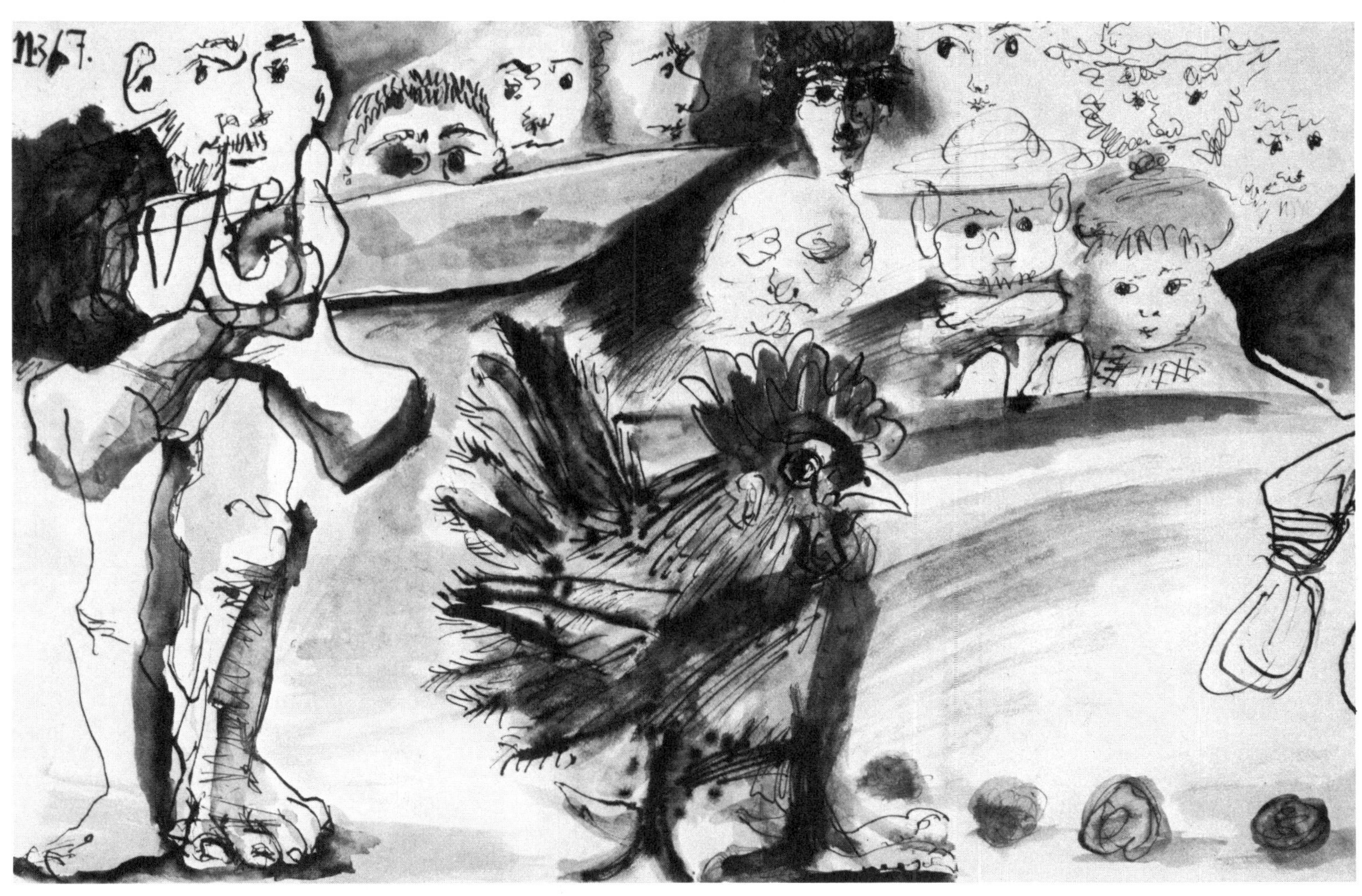

66
THE CIRCUS
wash 49.5×75.2
11.3.67

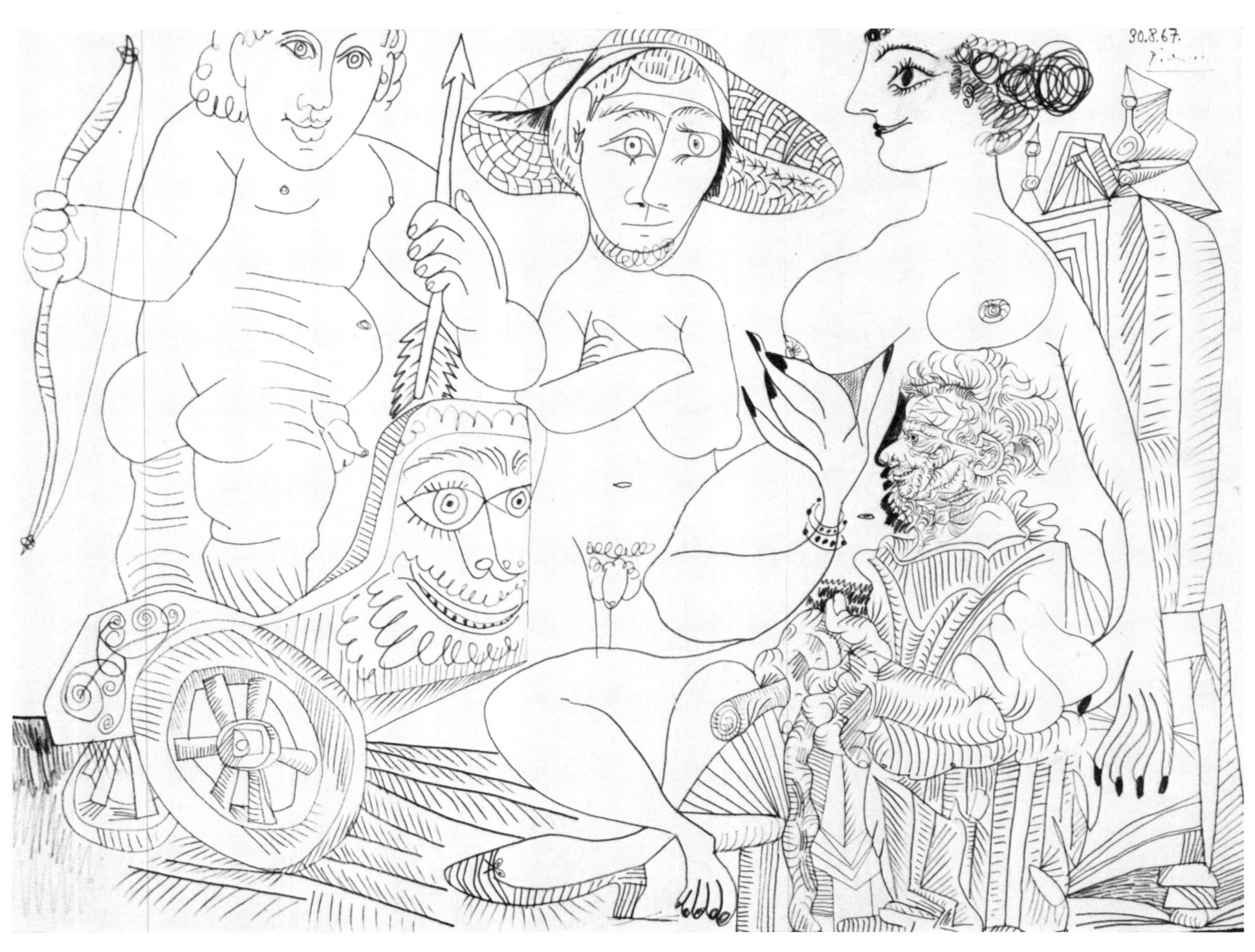

67
MYTHOLOGICAL SCENE
pencil 56.5×75
30.8.67

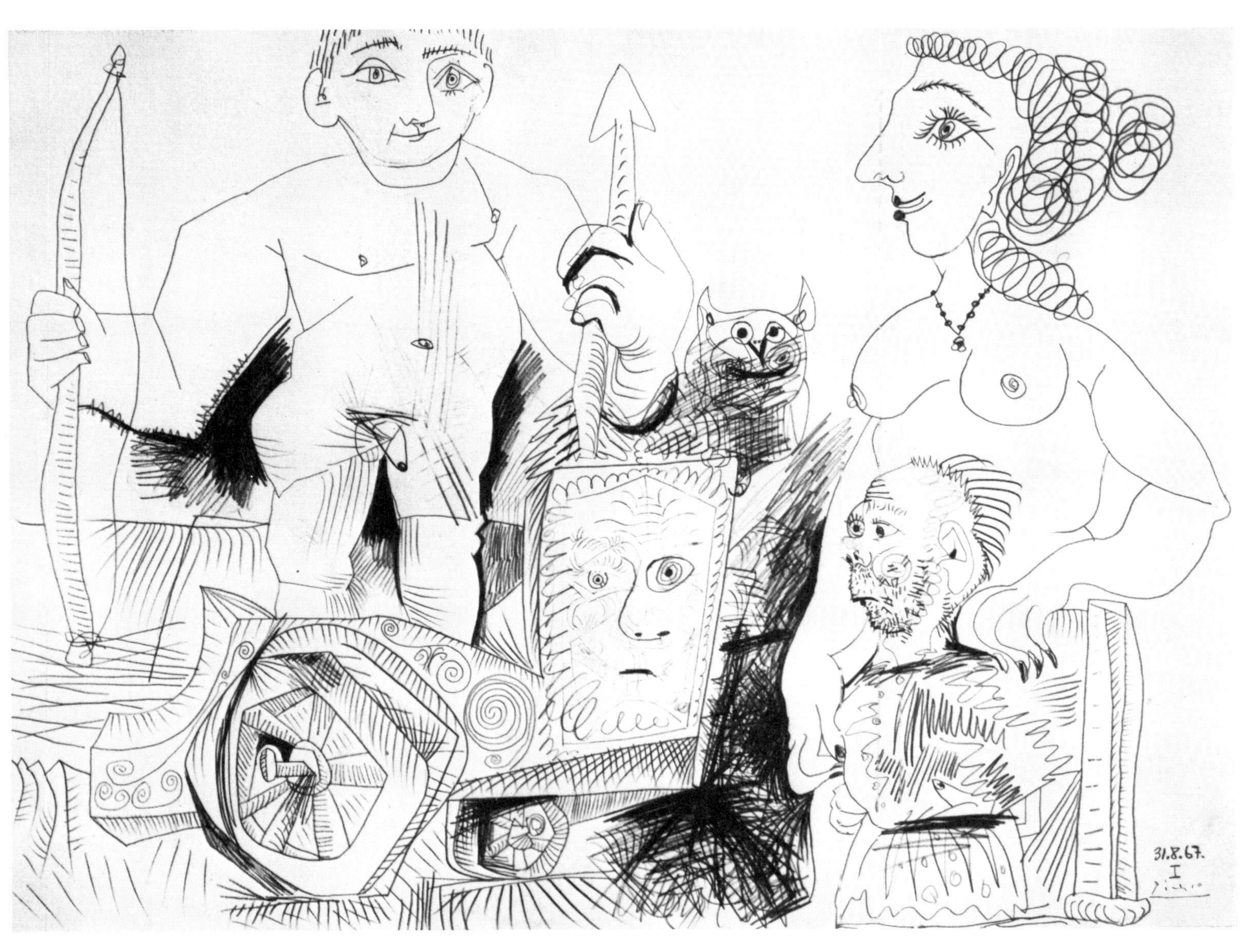

68
MYTHOLOGICAL SCENE
pencil 56.5×75
31.8.67 I

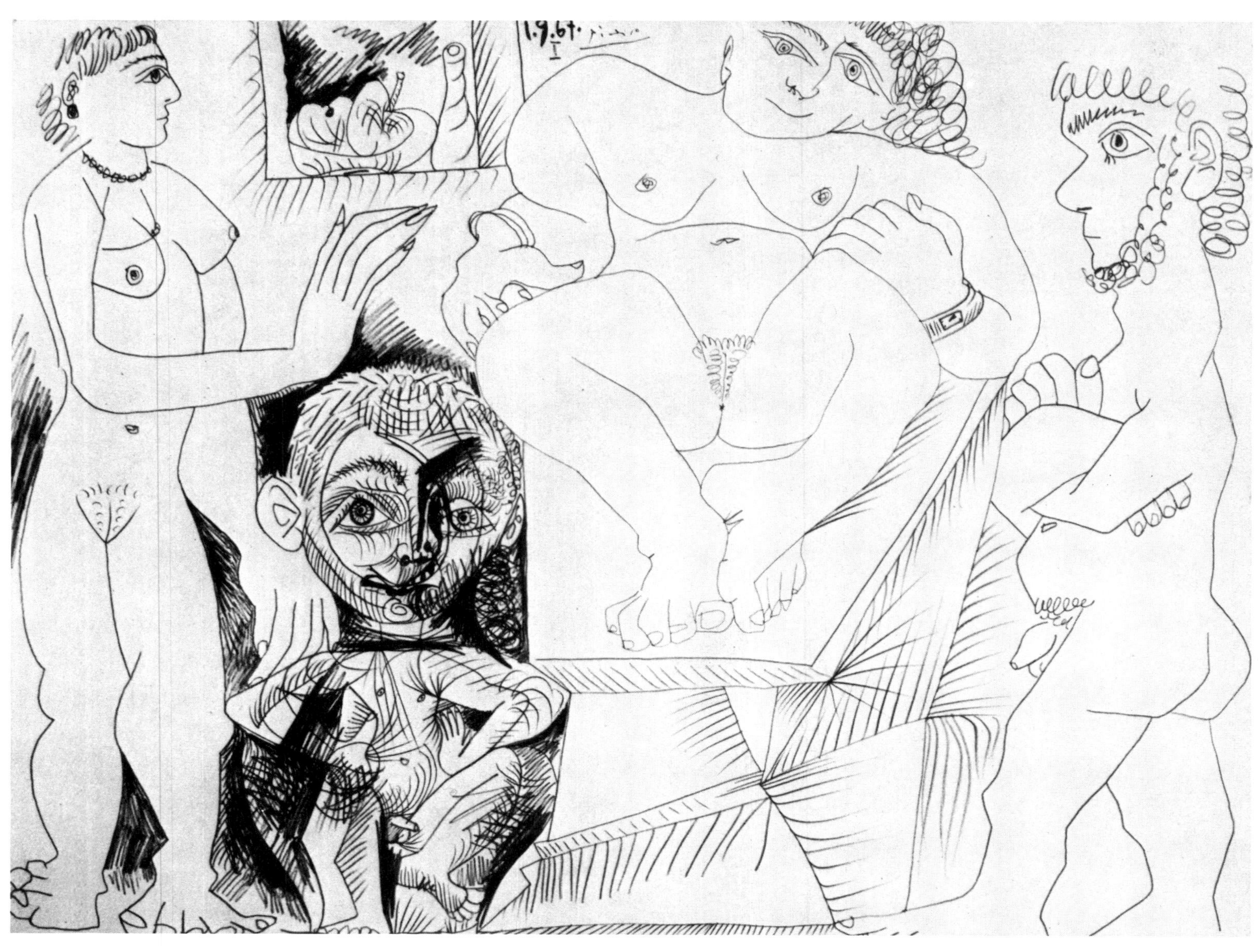

69
COURTSHIP SCENE
pencil 56.5×75
1.9.67 I

70
THE THREE GRACES
pencil and gouache 75×56.5
3.9.67 II and 4.9.67

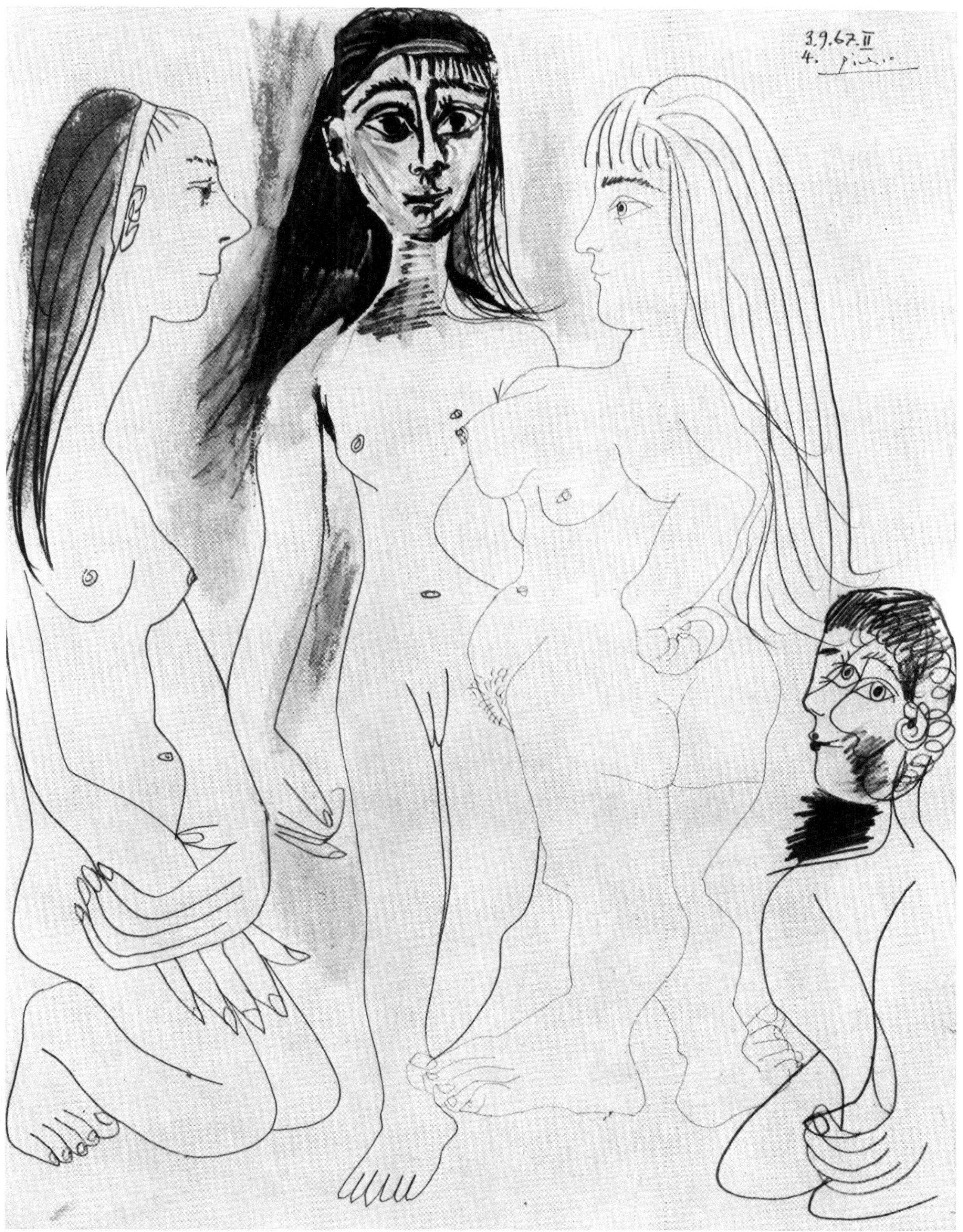
3.9.67.II
4.

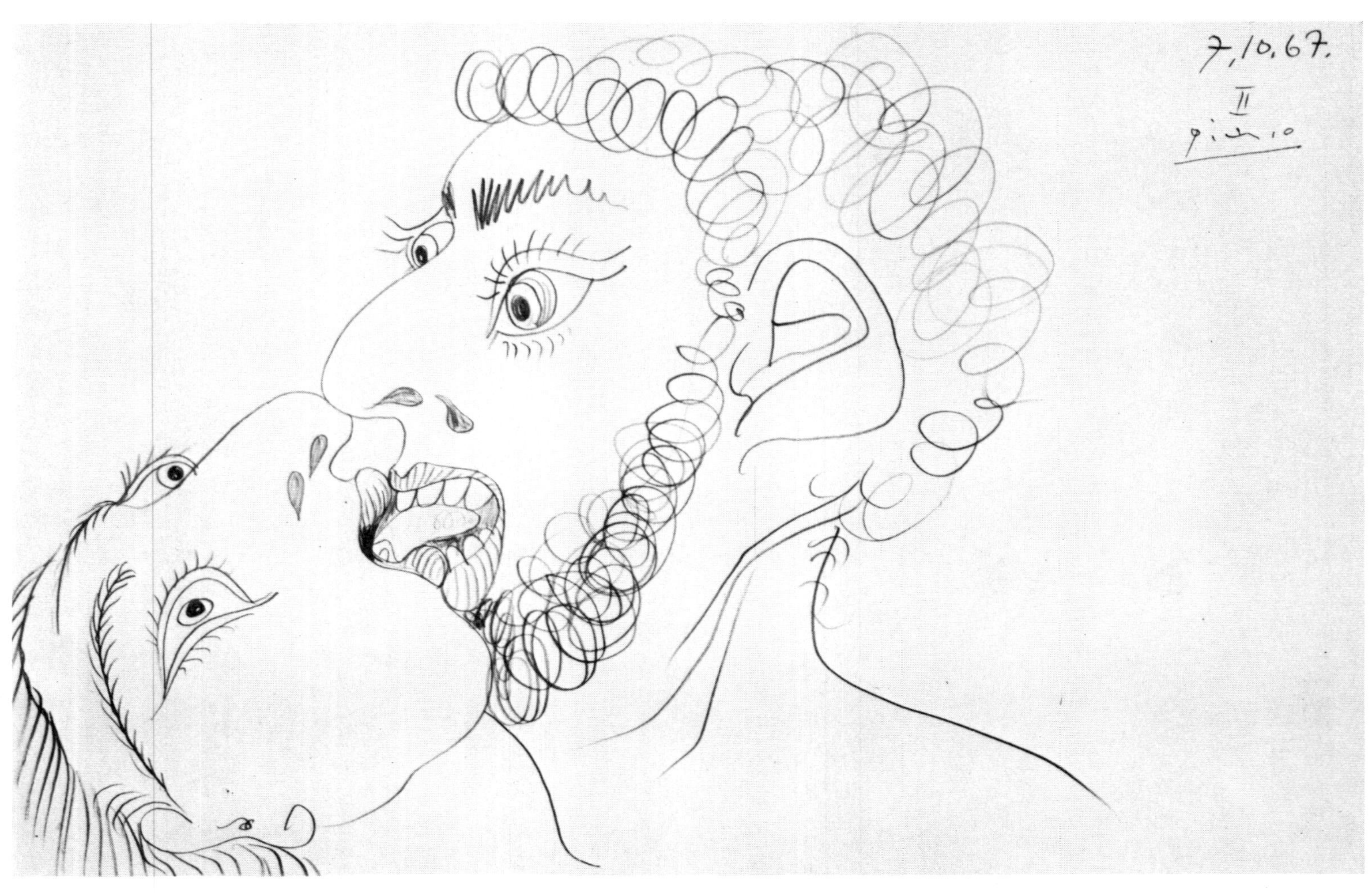

71
THE KISS
pencil 33×50.5
7.10.67 II

72
SIX NUDE FIGURES
Indian ink and gouache 65×58
8.11/14.11.67 and 25.12.67

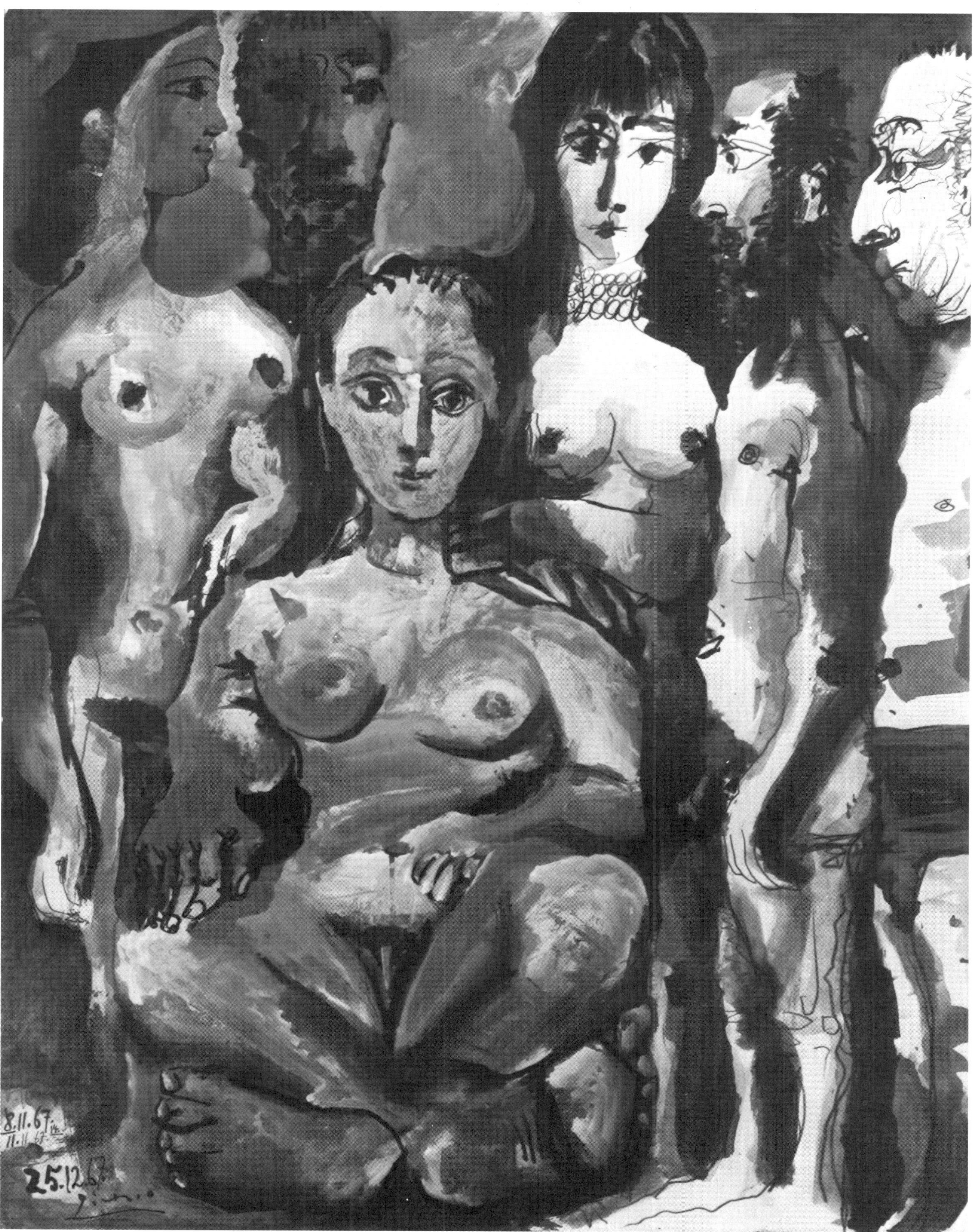
8.11.67
25.12.67

VII
SMOKER
pencil and coloured chalk
22.5.64 II

VIII
SMOKER
pencil and coloured chalk
22.5.64 III

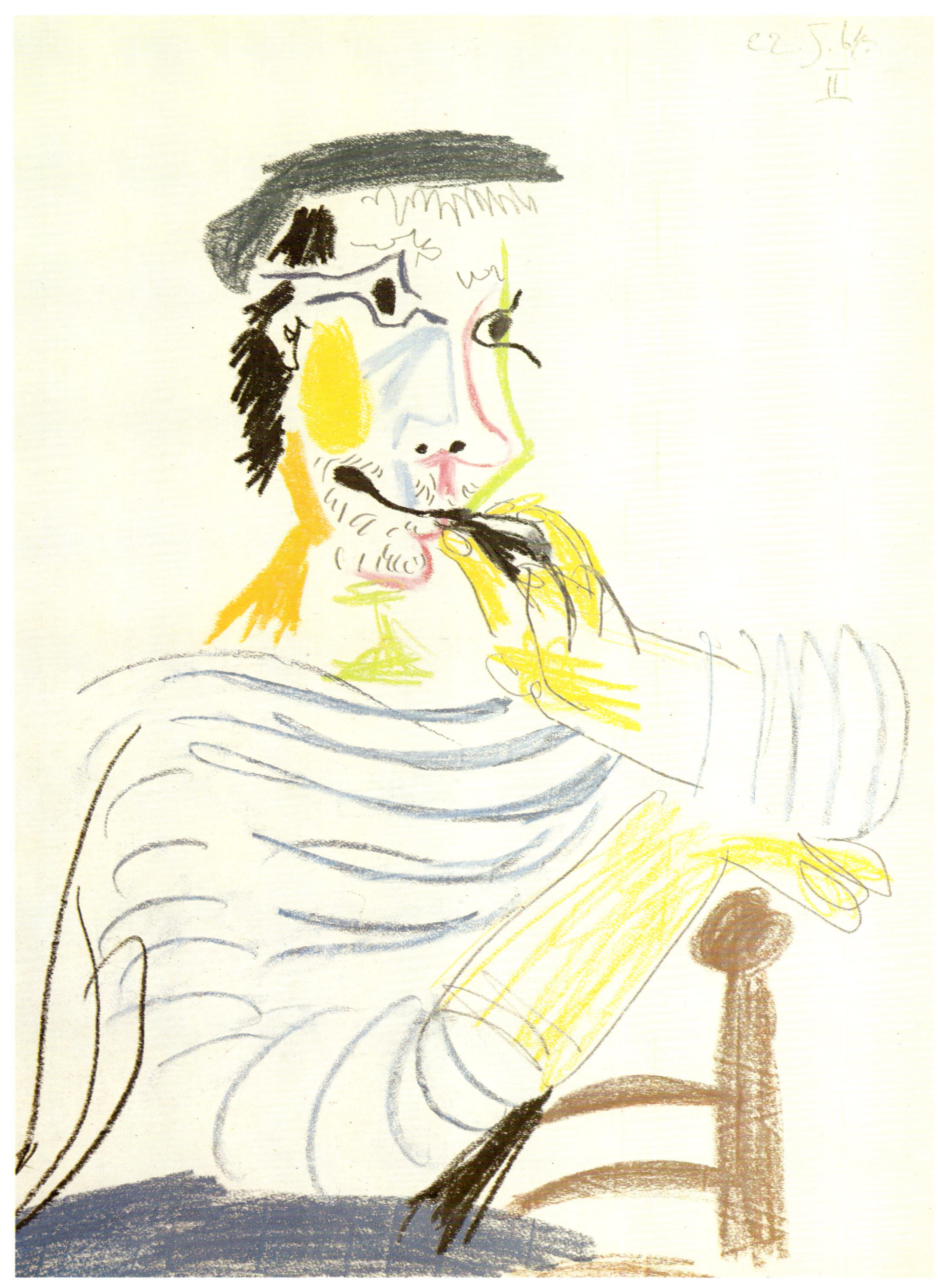
22.5.64.
II

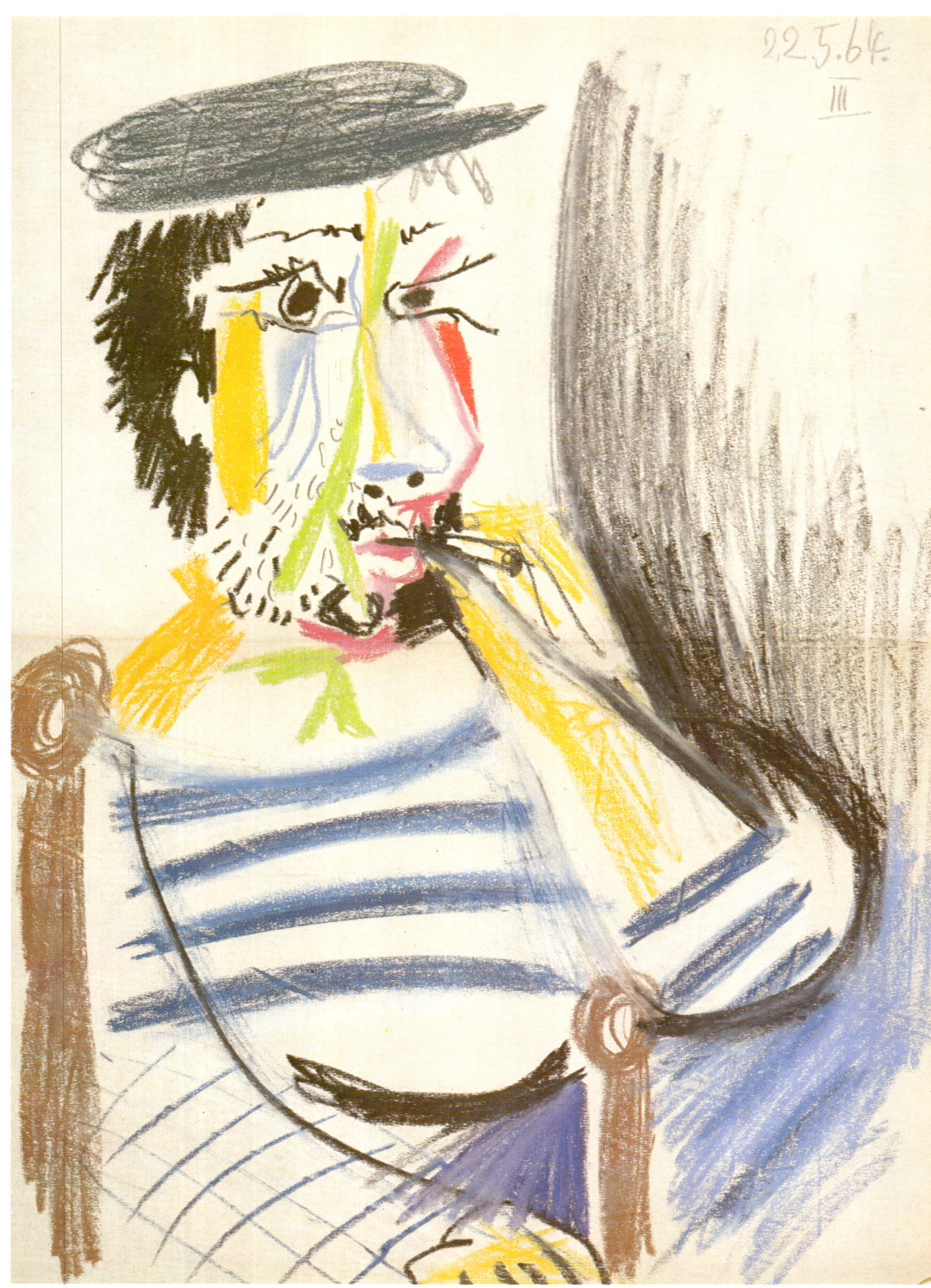
22.5.64.
III

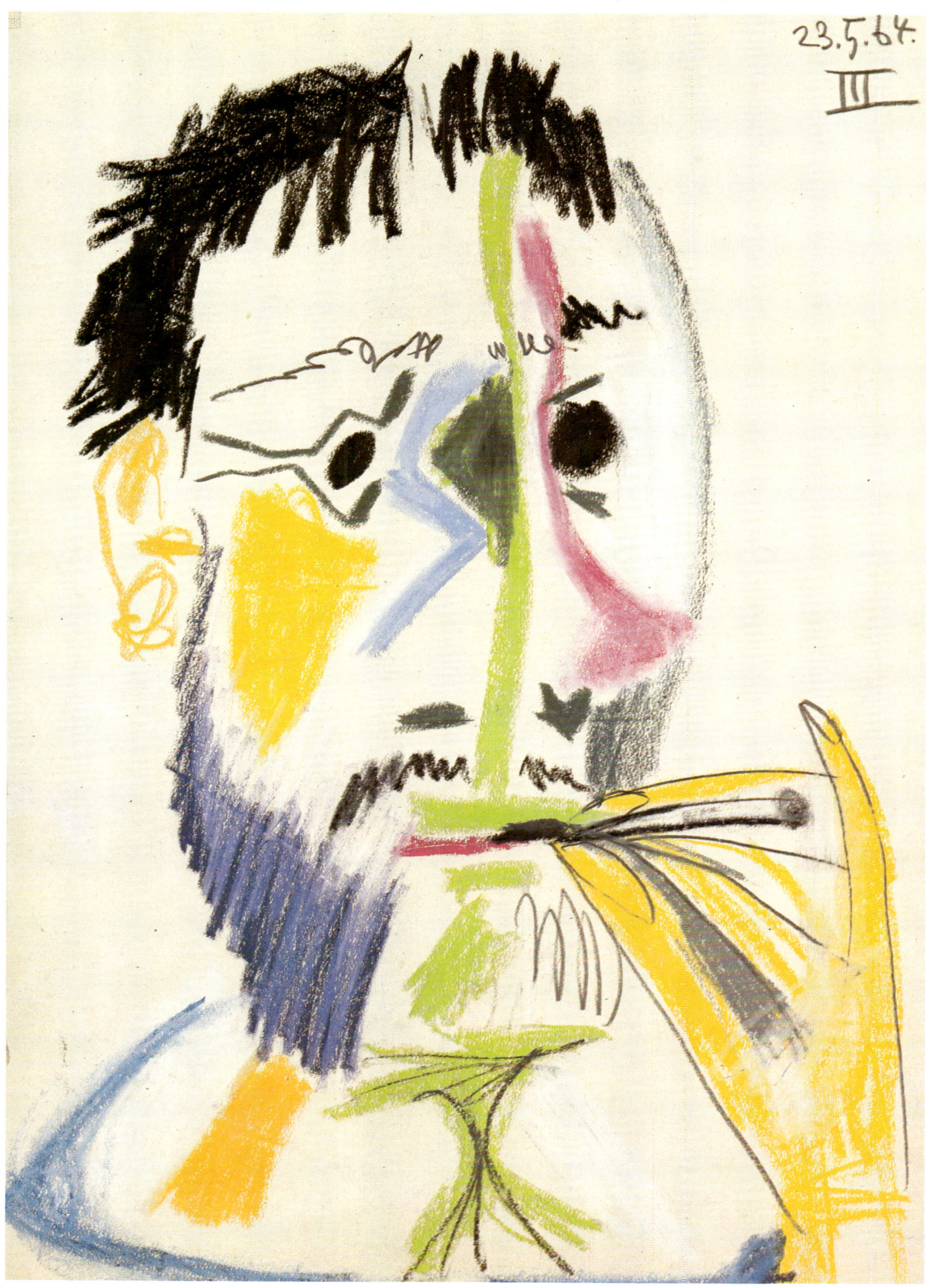
23.5.64.
III

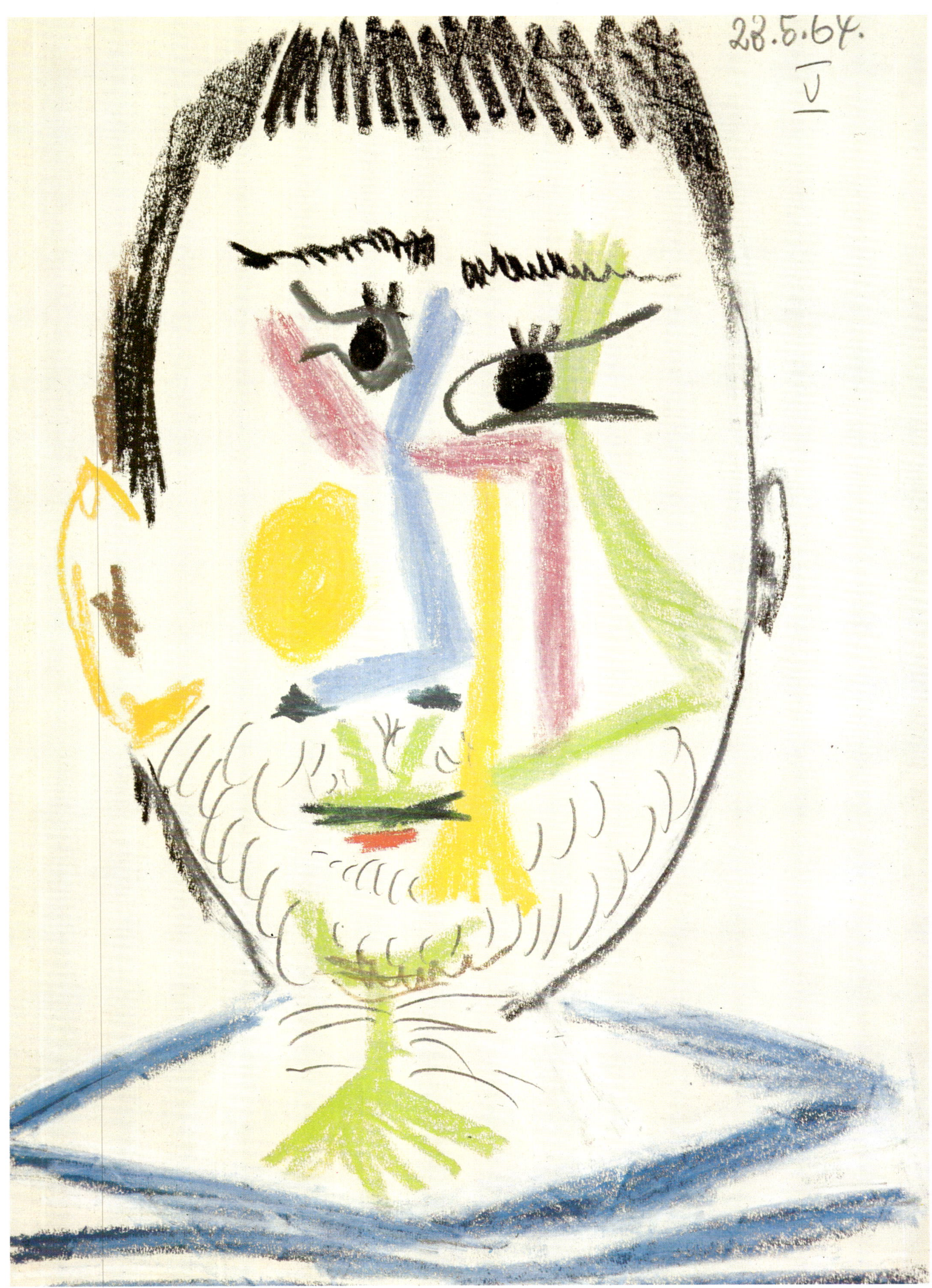
28.5.64.
V

XI

EROS ETERNAL

We have chosen a few series of drawings here from among several hundreds. On 8 October 1964, on the pages of a spiral bound sketch-book of the kind he particularly liked, Picasso drew a man intimately admiring a woman. He looks at her, touches her, strokes her, kisses her breasts. She seems frightened, hides her face, covers her genitals with her hands. How can she do all that? Because Picasso has given her three hands! The male figure is not identical from one drawing to the next, but the action of adoration is eternal. The line here is of apparently total spontaneity, clear and innocent as the scene it is describing.

In the same vein, another very linear series drawn on 26 November 1969 depicts a passionate embrace. Is the woman resisting the man, who seems to be using almost irresistible force? Here too the man's appearance changes from page to page. The same scene is drawn and redrawn time and time again and we shall not hazard a guess at the meaning of these transformations. Picasso may simply have been amusing himself, his mood may have changed . . . We can offer no other explanation.

It is nevertheless disconcerting to see the mature, strong, bearded man replaced by a frail youth, while a delicate young girl takes the place of the full-blown woman. One generation succeeds another. It is a thought-provoking comparison.

Here too, the line is elegant and expressive, in arabesques translating movement and expression all the virile strength of the actions.

The same passion, the same expressive line is to be seen in the series of passionate kisses from which we feature the one drawn on 7th October 1967.

He used the same linear treatment, which bears comparison with

IX
SMOKER
pencil and coloured chalk
23.5.64 III

X
SMOKER
pencil and coloured chalk
23.5.64 V

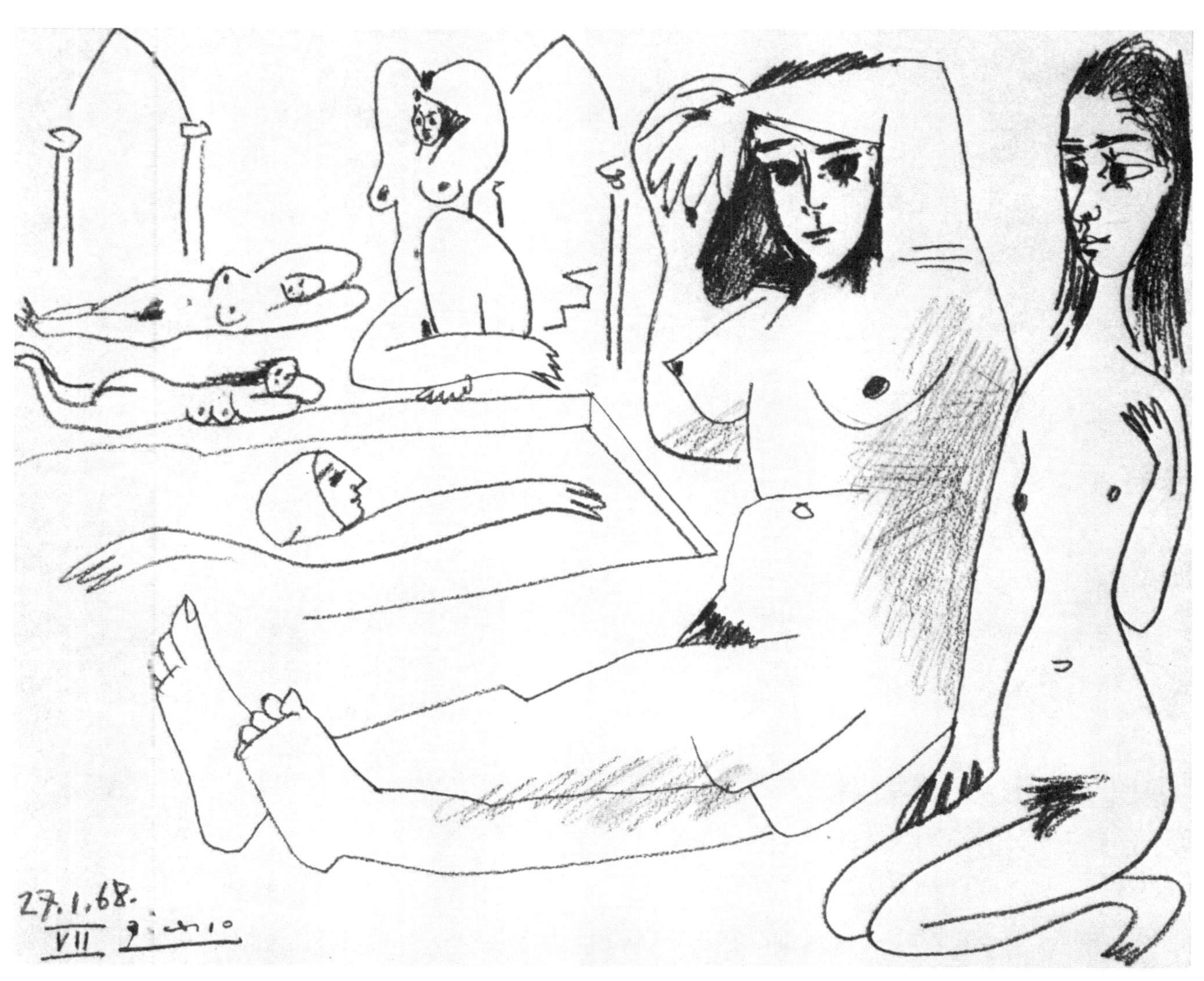

73
THE SWIMMING POOL
pencil 23.8×29.4
27.1.68 VII

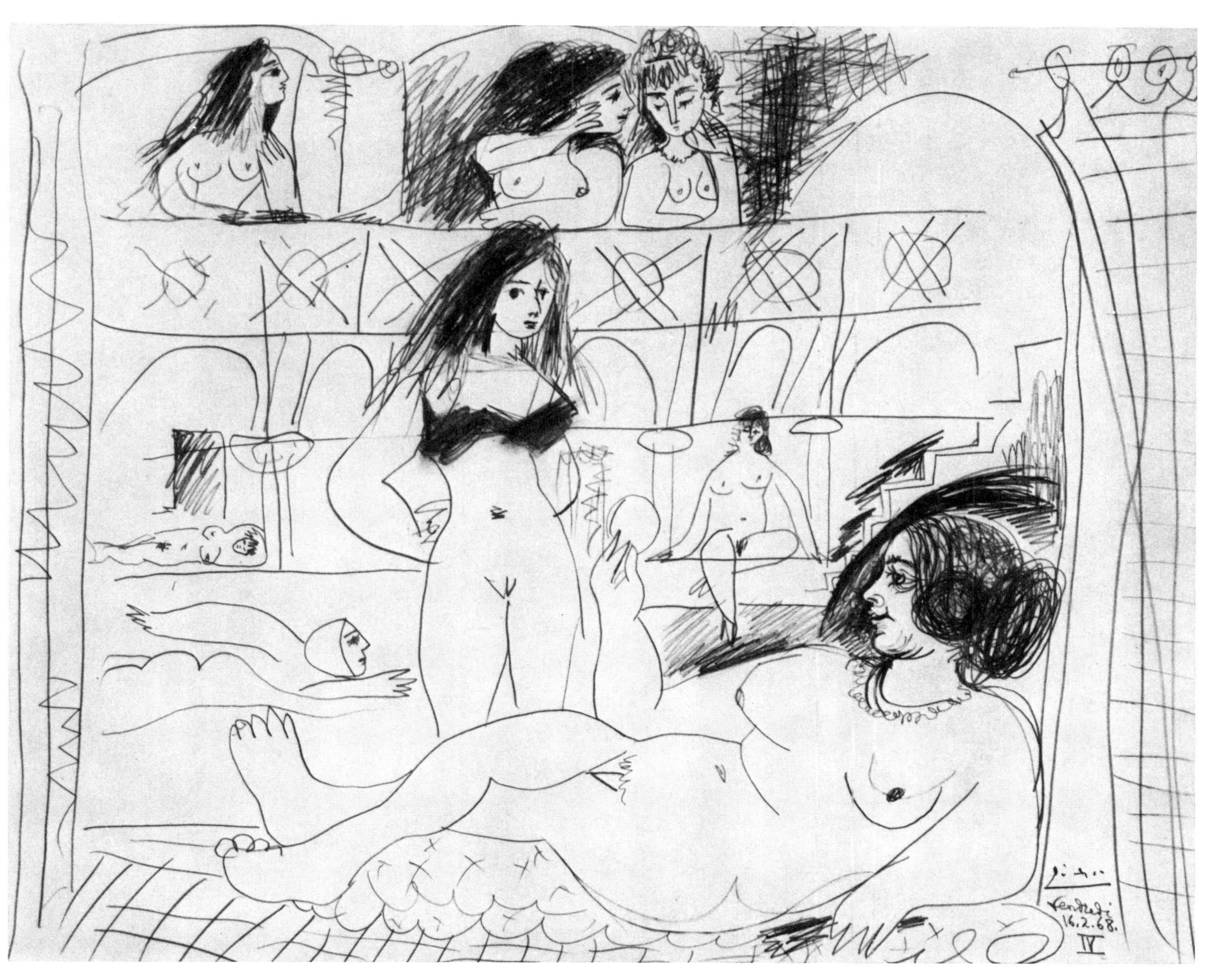

74
THE SWIMMING POOL
pencil 48×59
16.2.68 IV

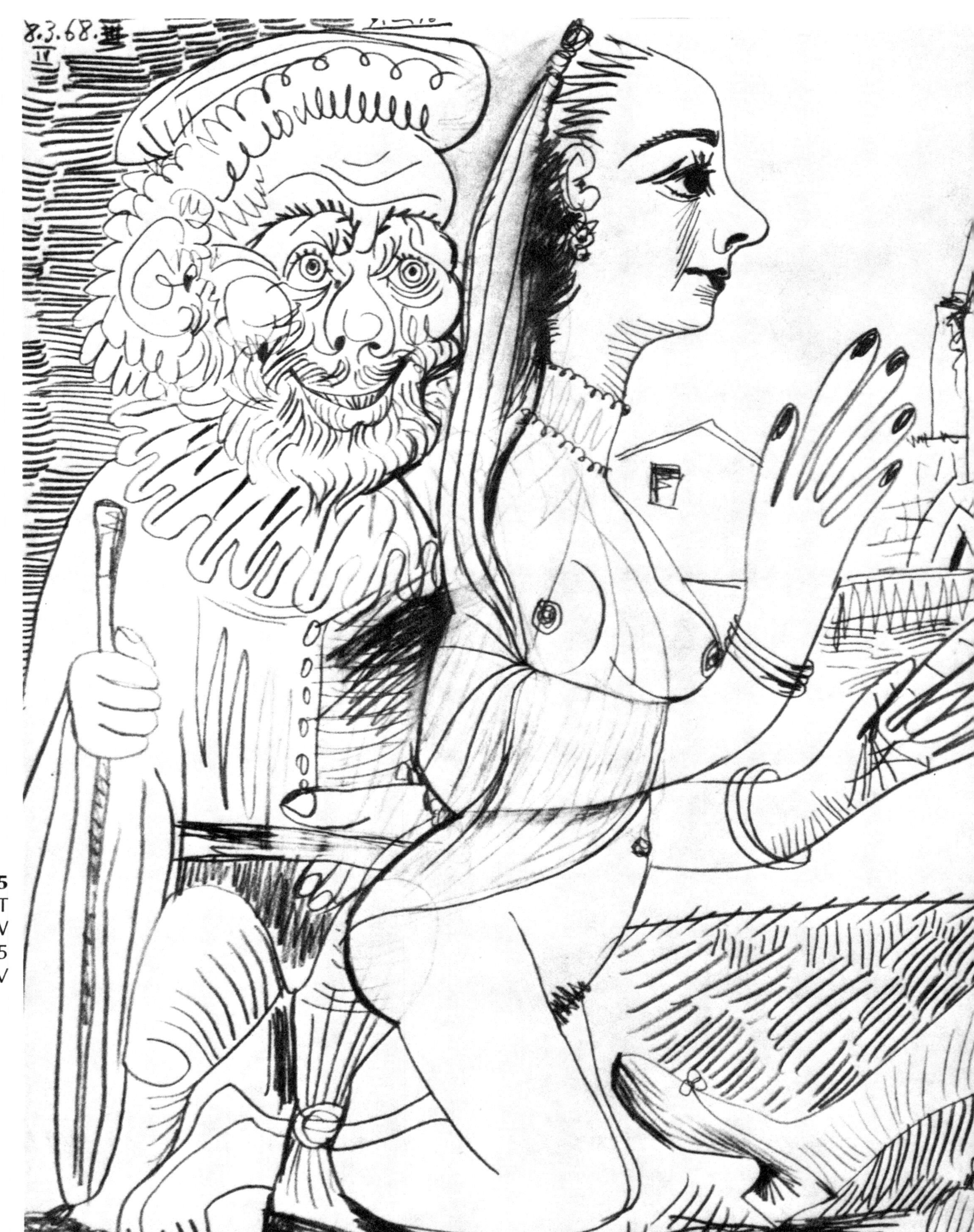

75
FIGURES AT THE WINDOW
pencil 49.2×75.5
8.3.68 IV

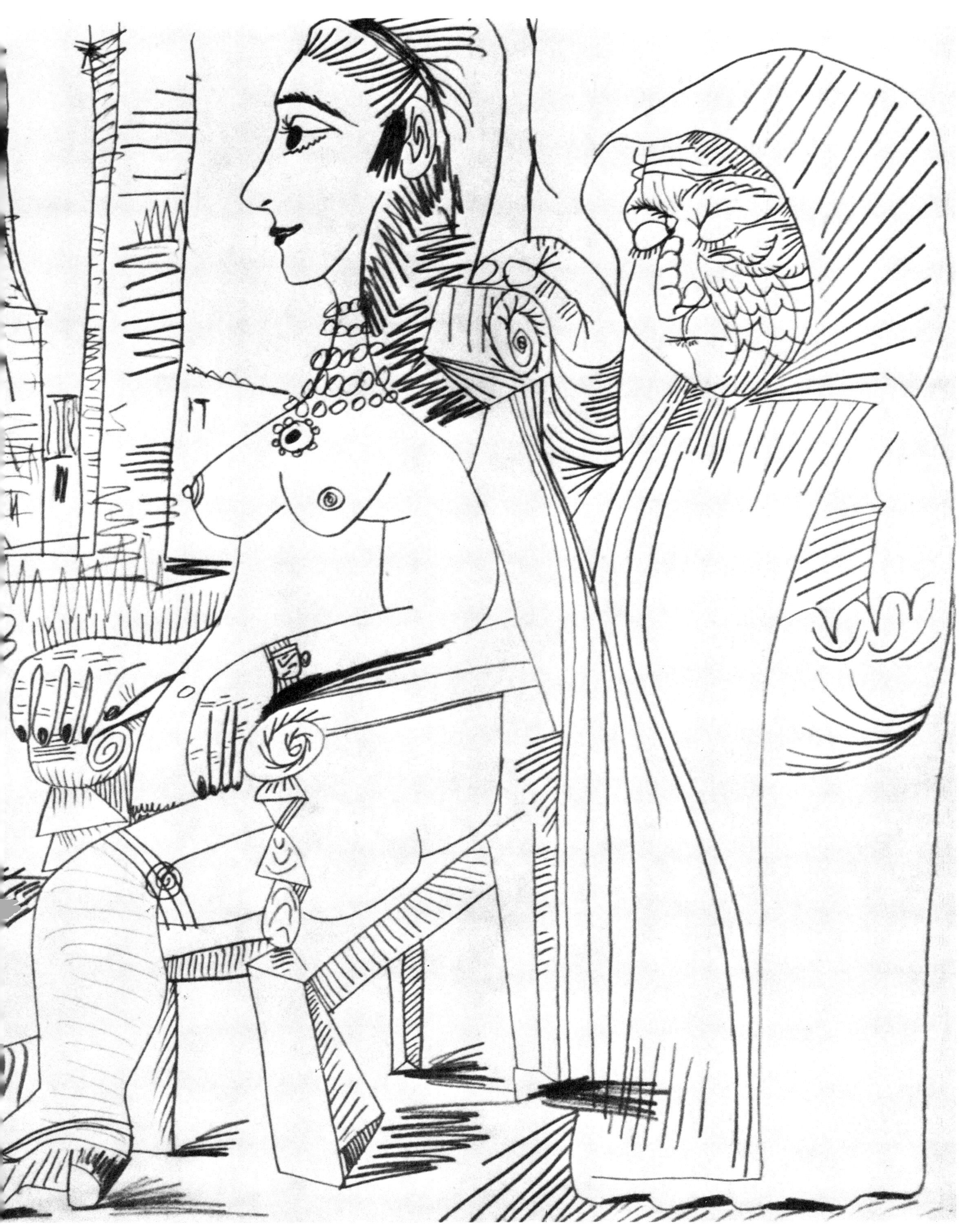

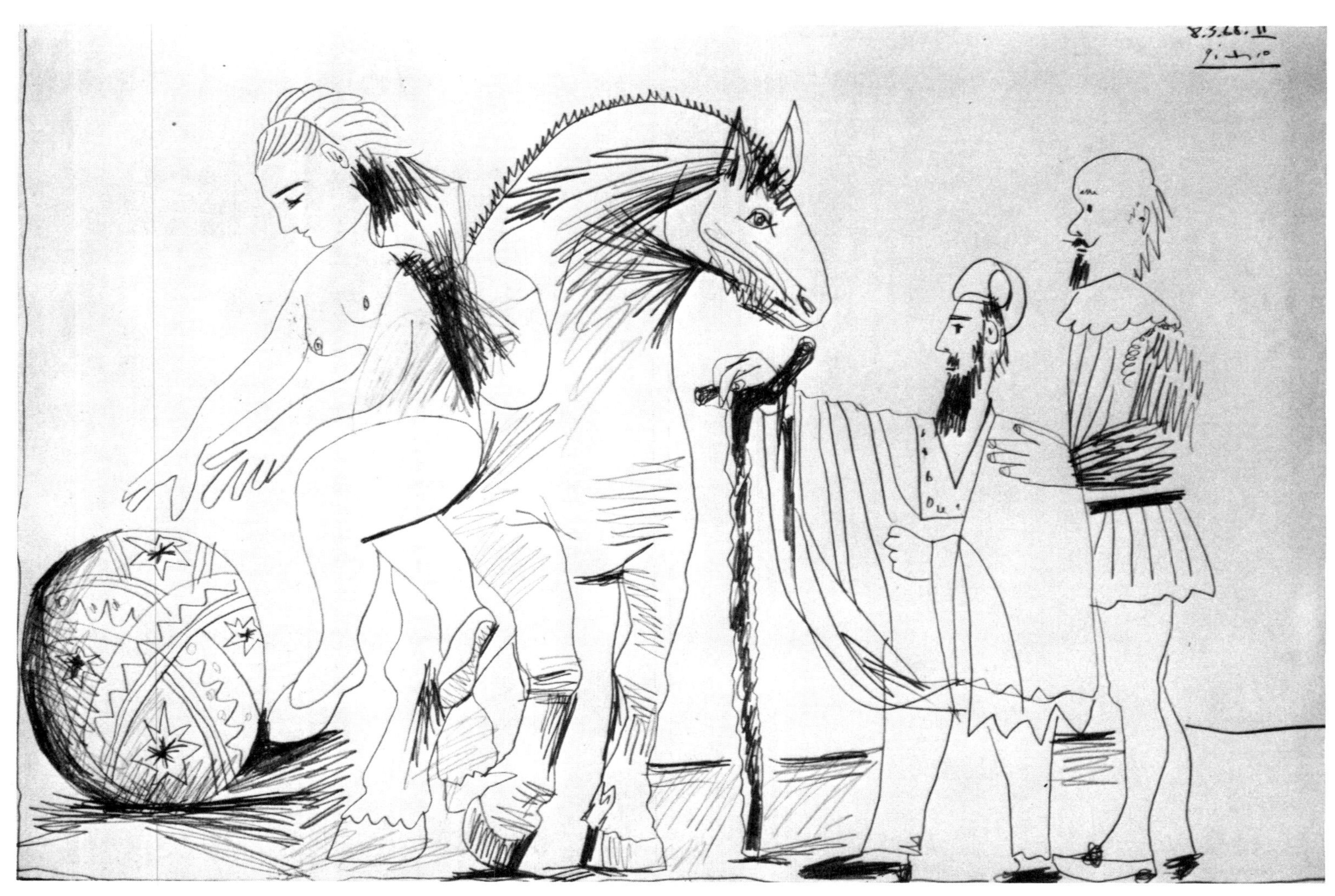

76
HORSEWOMAN WITH BALL
pencil 49.2×76
8.3.68 II

77
TWO WOMEN
coloured pencil 44×31.5
4.2.69 III

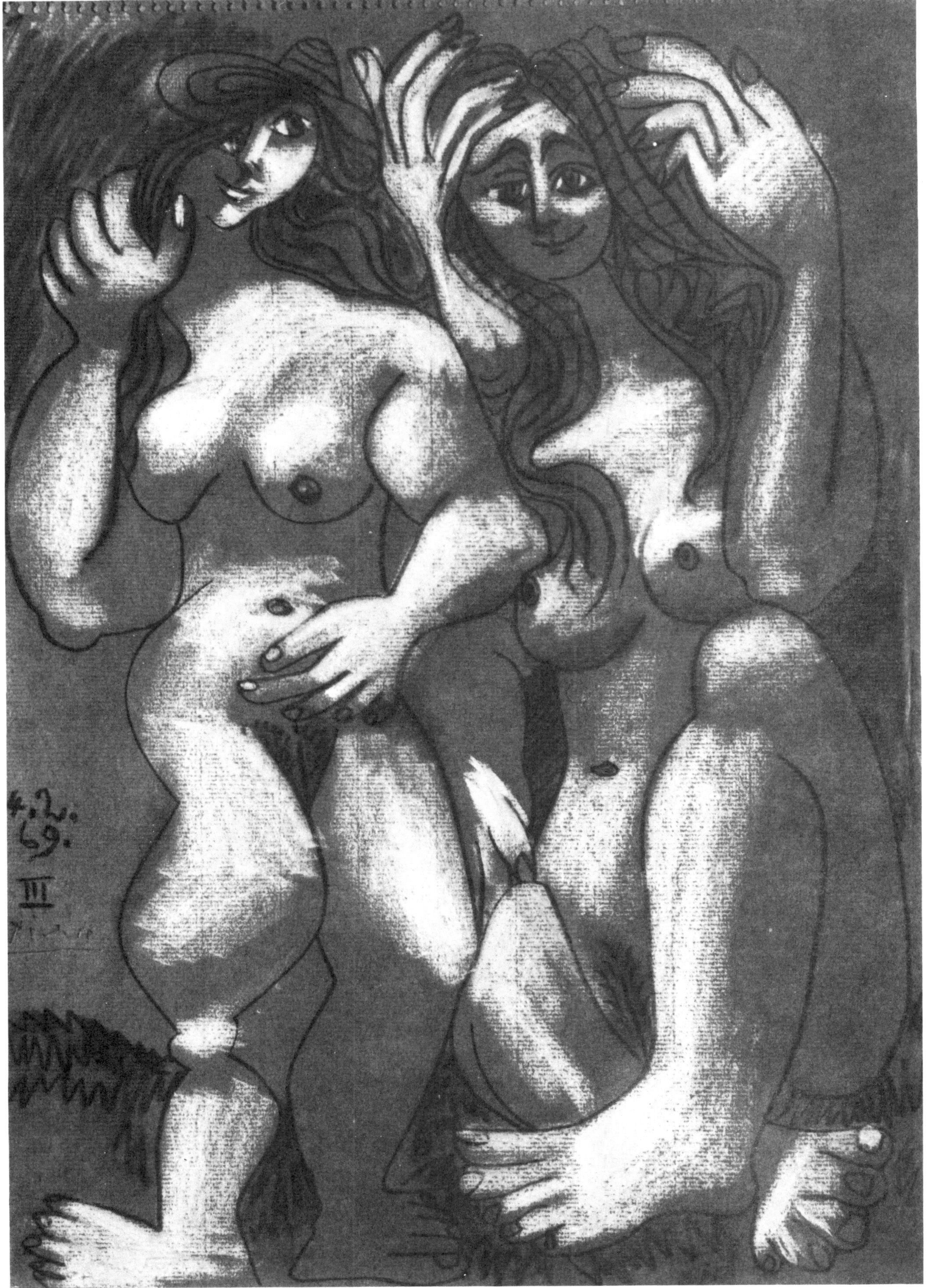
4.2.
69.
III

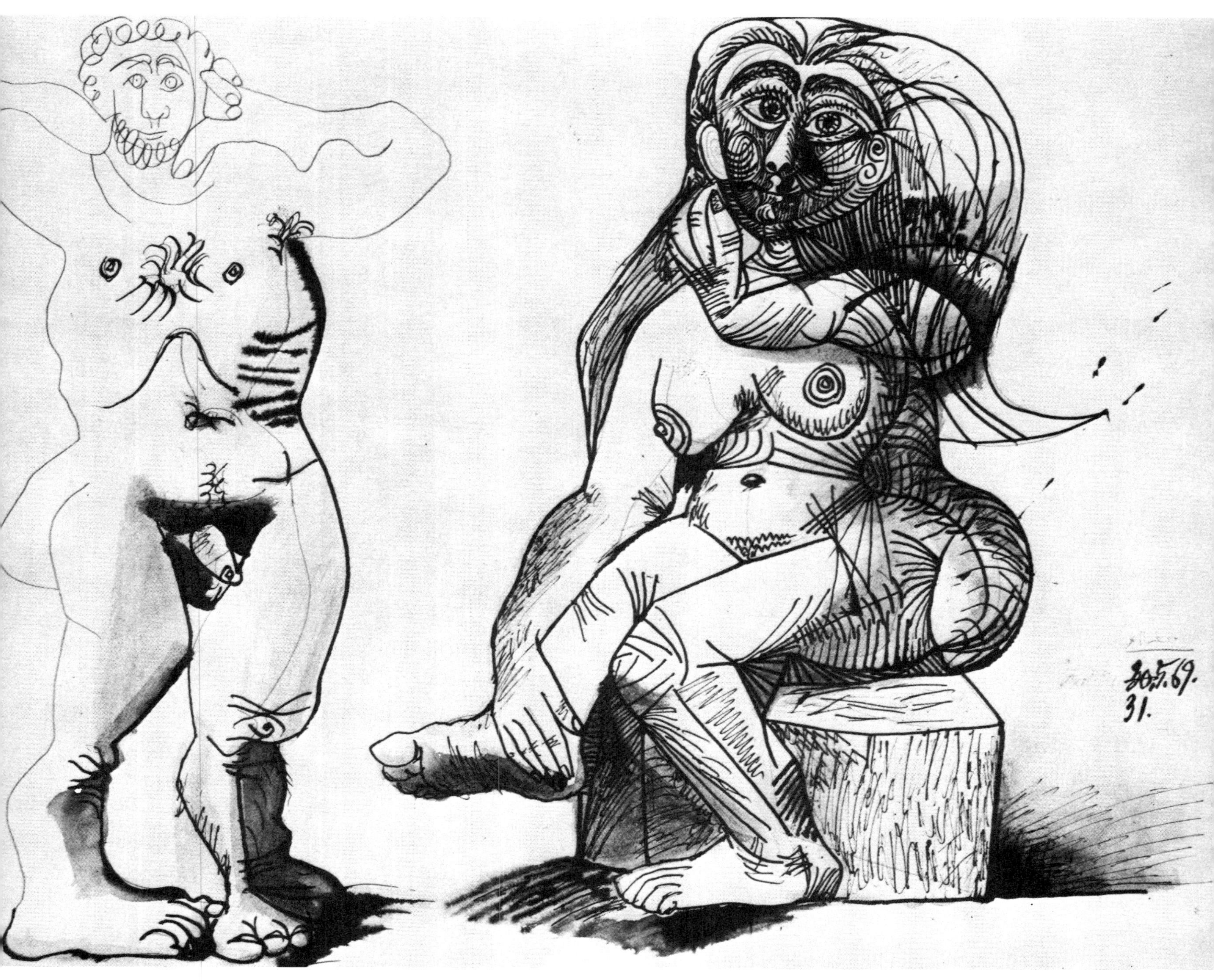

78
MAN AND WOMAN
Indian ink 50.8×65.2
31.5.69

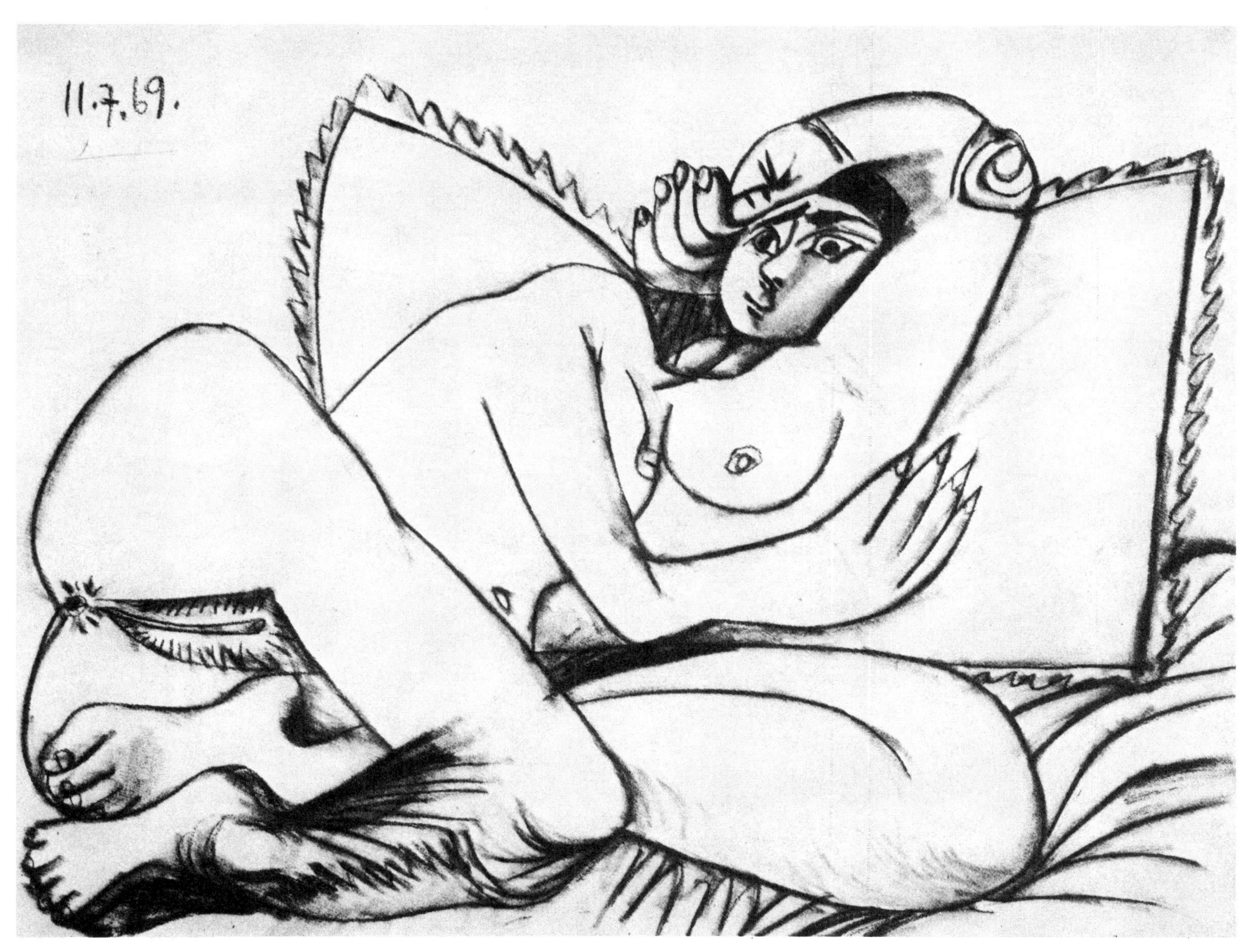

79
RECLINING WOMAN
charcoal 50.57×65.5
11.7.69

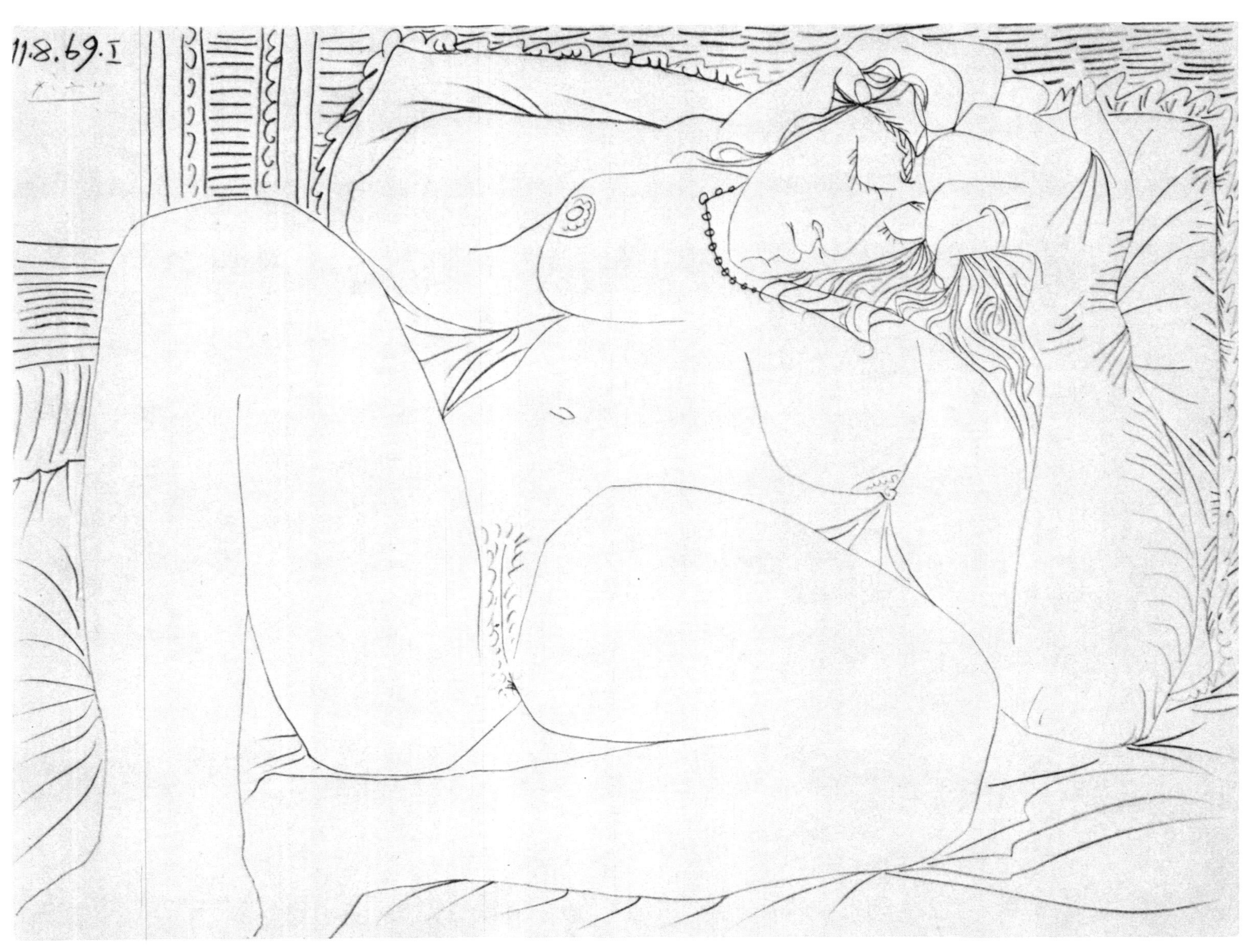

80
RECLINING WOMAN
pencil 50.57×65.5
11.8.69 I

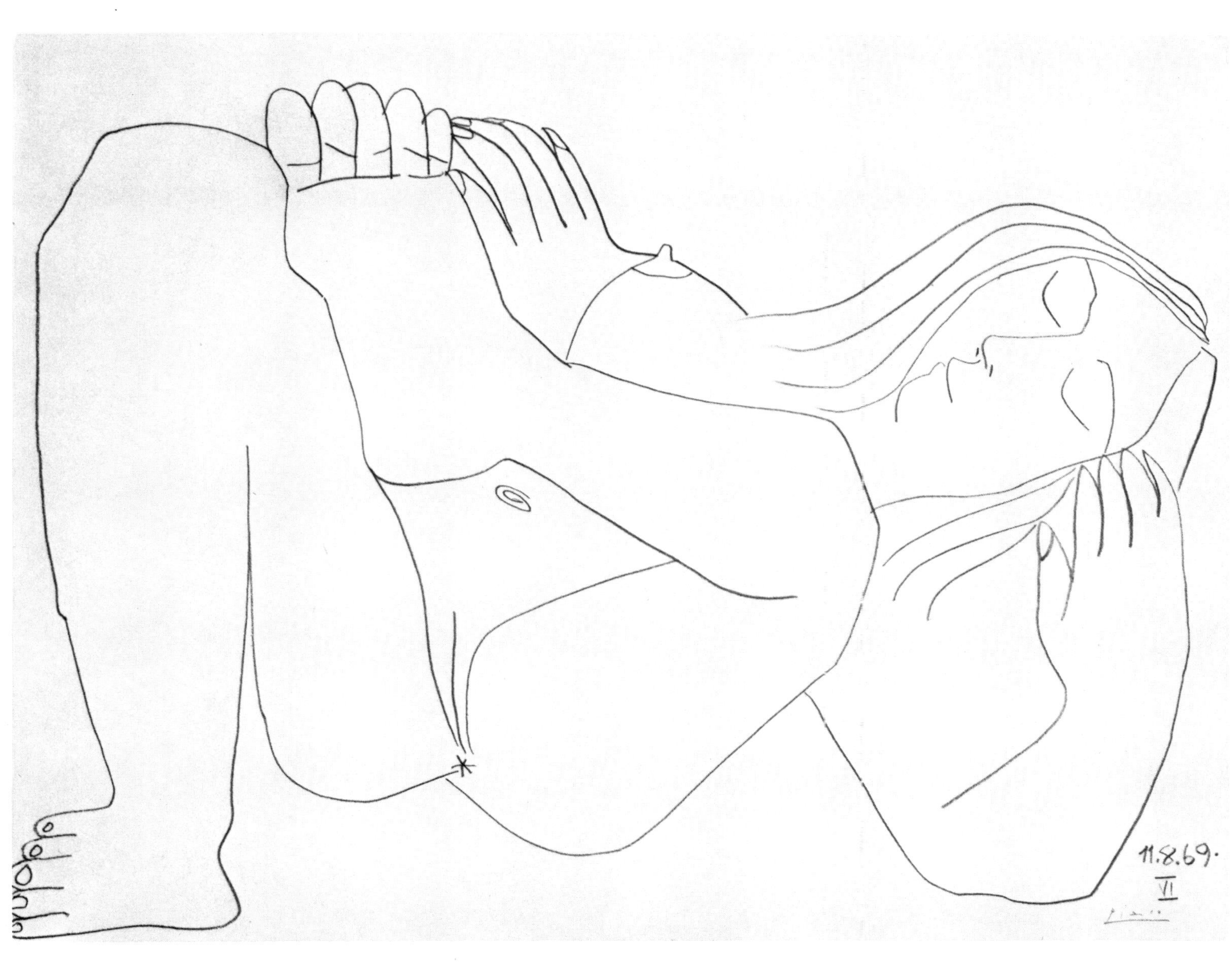

81
RECLINING WOMAN
coloured pencil 50.57×65.5
11.8.69 II

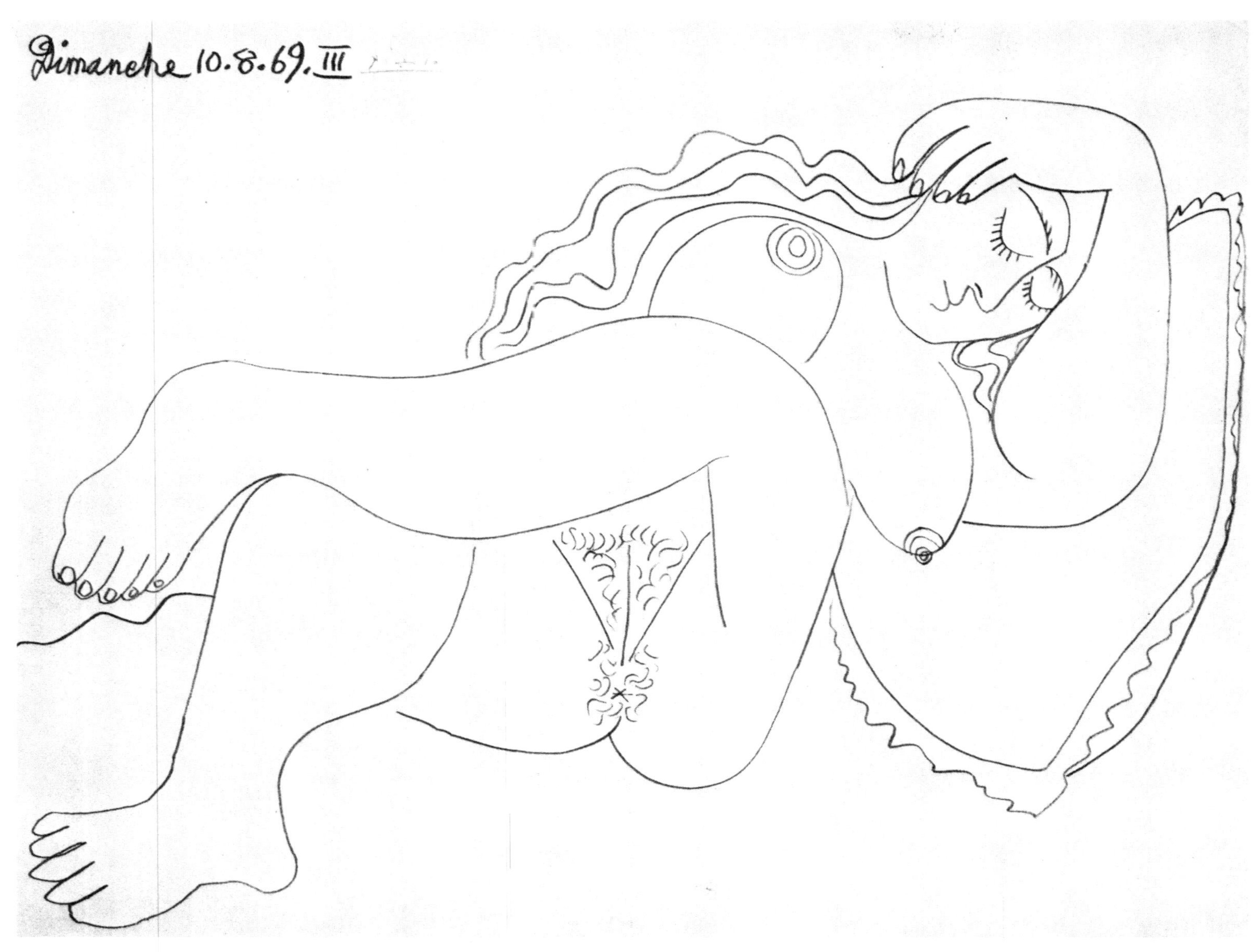

82
RECLINING WOMAN
pencil
Sunday 10.8.69 III

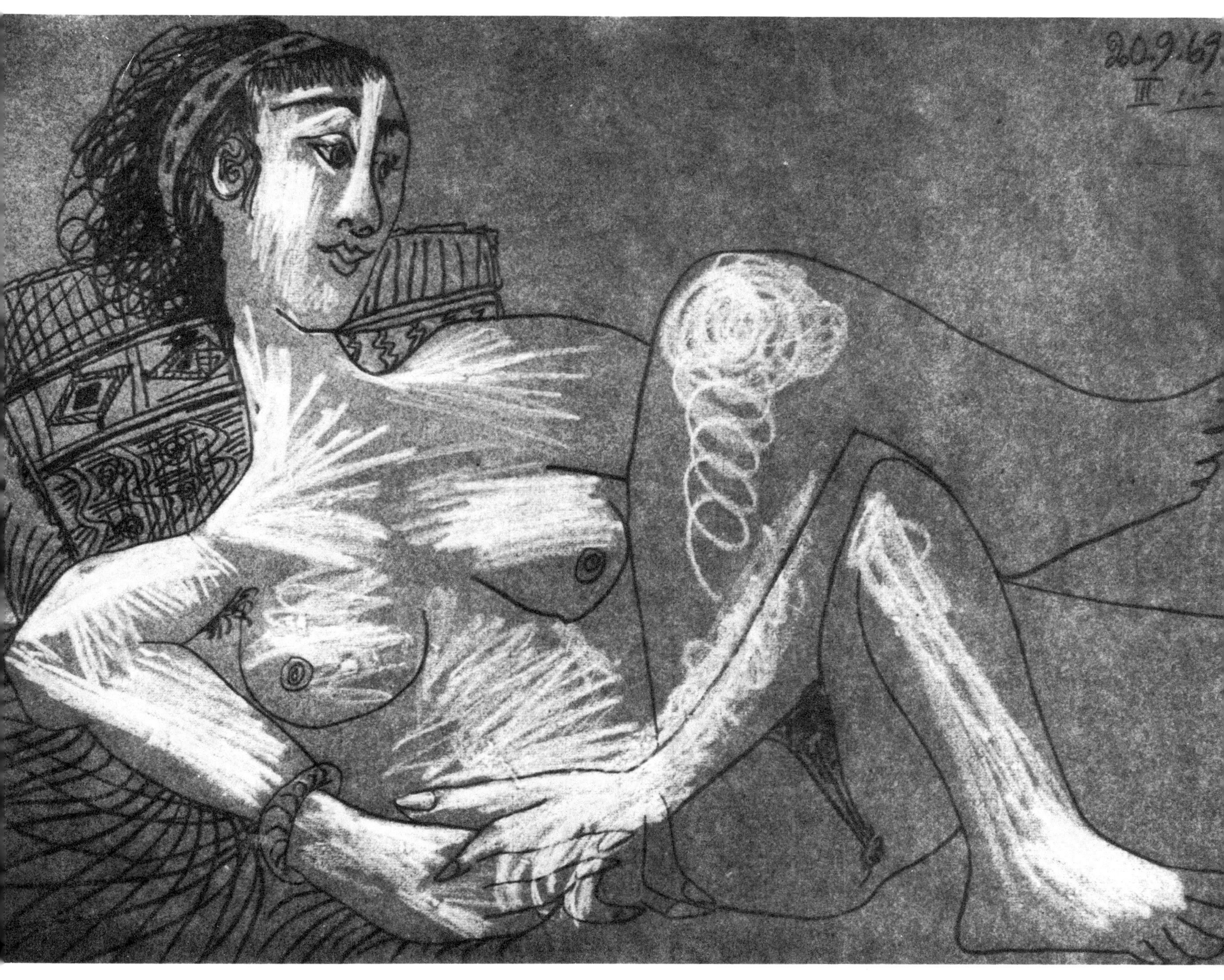

83
RECLINING WOMAN
pencil and chalk 48×63.5
20.9.69 III

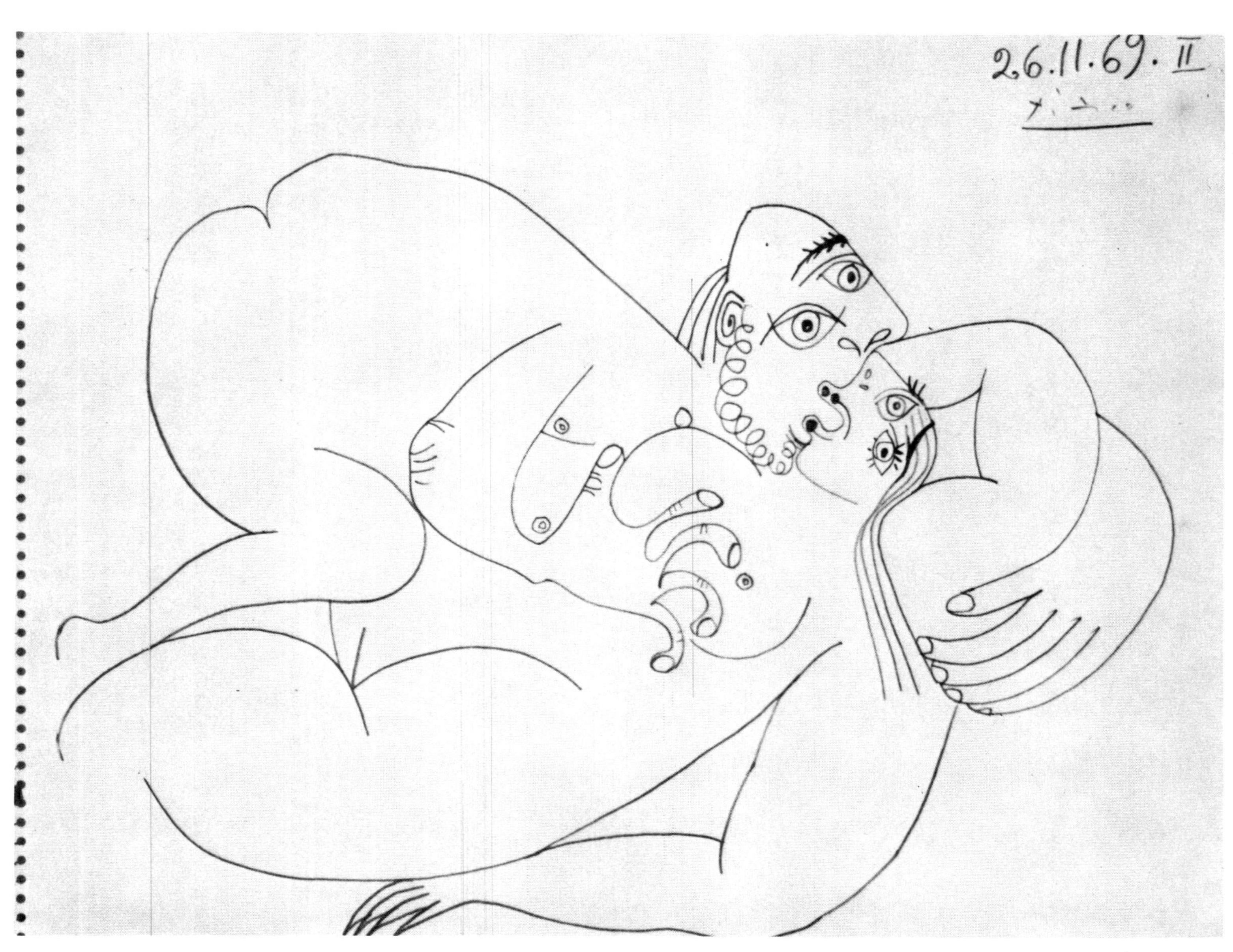

84
COUPLE EMBRACE (sketchbook page)
pencil 21×30.5
26.11.69 II

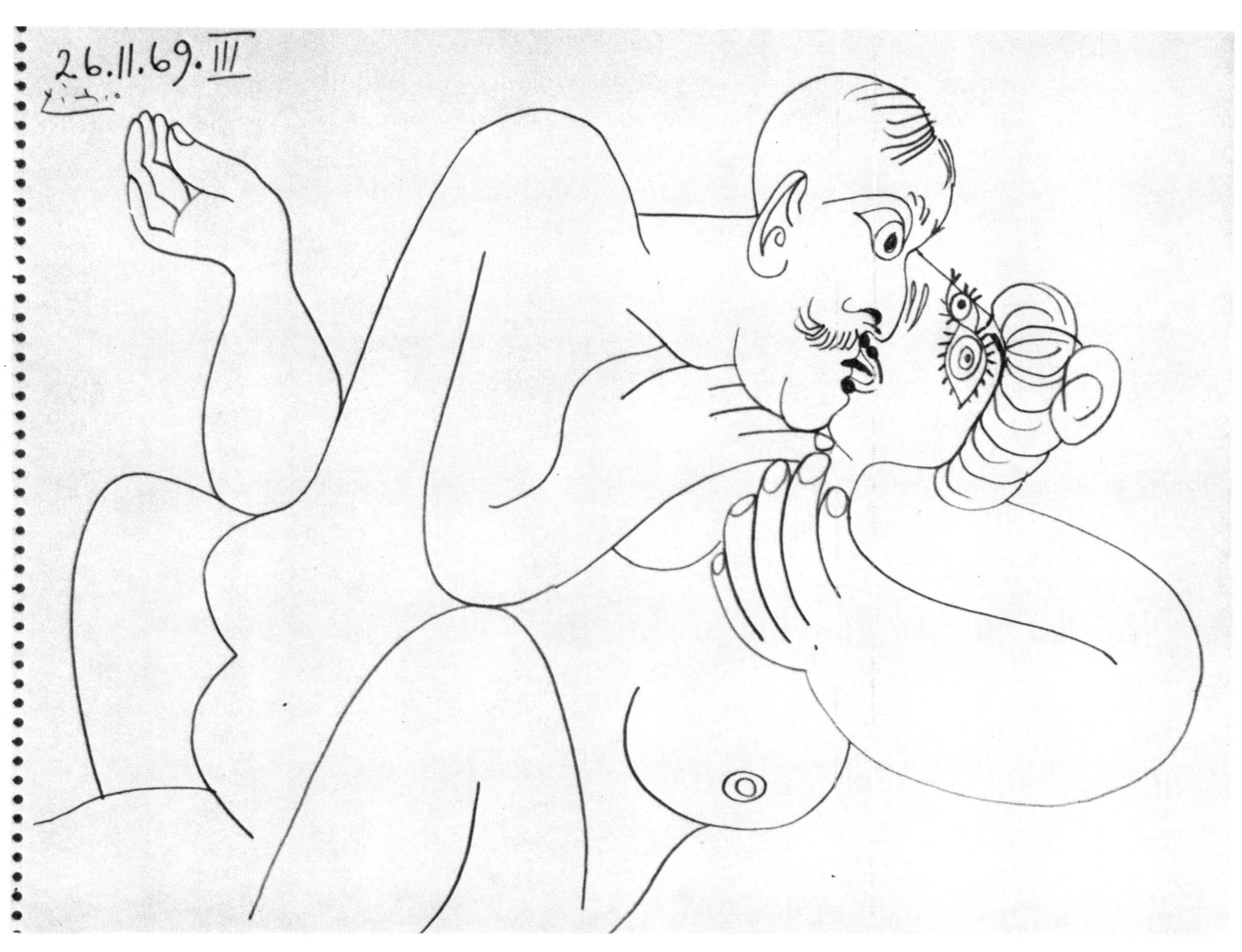

85
COUPLE EMBRACE (sketchbook page)
pencil 21×30.5
26.11.69 III

that of Matisse, for the *Sleeping Women* of August 1969, who reveal their most intimate parts, those that the painter saw as the very centre of womanhood: he brought his utmost artistry to bear in the stylished dressing of their pubic hair.

In September of the same year, Picasso relapsed into a quite different technique. He worked in black and white on grey card, using chalk, black and coloured pencil and Indian ink, occasionally heightened with gouache. The tinted ground lends the drawing body and relief; drawing tends towards painting. The characters too acquire individuality. They are no longer simply objects, excuses for a stylistic exercise. They look the spectator in the eye, they are alive. They are no longer isolated either, they are part of scenes where men and women mingle with mysterious figures of gnomes, old men dressed in sackcloth or in sumptuous doublets, sometimes even in ancient tunics. Picasso organised 'happenings' on paper. He brought historical figures who could never have met face to face with each other and imagined what they might have done together. His visions are comical, disturbing and strange. Imagination makes everything possible. But one thing is certain: these people are enjoying each other's company as much as Picasso enjoyed drawing them.

There are two bath scenes to end with. In one (12 February 1968), a young woman adjusts her brassiere in what looks like a Paris swimming pool. The other (27 January 1968) appears to be set in a Turkish bath. Each one poses the question of whether the scene was drawn from memory or from imagination.

To crown this anthology, we have chosen a work that is dramatic in its profund humanity. It is Picasso's last self-portrait, which was exhibited at the Galerie Louise Leiris in December 1968. One is lost for words in front of this picture, dumbfounded by its prescient and transcendental vision. Pierre Daix wrote:

XI
SMOKER
pencil and coloured chalk
23.5.64 VI

XII
SMOKER
pencil and coloured chalk
31.5.64 II

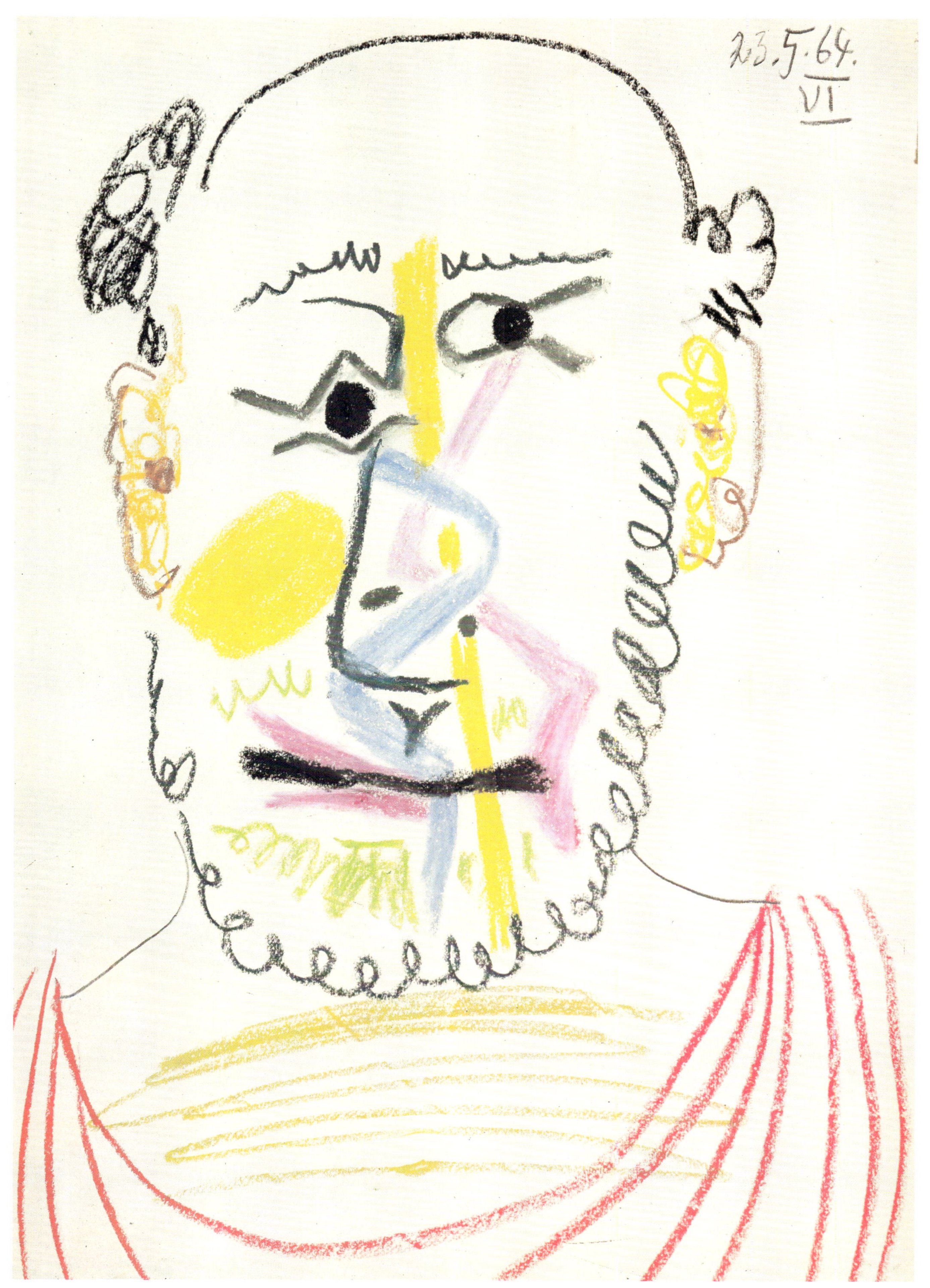
23.5.64.
VI

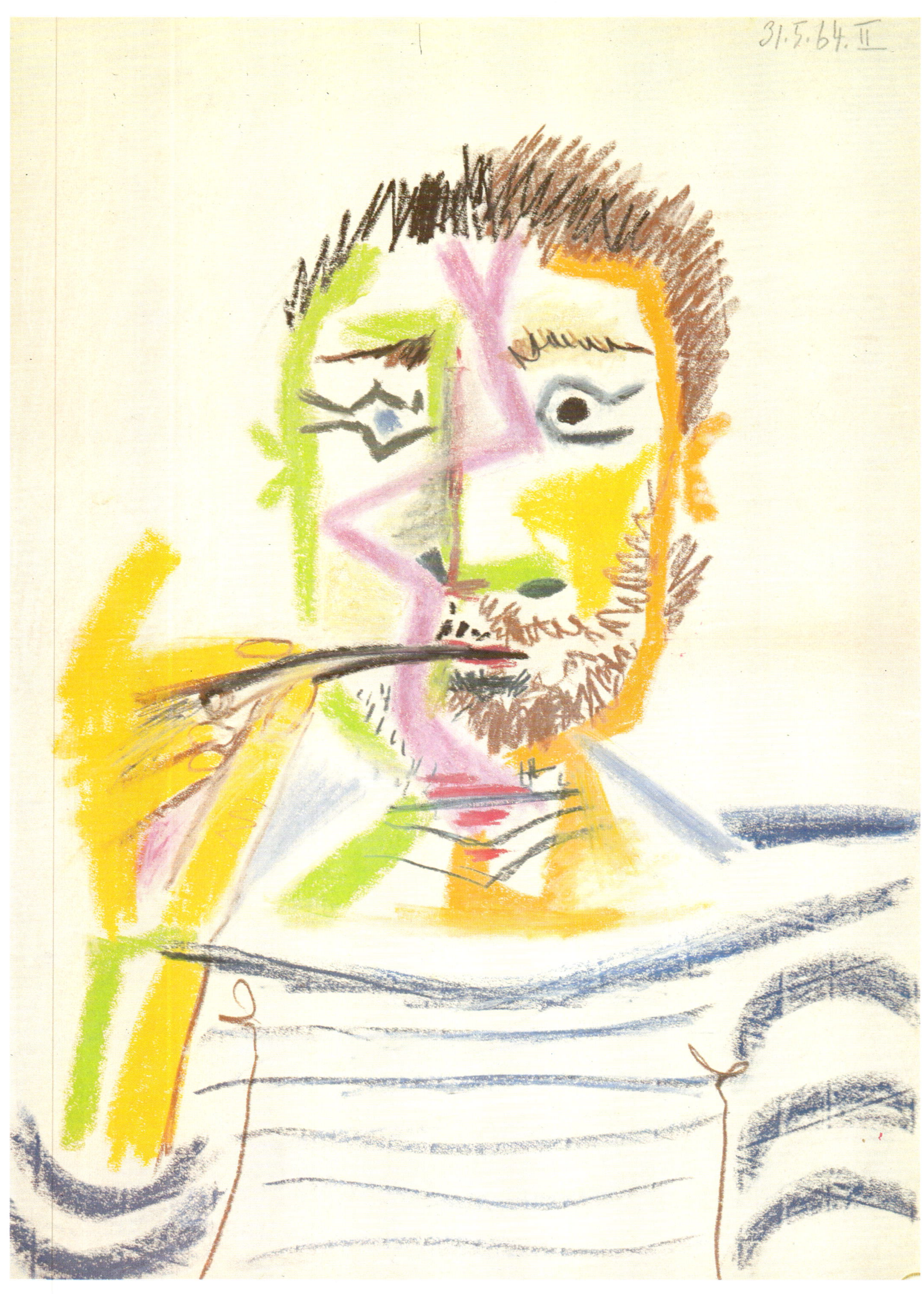
31.5.64. II

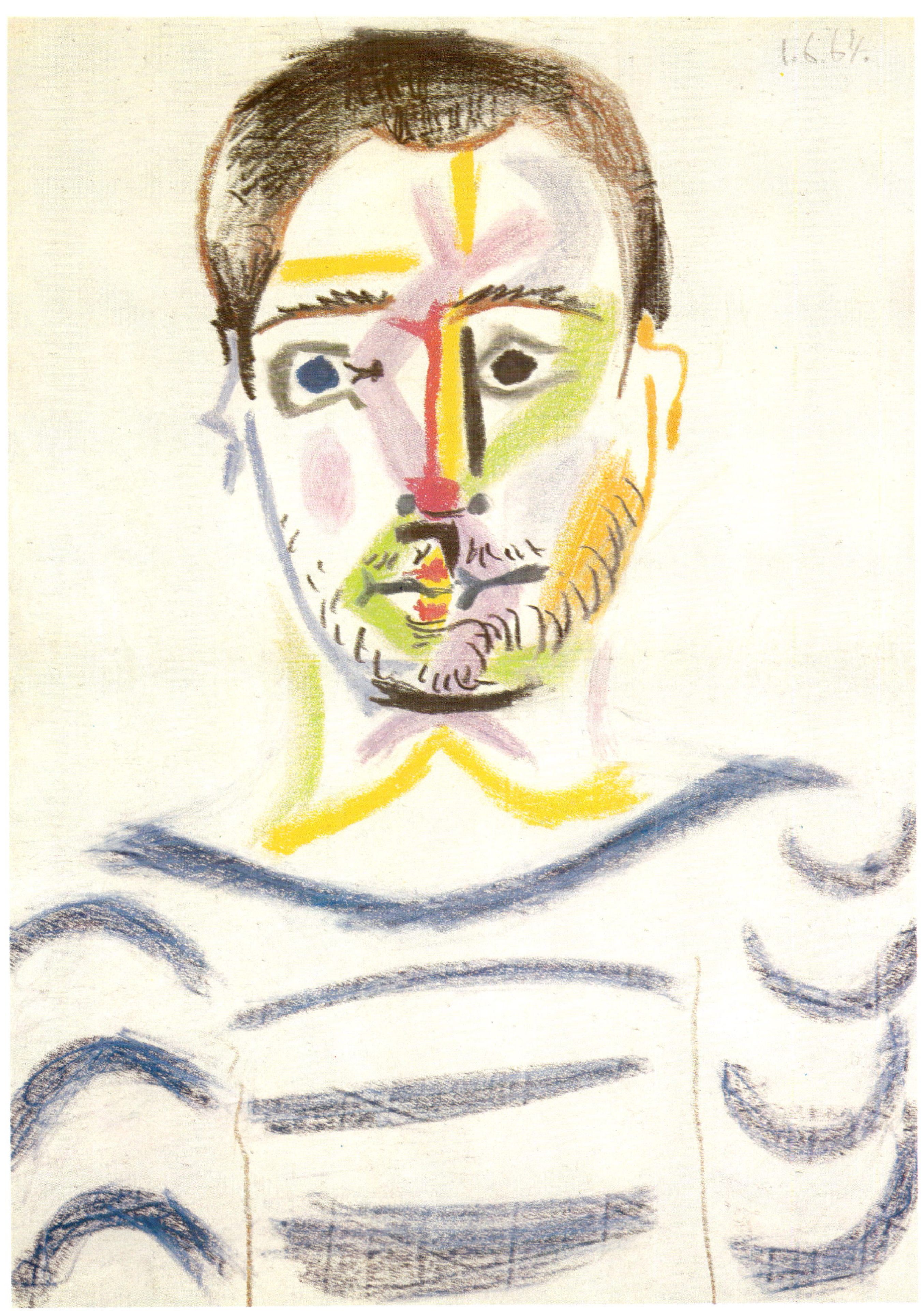
1.6.64.

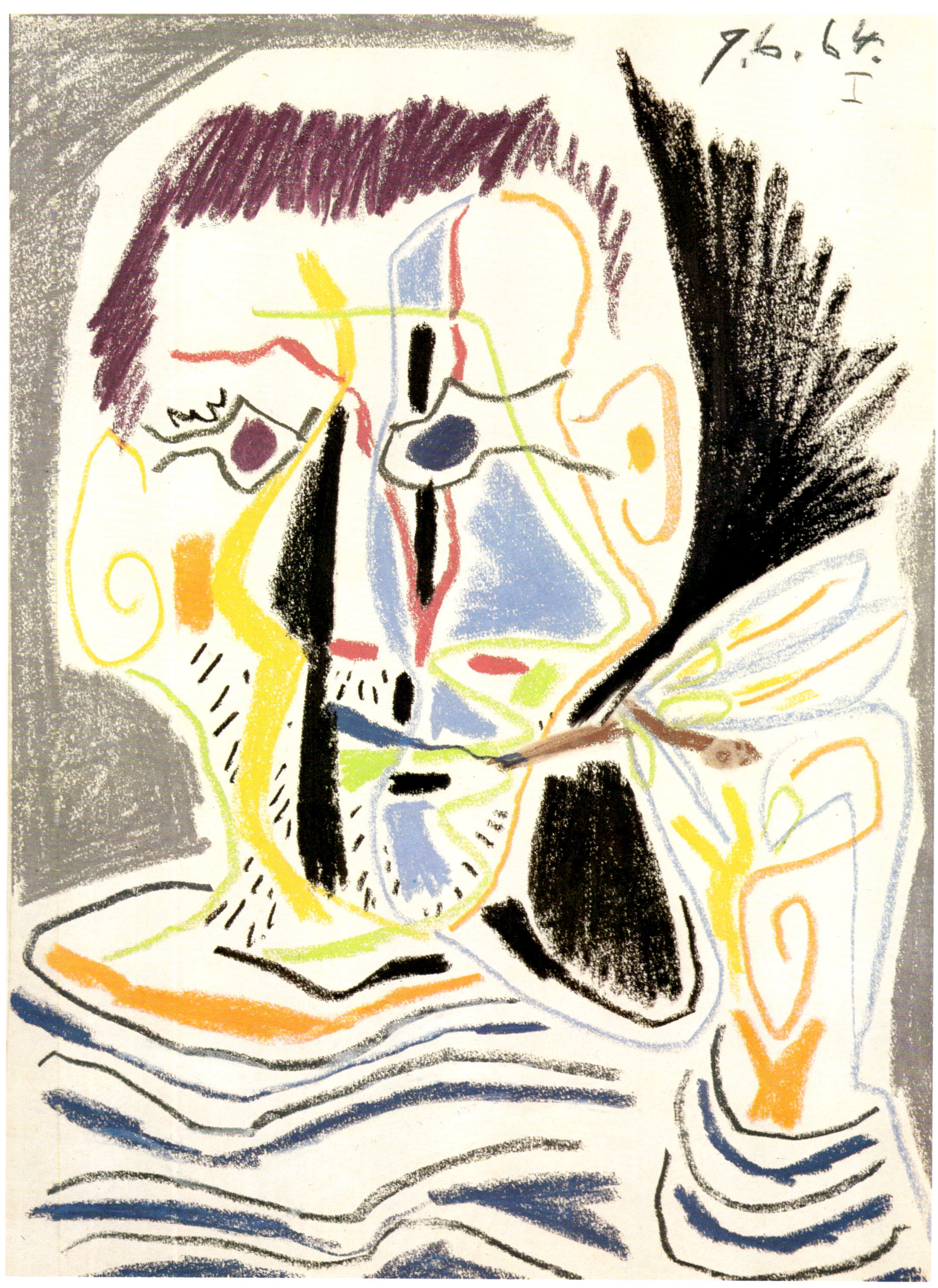
9.6.64.
I

'It was on the 30 June 1972 that he drew himself looking his own death in the face.

'Because of the holiday, I arrived at Picasso's the following day . . . Usually he would go no further than to answer the questions I asked him and talk about whatever thoughts and memories they evoked. That afternoon I was struck by his desire to confide in me . . . He took me to his studio, and as we were crossing the one adjacent to the living room, which was in half-darkness as usual, he said to me almost incidentally: "I did a drawing yesterday, I think I may have touched on something there . . . It doesn't look like anything I've ever done before." The drawing was half rolled-up on a chair. As he unrolled it, I saw the staring anguished face emerge, the face of Picasso as I had never seen him. He held the drawing up next to his face and then put it down again. I was overwhelmed . . . Three months later . . . he brought me back to look at the self-portrait again. I understood that he wanted me to tell him what I was feeling and that I must hide nothing. I told him that they were the colours of the still life after the death of Gonzalez. He didn't bat an eyelid. It suddenly struck me that he was looking his death in the eye, like a good Spaniard.'

XIII
SMOKER
pencil and coloured chalk
1.6.64

XIV
SMOKER
pencil and coloured chalk
9.6.64 I

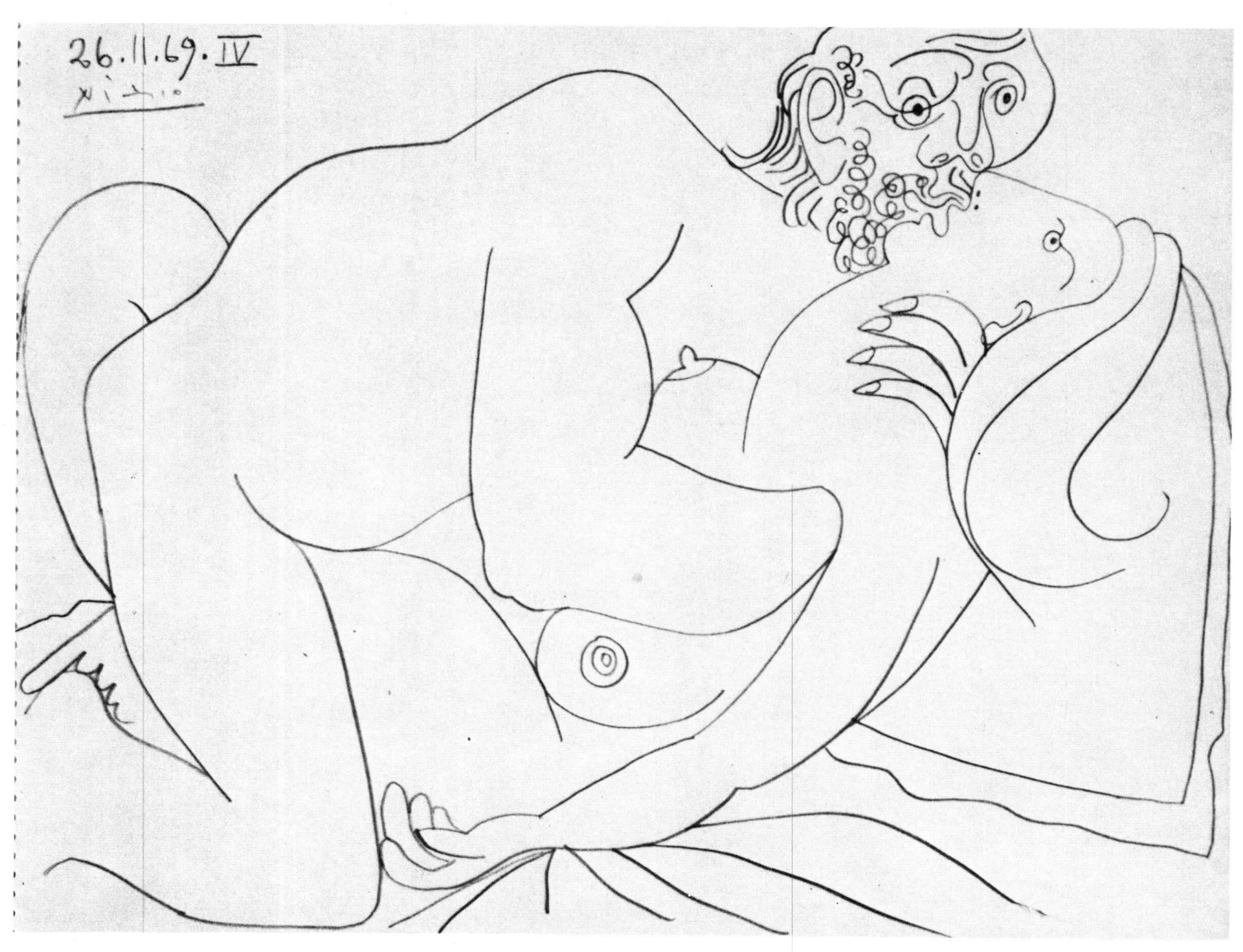

86
COUPLE EMBRACE (sketchbook page)
pencil 21×30.5
26.11.69 IV

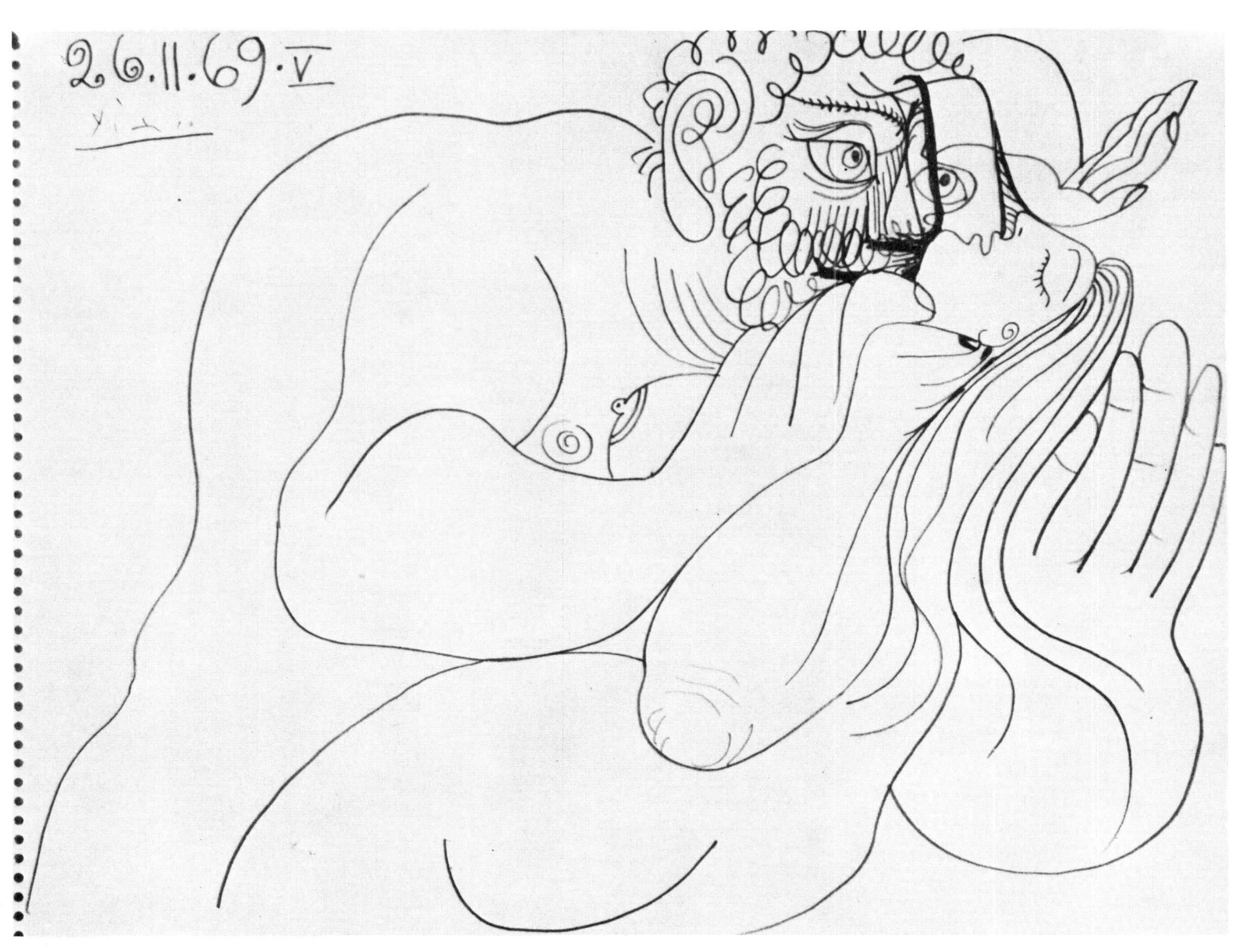

87
COUPLE EMBRACE (sketchbook page)
pencil 21×30.5
26.11.69 V

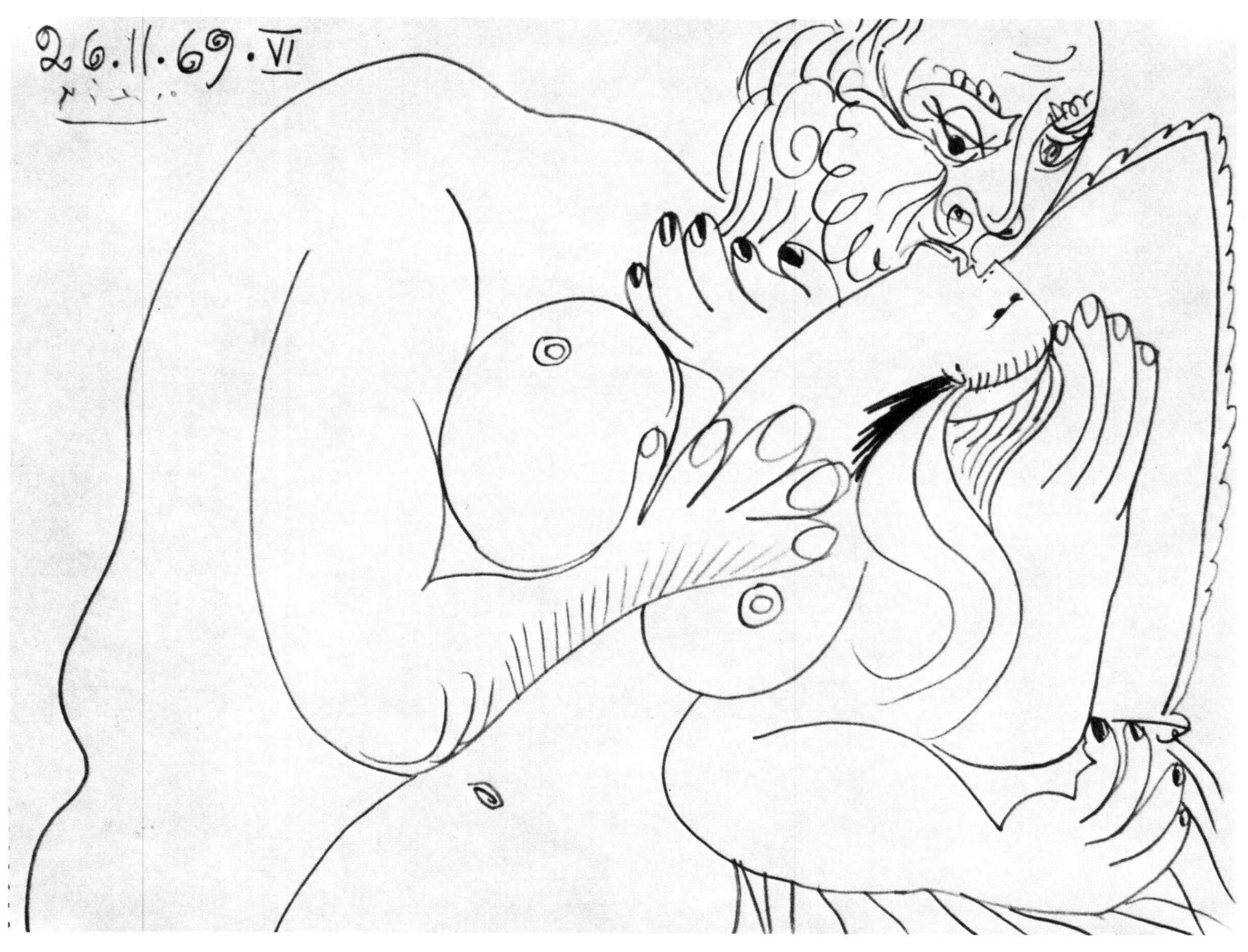

88
COUPLE EMBRACE (sketchbook page)
pencil 21×30.5
26.11.69 VI

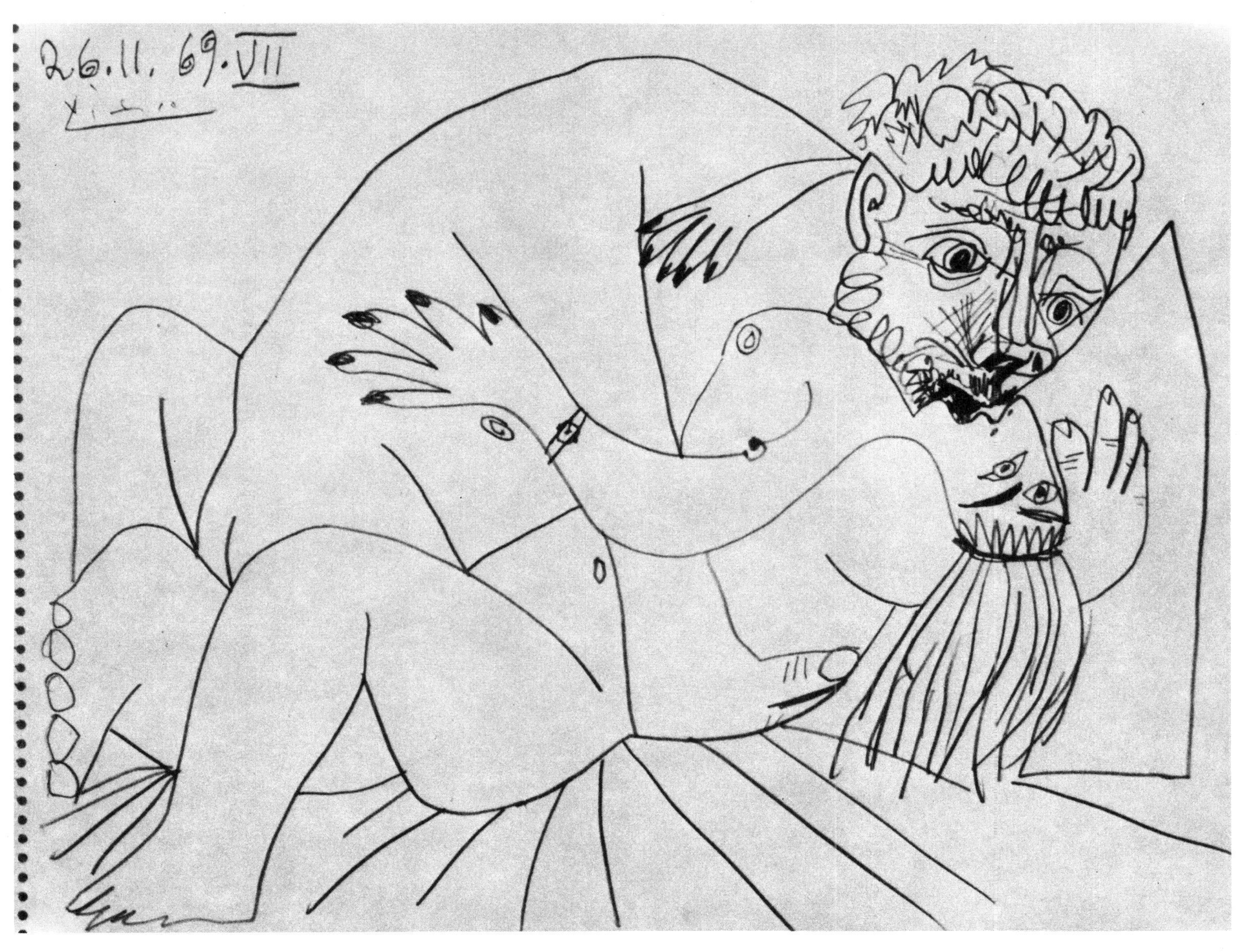

89
COUPLE EMBRACE (sketchbook page)
ink 21×30.5
26.11.69 VII

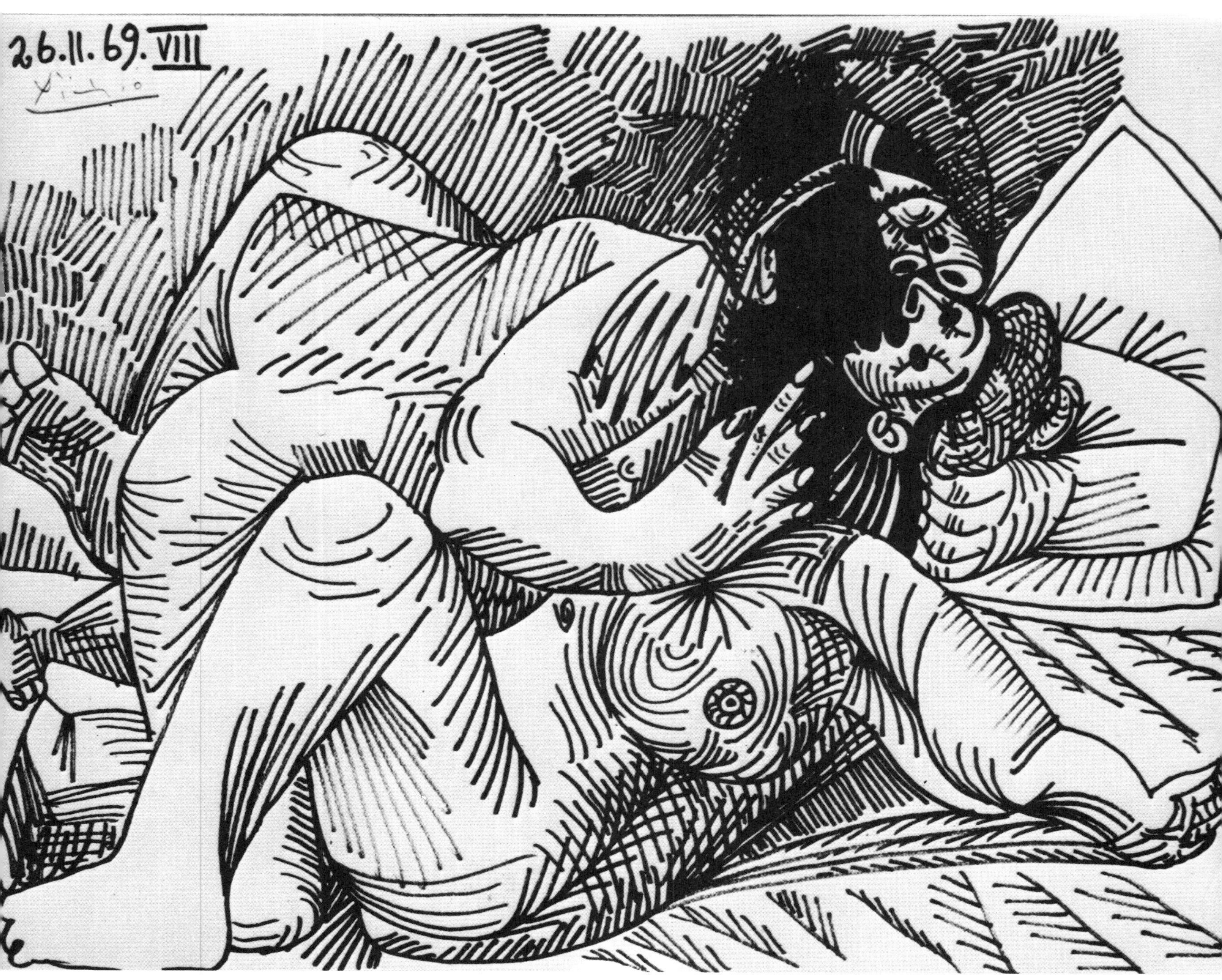

90
COUPLE EMBRACE (sketchbook page)
ink 21×30.5
26.11.69 VIII

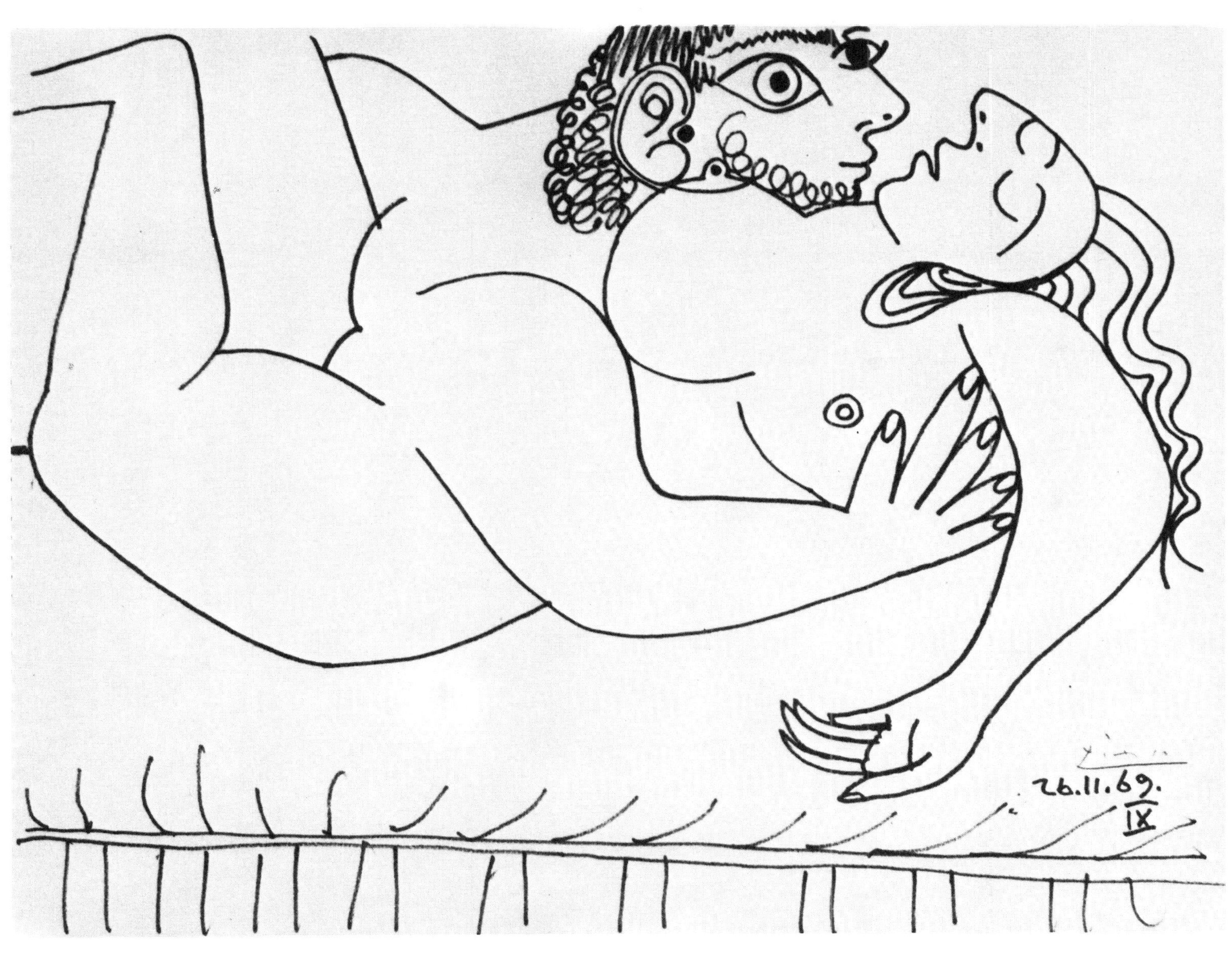

91
COUPLE EMBRACE (sketchbook page)
ink 21×30.5
26.11.69 IX

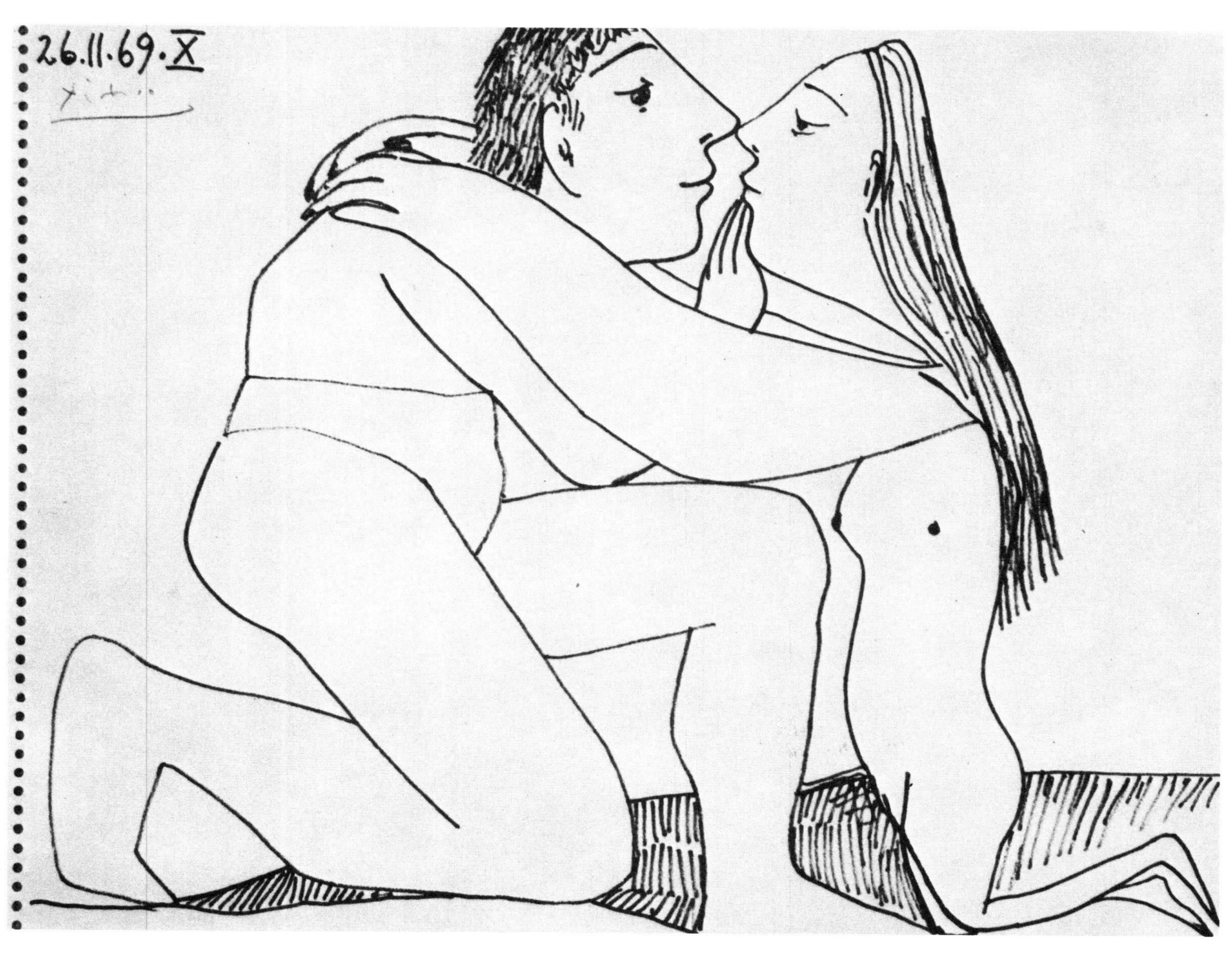

92
COUPLE EMBRACE (sketchbook page)
ink 21×30.5
26.11.69 X

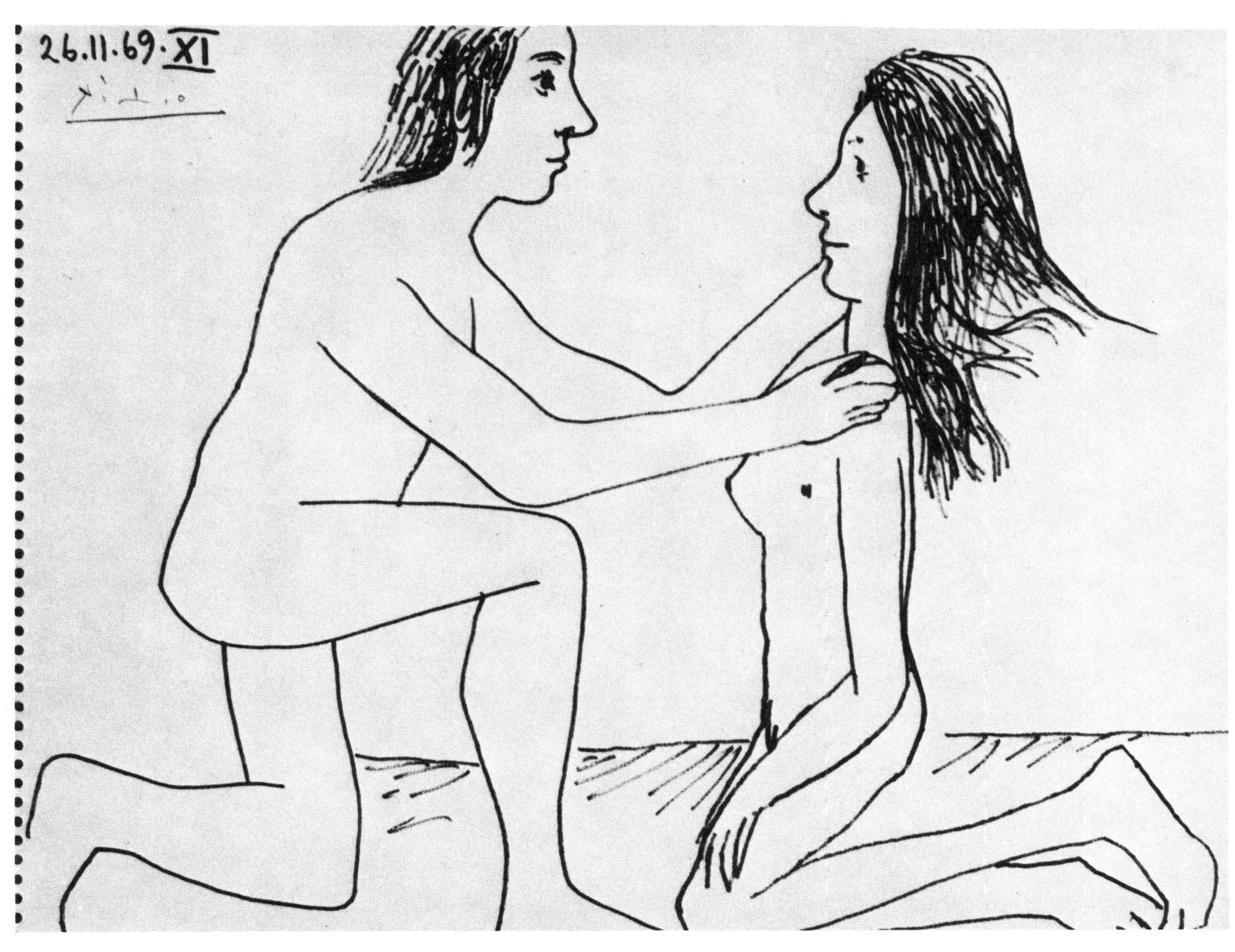

93
COUPLE EMBRACE (sketchbook page)
ink 21×30.5
26.11.69 XI

XII CONFRONTING THE PRESENT

At the end of this panorama, one might have the impression that the majority of the drawings consist of two figures, of different sexes. What could be more natural? Those couples gazing at each other, touching and kissing each other or making love reflects the preoccupations of their creator. They are the continuation of the great number of series of drawings entitled *Painter and Model*. Can one compare them? What do they have in common, apart from the fact that they all represent two figures?

In relation to the unbridled eroticisms of the last period, *Painter and Model* was an ambitious theme. It involved the artist putting himself, although disguised as someone else, on to his canvas.

The image suggests a double dialectic: the relations between men and women; the relations between reality and the representation of reality, especially with the intervention of a third element, the canvas. In this sense, *The Studio* of 1933, the linear frenzy of the 1926 *Painter and Model*, or the 1931 *Sculptor* reveal Picasso's ambitions. These works challenge us and ask fundamental questions to which there are not always easy answers. What role does the artist play as mediator between the outside world and his creation? Is he merely an eye – we know that he is more than that – or a catalyst? What are the limits of his power and is it justifiable? Any possible answer to questions such as these must depend on a great number of variables, and in any case they are the concern of philosophers and sociologists rather than art critics. Picasso put forward his own solution very simply, but far from naively.

He had lived with these problems all his life and he dealt with them, by one of two means, in his own way every working day. When his aim was to transcribe an aspect of reality, he did what all artists had always done with more or less success, with more or less boldness.

With the *Painter and Model*, he went further and committed more of himself, even if the figure on the canvas was not exactly him.

As Gert Schiff writes (in the catalogue of the 'Last Years' exhibition at the Guggenheim Museum in 1983):' . . . he hardly worked with live models, because he used the *Painter and Model* as a kind of metaphor for the conceptual nature of his art, for the transformation of things into signs, for the paradoxical relationship between artistic and pragmatic truth.'

In the face of such ambitions, the couples that pass one after another before our eyes do so simply to give us pleasure, as they gave pleasure to the artist when he captured them on paper. Yet one cannot help thinking about the mechanisms that impelled Picasso to perform these mental and graphic gymnastics.

There are many opinions on the subject. *Susanna and the Elders* has been cited on several occasions as evidence for the notion that voyeurism is a masculine tendency that develops with age. But knowing Picasso's life, his affairs, his passions, one would imagine other forms of behaviour. There was always something 'macho' about his way of depicting a woman. She always became more or less an object, an object of desire, of possession – or an object of an artistic exercise.

As an adjunct to the macho approach, his way of portraying a woman was a permanent incitement to rape. These are the views of a man who met Picasso a number of times and has given a great deal of thought to his creative processes and to those of other contemporary artists.

Gert Schiff's interpretation of Picasso in his last years is a surprising one. He believes that Picasso was developing a dream, a dream of living as natural a life as possible, surrounded by women, like a kind of primitive, but a life in which art would continue to be an important part. He lived out this dream, of being a sort of Paul Gauguin in the

94
SELF-PORTRAIT
pencil and coloured pencil 65.7×50.5
30.6.72
Fuji Television Gallery collection, Tokyo

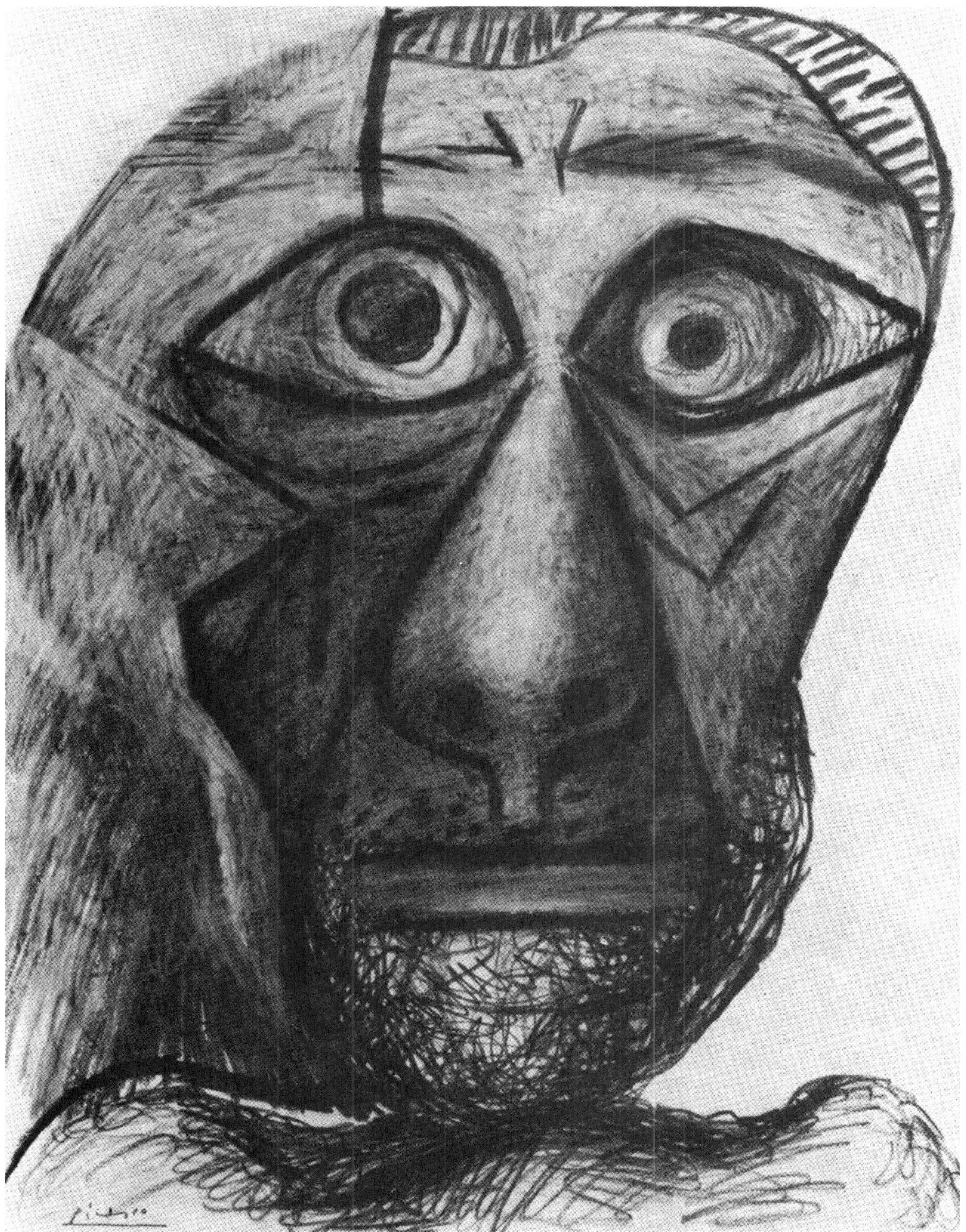

Marquesas, in his own way at Notre-Dame-de-Vie and committed his vision of it on to paper and canvas.

Schiff pursues the argument further, to a point where his hypothesis becomes incompatible with what we know of Picasso in these years. Schiff describes Picasso in his last period as a kind of guru figure, dreaming of nature, sex and music. He also inquires whether certain particularly detailed drawings of female genitalia are to be regarded as scrupulous renditions of the subject or as manifestations of childish curiosity. The reply is inherent in the question.

Do some of the series constitute 'an anthology of male frustration'? Leaving aside our indignation at such questions, Gert Schiff's replies to them are those of a man who knows Picasso and admires him in the light of his knowledge of his work.

We cannot but agree with Schiff that Picasso tackled every aspect of the problem 'without inhibition or self-pity', as a man of conscience and lucidity.

* * *

One final passage, roughly paraphrased from the first lines of Schiff's introduction to the catalogue, is worth noting.

'We can see today that the apparent carelessness of execution of some of his last works comprises a pictorial shorthand of striking expressive value, and that the most carelessly painted pictures reveal unerring plastic control.

What is more, we can understand that this exploitation of simultaneity continually gives rise to most unexpected solutions. By constantly reinventing the human form, he constantly reveals new truths to us, even about ourselves.

'If we resist his attacks on our optic nerves, we will be rewarded by considerable enhancement of our visual sensitivity. As long as we remain civilised people, conscious of our own cultural standing, we shall be grateful for his re-creations of the history of art in a language that touches on our sensibility.

'Picasso was a genius. He was also a man endowed with an ardent soul, with passions and energy that were stronger and more tenacious than those of most men. At the end, he threw all his humanism and his passionate humanity into his art. Thus, his last works teach us something that is not to be found in the late works of the other giants.

By pushing back the limits of our self-conscience a little further, Picasso saps our moral complacency in the name of his personal humanism 'without fear and without reproach'. Often he does it with disarming naivety and exquisite humour.

For all these reasons, his last period holds a special place in his evolution. It is not a swan-song, but the apotheosis of a career.'

Picasso was an integral part of our age and, at the same time, stood outside its prevailing streams. In his work he was, however numerous his imitators, a solitary figure. To parody Paul Valéry, writing about one of the greatest draughtsmen of all times, 'Rembrandt knew that flesh is mud which light turns into gold', one could say, 'Picasso knew that flesh was gold and with light he turned it into air.'

Not simply 'art', but a feature of civilisation. His work is always meaningful for its content is humanistic. He had faith in mankind and in life and that was the sole subject of his art. That is the reason why his philosophy took on a political significance and why, strictly speaking, he has no aesthetic heirs. The power of his art and the originality of his style have discouraged those who would follow in his footsteps. His legacy is a moral one, safe from the ravages of time and fashion.

XV
SMOKER
pencil and coloured chalk
12.6.64

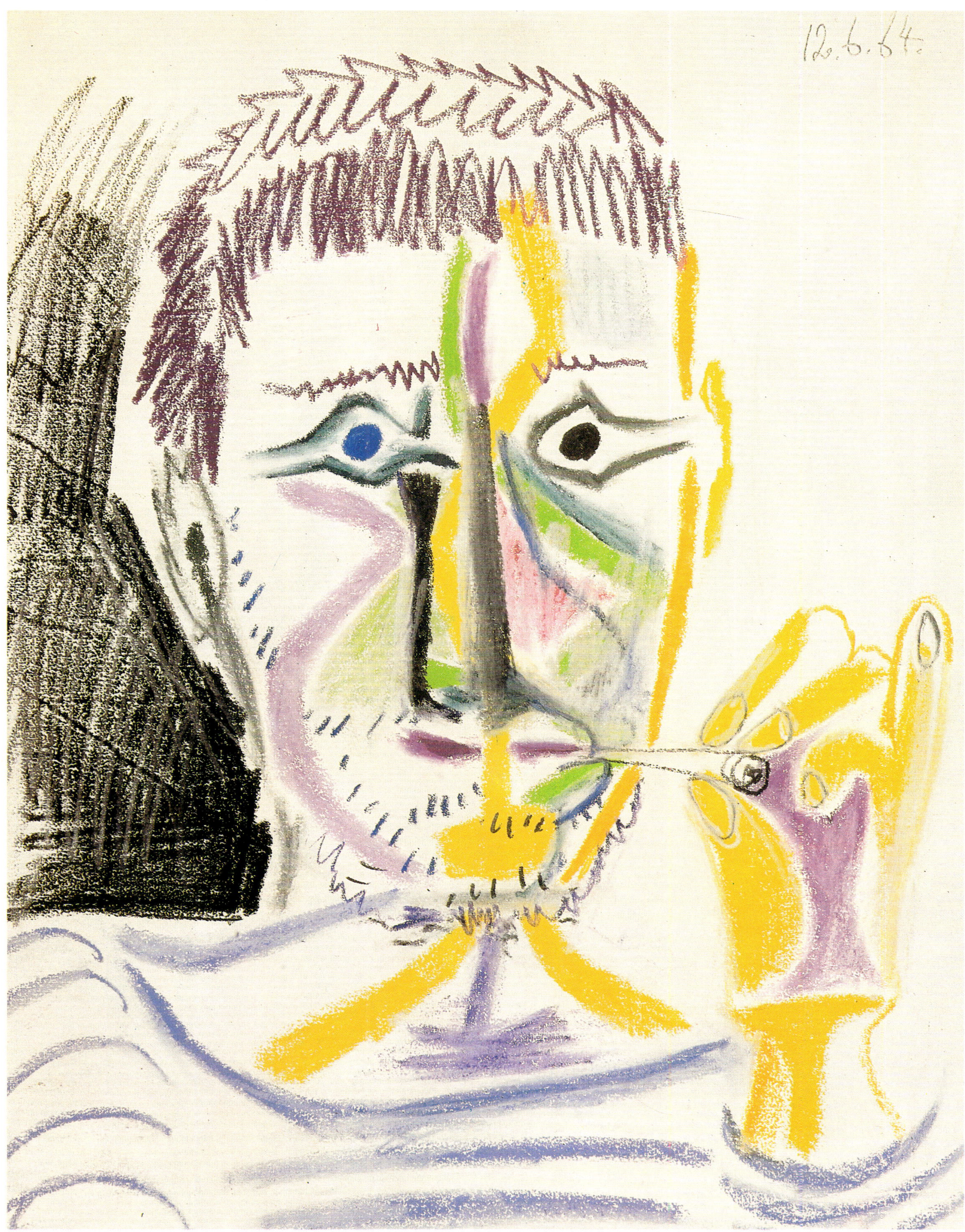
12.6.64.

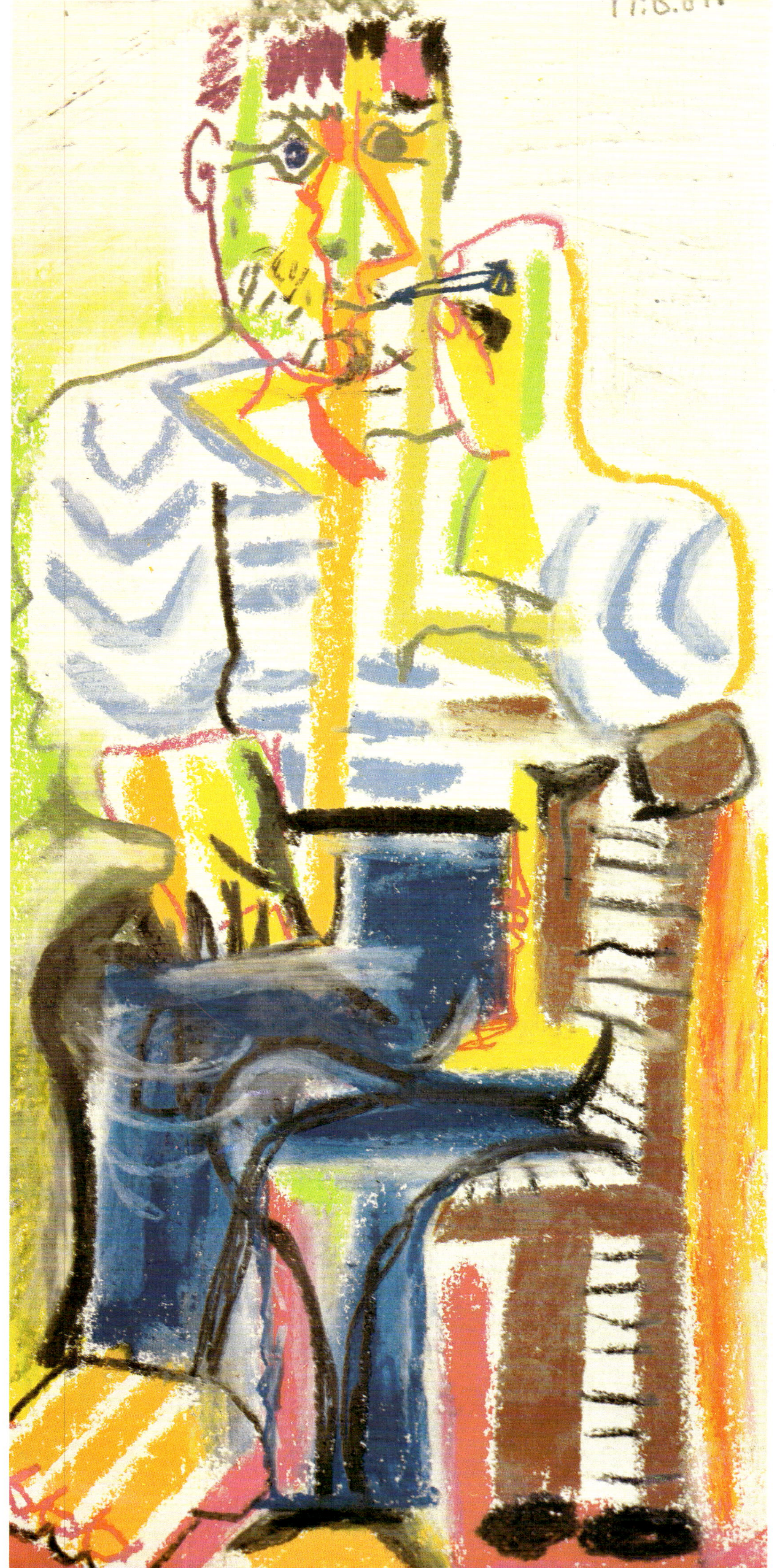

CHRONOLOGY

1881 : Pablo, son of Don José Ruiz Blasco, an art teacher, and Maria Picasso López is born in Malaga on 25 October.
1891–2 : The Ruiz-Picasso family moves to La Coruña. Pablo enters the School of Fine Arts.
1895 : Don José Ruiz is appointed to the School of Fine Arts in Barcelona, which Pablo attends. *The First Communion.*
1897 : Accepted at the San Fernando Academy in Madrid. Exhibits *Science and Charity* at the Fine Arts in Madrid.
1898 : Leaves to spend seven months in the village of Horta de Ebro with his friend Pallares.
1899 : Returns to Barcelona. Joins the artistic and literary circle of the Els Quatre Gats and makes friends with Jaime Sabartes and Casagemas.
1900 : Exhibits at Els Quatre Gats. One piece (*Science and Charity*?) is selected for the International Exhibition in Paris. Arrives in Paris with Casagemas and lodges in Montmartre. Meets art dealers Pedro Manach and Berthe Weill. Returns to Barcelona at the end of the year.
1901 : Casagemas commits suicide. Picasso leaves for Paris in April. Instals himself in Casagemas's studio on the boulevard de Clichy. First Blue Period portraits. *Motherhoods.*
1902–3 : Goes back to Barcelona but returns to France in the autumn. Berthe Weill organises an exhibition of his work. Leaves for Barcelona in January 1903. *Life.*
1904 : Goes to live at the Bateau Lavoir in Paris in April. Meets Guillaume Apollinaire, André Salmon and Fernande Olivier.
1905–6 : The first Rose Period canvases are exhibited at the Serrurier gallery. Series on *The Jugglers.* Meets Gertrude and Leo Stein who introduce him to Matisse. Vollard buys most of the Rose canvases. Leaves in May 1906 with Fernande for Barcelona, then for Gosol. *Portrait of Gertrude Stein.*
1907 : *Les Demoiselles d'Avignon. Nude with drapery.* Kahnweiler comes to the Bateau Lavoir. Braque visits his studio.
1908–9 : Spends August at Rue-des-Bois, paints landscape. Leaves in May 1909 for Horta de Ebro with Fernande. Back to Paris, moves into 11 boulevard de Clichy.
1910 : Summer in Spain with Fernande. Portraits of *Vollard, Udhe* and *Kahnweiler.*
1911 : Exhibition of 36 canvases at the Photo Secession Gallery in New York. Summer in Ceret, alone then with Fernande and Braque. Does not take part in the Cubist exhibit at the Salon d'Automne. Meets Eva Gouel.
1912–13 : First collage, *Still Life with Chair Caning* and first collations: *Guitar.*

XVI
SMOKER
pencil and coloured chalk
14.6.64

Summer in the Midi at Ceret, Avignon and Sorgues, with Eva, Braque and his wife. Braque's first *papier collé* in September, then first coloured paper collages and *papiers collés* by Picasso in October and November. Signs contract with Kahnweiler. Spends much of 1913 in Cernet with Eva.

1914–15 : Stays in Avignon. Returns to Paris at the end of the year. Eva dies on 14 December 1915. *The Glass of Absinthe*.

1916–17 : Meets Diaghilev through Cocteau. Designs his first scenery for Cocteau's *Parade*. Spends time in Italy. Meets Stravinsky and Olga Kokhlova. First performance of *Parade* on 18 May in Paris. Goes with the Russian Ballet to Spain. In November 1917, Olga and Picasso move to Montrouge.

1918–19 : Matisse-Picasso exhibition at the Paul Guillaume Gallery. Marries Olga on 12 July. Cocteau, Max Jacob and Apollinaire are his witnesses. Moves into 23 rue de la Boétie. Visited by Joan Miró in spring 1919. Designs sets for ballet *The Three-Cornered Hat*. Spends summer in Saint-Raphaël with Olga.

1920 : Ballet *Pulcinella*. Summer in Juan-les-Pins with Olga.

1921 : Birth of his son Paulo on 14 February. Ballet *Cuadro Flamenco*. Summer in Fontainebleau. First monograph by Maurice Raynal.

1922 : Jacques Doucet buys Les *Demoiselles d'Avignon*. Summer in Dinard.

1923 : Summer at Cap-d'Antibes. *Pipes of Pan*.

1924 : Exhibition at Paul Rosenberg Gallery. Ballets *Mercury* and *Le Train Bleu*. Summer in Juan-les-Pins.

1925–26 : *La Danse*. Takes part in the first Surrealist exhibition. Exhibits at Paul Rosenberg Gallery in June 1926.

1927 : Meets Marie-Thérèse Walter.

1928–29: Summer in Dinard. Steel sculptures: *Constructions*.

1930 : *Seated Bather*. Marie-Thérèse lives at 44 rue de la Boétie.

1931 : First retrospective in London. Moves to Boisgeloup in Normandy.

1932 : Retrospective at the Georges Petit Gallery in Paris, then at the Zurich Kunsthaus. Summer at Boisgeloup. Publication of the first volume of the Zervos catalogue.

1933 : Illustrates the cover of the first edition of the *Minotaur*. Summer in Cannes with Olga and Paulo.

1935 : Exhibits *papiers collés* at the Pierre Gallery. Separation from Olga. Maya, daughter of Marie-Thérèse Walter, is born on 5 October.

1936 : Exhibits in Barcelona. Designs the curtain for Romain Rolland's *14th of July*. Summer in Mougins with Dora Maar. Moves into a studio at Tremblay-sur-Mauldre with Marie-Thérèse and Maya.

1937 : Rents studio at 7 rue des Grands-Augustins. Guernica is bombed on 26

April. Works at the canvas of *Guernica* from 1 May to 4 June. First appearance of *Les Demoiselles d'Avignon* in an official exhibition at the Petit Palais. Meets Paul Klee in Switzerland. Summer in Mougins with Dora Maar.
1939 : Summer with Man Ray in Antibes with Dora Maar. *Night Fishing at Antibes.* Exhibition in New York at the Museum of Modern Art: 'Picasso, Forty Years of his Art'.
1940 : To and fro between Royan and Paris. Marie-Thérèse and Maya return to Paris in the autumn.
1943 : *Man Carrying a Sheep.* Meets Françoise Gilot.
1944 : Private performance of *Desire Caught by the Tail* with Jean-Paul Sartre, Simone de Beauvoir, Michel Leiris and Louise Leiris. Joins the French Communist party on 5 October. On 7 October, retrospective at the autumn Salon.
1946 : Visits Matisse in Nice. Retrospective at the Museum of Modern Art in New York: 'Picasso, Fifty Years of his Art'. Summer with Françoise at Menerbes and with Louis Fort in Golfe-Juan. Works at the castle in Antibes which has been put at his disposal by Romuald Dor de la Souchère. *Flower-Woman.*
1947 : Claude, his son by Françoise Gilot, is born on 15 May. Works in ceramics with Suzanne and Georges Ramie.
1948 : Takes part in the first Peace Congress in Poland.
1949 : Aragon chooses *The Dove* for the Peace Congress poster. Birth of Paloma on 19 April. Buys the Fournas studios in Vallauris.
1950 : Lives in the Midi. Awarded the Lenin Peace Prize.
1951 : *Massacre in Korea.*
1953 : Retrospectives in Milan and Lyon.
1954 : *Portraits of Sylvette David.* Meets Jacqueline Roque. Begins the *Women of Algiers* series.
1955 : Olga dies. Moves permanently to the Midi with Jacqueline Roque. Retrospective at the Museum of Decorative Arts in Paris. Settles in 'La Californie' in Cannes. Henri-Georges Clouzot films *The Picasso Mystery.*
1957 : Alfred Barr organises an exhibition at the New York Museum of Modern Art for his 75th birthday. Works at the series *Las Meninas.*
1958 : Moves to the Château de Vauvenargues.
1959 : The *Déjeuners sur l'herbe.*
1960 : Retrospective at the Tate Gallery in London.
1961 : Marries Jacqueline on 2 March at Vallauris. Moves into the villa Notre-Dame-de-Vie at Mougins.
1962 : Exhibition at the New York Museum of Modern Art: 'Picasso, an American Tribute'.

1966 : Retrospective in Paris at the Grand and Petit Palais.
1968 : Exhibition of 347 recent etchings at the Louise Leiris Gallery.
1970 : Exhibition at the Palais des Papes in Avignon.
1971 : Exhibition of 194 new drawings at the Louise Leiris Gallery.
1973 : Exhibition of 156 etchings from 1970 to 1972 at the Louise Leiris Gallery. Picasso dies on 8 April. Exhibition of 201 canvases at the Palais des Papes in Avignon.

SELECT BIBLIOGRAPHY

Picasso – The Man

Brassaï, *Conversations avec Picasso*, Paris, Gallimard, 1964.

Champris, Pierre de, *Picasso, ombre et soleil*, Paris, Gallimard, 1960.

Duncan, David Douglas, *The Private World of Pablo Picasso,* New York, 1957.

Duncan, David Douglas, *Goodbye Picasso*, London, Times Books, 1974.

Duncan, David Douglas, *The Silent Studio*, London, Collins, 1976.

Duncan, David Douglas, *Viva Picasso, a Centennial celebration 1881-1981*, New York, The Viking Press, 1980.

Eluard, Paul, *Pablo Picasso*, London, Secker and Warburg, 1947.

Gilot, Françoise, and Lake, Carlton, *Life with Picasso*, London, Nelson, 1965; London, Penguin, 1966.

Kahnweiler, Daniel-Henry, *My Galleries and Painters: The Documents of 20th Century Art*, London, Thames and Hudson, 1971.

Kahnweiler, Daniel-Henry, *Confessions esthétiques*, Paris, Gallimard, 1963.

Malraux, André, *Picasso's Mask* (trans. by June and Jacques Guicharnaud), London, Macdonald and Jane's, 1976.

Olivier, Fernande, *Picasso and his Friends*, London, Heinemann, 1964.

Parmelin, Hélène, *Picasso Plain: An Intimate Portrait*, London, Secker and Warburg, 1963.

Parmelin, Hélène, *Picasso Says* (trans. by Christine Trollope), London, Allen and Unwin, 1969.

Parmelin, Hélène, *Voyage en Picasso*, Paris, Robert Laffont, 1980.

Quinn, Edward, *Picasso at Work, an Intimate Photographic Study*, text by Roland Penrose, London, W.H. Allen, 1965.

Sabartés, Jaime, *Picasso: An Intimate Portrait*, London W.H. Allen, 1949.

Sabartés, Jaime, *Picasso: Documents iconographiques,* Geneva, Pierre Callier, 1954.

Salmon, Pierre, *Souvenirs sans fin*, Paris, Gallimard, 1955-56, 2 vol.

Stein, Gertrude, *The Autobiography of Alice B. Toklas*, London, Penguin, 1977.

Tzara, Tristan, *Picasso et les chemins de la connaissance,* Paris, Skira, 1948.

Verdet, André, *Pablo Picasso*, Photographs by Roger Hauert, Geneva, René Kister, 1956.

Weill, Berthe, *Pan! Dans l'oeil! ou trente ans dans les coulisses de la peinture contemporaine, 1900-1930,* Paris, Lipschutz, 1933.

Works of Reference

Bloch, Georges, *Pablo Picasso, Catalogue de l'oeuvre gravé et lithographié*, 4 vol., Berne, Kornfeld et Klipstein, 1968-1979.

Cachin, Françoise, and Minervino, Fiorella, *Tout l'oeuvre peint de Picasso, 1907-1916*, Paris, Flammarion, 1977.

Czwiklitzer, Christophe, *Les affiches de Pablo Picasso*, Basle-Paris, Art-C.C., 1970.

Daix, Pierre, and Boudaille, Georges, *Picasso 1900-1906, catalogue raisonné de l'oeuvre peint*, Neuchâtel, Ides et Calendes, 1966.

Duncan, David Douglas, *Picasso's Picassos,* London, Macmillan, 1970.

Geiser, Bernhard, *Picasso peintre-graveur*, 2 vol., Berne, publ. by the author, 1933; Kornfeld et Klipstein, 1968.

Goeppert, Sebastian, Goeppert-Frank, Herma and Cramer, Patrick, *Pablo Picasso, catalogue raisonné des livres illustrés,* Geneva, Patrick Cramer, 1983.

Moravia, Alberto, Lecaldano, Paolo, and Daix, Pierre, *Tout l'oeuvre peint de Picasso, périodes bleue et rose*, Paris, Flammarion, 1980.

Mourlot, Fernand, *Picasso lithographe,* 4 vol., Monte-Carlo, André Sauret, 1949-1964.

Palau i Fabre, Josep, *Picasso: Life and Work of the Early Years*, Oxford, Phaidon, 1981.

Ramié, Georges, *Picasso's Ceramics*, London, Secker and Warburg, 1975.

Spies, Werner, *Picasso Sculpture: With a Complete Catalogue* (trans by J. Maxwell Brownjohn), London, Thames and Hudson, 1972.

Zervos, Christian, *Pablo Picasso,* Paris, Cahiers d'Art, vol. 1, 1932, to vol. XXXIII, 1978.

Monographs

Barr, Alfred Hamilton, *Picasso, Fifty Years of his Art*, London, Secker and Warburg, 1975.

Berger, John, *The Success and Failure of Picasso*, London, Writers and Readers, 1980.

Boeck, Wilhelm, and Sabartés, Jaime, *Picasso*, London, Thames and Hudson, 1955.

Boudaille, Georges, and Moulin, Raoul-Jean, *Picasso*, Paris, Nouvelles Editions Françaises, 1971.

Cabanne, Pierre, *Le siècle de Picasso*, Paris, Denoël, 1975, 2 vol.

Cabanne, Pierre, *Picasso*, Neuchâtel, Ides et Calendes, 1981.

Cassou, Jean, *Picasso* (trans. by M. Chamot), Paris, Hyperion Press, 1940.

Cassou, Jean, *Pablo Picasso*, Paris, Somogy, 1975.
Daix, Pierre, *Picasso*, London, Thames and Hudson, 1965.
Daix, Pierre, *La vie de peintre de Pablo Picasso*, Paris, Le Seuil, 1977.
Dmitrieva, Nina Alexandrovna, *Pikasso*, Moscow, Nauka, 1971.
Elgar, Frank, and Maillard, Robert, *Picasso: A Study of His Work* (trans. by Francis Scarfe), London, Thames and Hudson, 1972.
Fermigier, André, *Picasso*, Le Livre de Poche, 1969.
Leymarie, Jean, *Métamorphoses et Unité,* Geneva, Skira, 1971.
Palau i Fabre, Josep, *Picasso*, London, Academy Editions, 1987.
Penrose, Roland, *Picasso: His Life and Work,* London, Paladin, 1981.
Perry, Jacques, *Yo Picasso*, Paris, J.-C. Lattès, 1982.
Picasso, coll. Génies et Réalités, Paris, Hachette, 1967.
Raynal, Maurice, *Picasso,* Geneva, Skira, 1953.
Schiff, Gert (ed.), *Picasso in Perspective*, London, Prentice-Hall, 1976.
Stein, Gertrude, *Picasso*, new ed., New York, Dover, 1985.
Vallentin, Antonina, *Picasso*, London, Cassell, 1963.

At the Beginning: 'Blue' and 'Pink' Periods

Cirici-Pellicer, Alexandre, *Picasso avant Picasso,* Geneva, Pierre Cailler, 1950.
Cirlot, Juan Eduardo, *Picasso: Birth of a Genius*, London, Elek, 1972.
Lieberman, William S., *Pablo Picasso: Blue and Rose Periods*, London, Thames and Hudson, 1954.
Palau i Fabre, Josep, *Picasso en Catalogne,* Paris, Société Française du Livre, 1979.

Cubism

Golding, John, *Cubism: A History and an Analysis, 1907-1914*, 2nd ed., London, Faber, 1968.
Paulhan, Jean, *La peinture cubiste*, Paris, Denoël, 1971.

1917-1925

Cooper, Douglas, *Picasso et le théâtre*, Paris, Cercle d'Art, 1960.

1925-1936

Glozer, Laszlo, *Picasso und der Surrealismus*, Cologne, DuMont Schauberg, 1974.
Penrose, Roland, 'Beauty and Monster', *Picasso 1881-1973*, London, Elek, 1973, pp. 156-195.

Ries, Martin, 'Picasso and the Myth of the Minotaur', *Art Journal,* Winter 1972-1973, pp. 142-145.
Rubin, William, *Dada and Surrealist Art,* London, Thames and Hudson, 1969.
Runnqvist, Jan, *Minotauros; en studie i for,* Stockholm, Bonnier, 1959.
Seckel, Curt, 'Picasso, Wege zur Symbolik der Minotauromachie', *Die Kunst und das schöne Heim,* May 1973, pp. 289-296.

1936-1945
Blunt, Anthony, *Picasso's Guernica,* London, Oxford University Press, 1969.
Cahiers d'Art, No. IV-V, 1937, special issue devoted to *Guernica.*
Ferrier, Jean-Louis, 'Elements pour Guernica', *XXe siècle,* special issue, 1971, pp. 48-51.
Guernica-Legado Picasso, Museo del Prado, 1981.

1945-1973
Cooper, Douglas, *Pablo Picasso's 'Les Déjeuners',* London, Thames and Hudson, 1963.
Dor de la Souchère, Romuald, *Picasso in Antibes* (trans. by W.J. Strachan), London, H. Lund, 1960.
Gallwitz, Klaus, *Picasso at 90: the Late Work,* London, Weidenfeld and Nicolson, 1971.
Parmelin, Hélène, *Picasso: Women, Cannes and Mougins, 1954-63* (trans. by Humphrey Hare), London, Weidenfeld and Nicolson, 1965.
Parmelin, Hélène, *Le peintre et son modèle,* Paris, Cercle d'Art, 1965.
Parmelin, Hélène, *Picasso: Intimate Secrets of a Studio at Notre-Dame-de-Vie,* New York, Abrams, 1968.
Roy, Claude, *La Guerre et la Paix,* Paris, Cercle d'Art, 1952.
Sabartés, Jaime, *Les Ménines et la vie,* Paris, Cercle d'Art, 1958.

Collages
Exhibition Catalogue *Georges Braque, les papiers collés,* Paris, Centre Pompidou, Musée National d'Art Moderne, 17 June-27 September 1982.

Ceramics
Bloch, Georges, *Picasso, Ceramics Catalogue of the Printed Graphic Work, Series: Vol. III, 1949-1971,* New York, Wittenborn, 1972.

Drawings
Boeck, Wilhelm, *Picasso: Zeichnungen,* Cologne, DuMont Schauberg, 1973.

Boudaille, Georges (Introduction), *Pablo Picasso. Carnet de la Californie*, Paris, Cercle d'Art, 1959.
Boudaille, Georges, and Dominguin, Luis Miguel, *Pablo Picasso, Toros y Toreros*, Paris, Cercle d'Art, 1961.
Eluard, Paul, *Picasso. Dessins*, Paris, Braun, 1952.
George, Waldemar, *Picasso. Dessins*, Paris, Les Quatre Chemins, 1926.
Jardot, Maurice, *Picasso, Dessins d'un demi-siècle*, Paris, Berggruen, 1956.
Jardot, Maurice, *Pablo Picasso, Dessins*, Paris, Calmann-Lévy, 1959.
Lambert, Jean Clarence, *Picasso. Dessins de Tauromachie, 1917-1960*, Paris, Art et Style, 1960.
Leymarie, Jean, *Picasso, dessins*, Geneva, Skira, 1967.
Marcenac, Jean, *Picasso. Le goût du bonheur. A Suite of Happy, Playful and Erotic Drawings*, New York, Abrams, 1970.
Millier, Arthur, *The Drawings of Picasso*, Los Angeles, Borden, 1961.
Picasso, 145 dessins pour la presse et les organisations démocratiques, Paris, L'Humanité, 1973.
Picon, Gaëtan, *Pablo Picasso, 'La chute d'Icare'*, Skira, Les Sentiers de la Création, 1971.
Zervos, Christian, *Dessins de Picasso, 1892-1948*, Paris, Cahiers d'Art, 1949.

LIST OF COLOUR PLATES

As was his custom Picasso did not give any title to these pages from his sketchbook. We are therefore using the title SMOKER which is justified by Hélène Parmelin in the collection *Notre-Dame-de-Vie*, published by Editions Cercle d'Art in 1966.

I SMOKER, pencil and coloured chalk, 16.5.64 IV

II SMOKER, pencil and coloured chalk, 18.5.64 I

III SMOKER, pencil and coloured chalk, 18.5.64 II

IV SMOKER, pencil and coloured chalk, 18.5.64 VI

V SMOKER, pencil and coloured chalk, 19.5.64 II

VI SMOKER, pencil and coloured chalk, 19.5.64 III

VII SMOKER, pencil and coloured chalk, 22.5.64 II

VIII SMOKER, pencil and coloured chalk, 22.5.64 III

IX SMOKER, pencil and coloured chalk, 23.5.64 III

X SMOKER, pencil and coloured chalk, 23.5.64 V

XI SMOKER, pencil and coloured chalk, 23.5.64 VI

XII SMOKER, pencil and coloured chalk, 31.5.64 II

XIII SMOKER, pencil and coloured chalk, 1.6.64

XIV SMOKER, pencil and coloured chalk, 9.6.64 I

XV SMOKER, pencil and coloured chalk, 12.6.64

XVI SMOKER, pencil and coloured chalk, 14.6.64

LIST OF BLACK AND WHITE REPRODUCTIONS

1 MOTHER AND SMALL BOY charcoal coloured in oil 48×25.5, Barcelona 1903, private collection, New York

2 NUDE WITH LEGS CROSSED pastel 60×46, Barcelona 1903

3 WOMAN AND CHILD BY THE SEA pastel 1903, private collection, Paris

4 WOMAN WITH A CROW charcoal, pastel and watercolour, Paris 1904, The Toledo Museum of Art, Toledo, Ohio

5 WOMAN WITH HELMET OF HAIR gouache 42×30, Paris 1904, Art Institute, Chicago

6 MOTHER AND CHILD (studies) black crayon 36×26, Paris 1904, The Fogg Art Museum, Cambridge

7 LA COIFFURE drawing, Paris 1905

8 TWO NUDES, Paris 1906

9 WOMAN SITTING AND WOMAN STANDING drawing 61 × 46.4, Paris 1906

10 STUDY drawing 22.5×17.5, Paris 1907

11 STUDY FOR NUDE WITH DRAPERY (Moscow linen) 22.5×17, 1907

12 STUDY FOR THREE WOMEN drawing 62×47, Y. Zervos collection

13 NUDE WOMAN 48.5×31.5, spring 1910, private collection, New York

14 HEAD OF A MAN Conté pencil drawing 62.5×47, Paris 1912, private collection

15 BOTTLE, CUP, NEWSPAPER *papier collé* with drawing, Paris 1912–13

16 MAN WITH PIPE LEANING ON A TABLE drawing 32×24, Paris 1914

17 SLEEPING PEASANTS tempera, watercolour and pencil 31×48, Paris 1919

18 HEAD OF A WOMAN pastel 75×60, 1921, collection of Madame Cuttoli

19 HEAD OF A MAN pastel 77×60, 1921, collection of Madame Cuttoli

20 HEAD OF A WOMAN pastel 62×46, Fontainebleau 1921

21 TWO WOMEN WITH HATS pastel 105×75, Fontainebleau 1921

22 HEAD OF A YOUNG MAN Conté pencil 60×47, 11–12 February 1923

23 DRAWING charcoal, sketchbook, summer 1927

24 DRAWING charcoal, sketchbook, summer 1927

25 DRAWING charcoal, sketchbook, summer 1927

26 CRUCIFIXION Indian ink drawing 34.5×50.5, Boisgeloup 19 September 1932, Picasso Museum, Paris

27 THE STUDIO lead pencil 26×34.5, Paris 22 February 1933, Picasso Museum, Paris

28 MINOTAUR Indian ink 47×62, Boisgeloup 24 June 1933, private collection

29 BULL'S HEAD charcoal 50.5×34, 1933

30 BULLFIGHT Indian ink on wood panel 31.5×40.7, Boisgeloup 24 July 1934

31 NUDES charcoal 28×27, sketchbook, Paris 30 August 1934

32 COMPOSITION Indian ink 34.5×50.5, Paris 2 January 1934

33 DISEMBOWELLED HORSE pencil, Barcelona 1917

34 THE RESCUE charcoal 28×27, sketchbook, Paris 11 January 1933

35 WOMAN HOWLING IN PAIN pencil 29.3×21.2, private collection, Lucerne

36 STUDY FOR GUERNICA pencil 24×45, Paris 8 May 1937

37 STUDY FOR GUERNICA Indian ink 24×45, Paris 9 May 1937

38 STUDY FOR GUERNICA black and coloured pencil 45×24, Paris 13 May 1937

39 STUDY FOR GUERNICA black and coloured pencil and gouache on tracing linen, Paris 13 June 1937, Prado Museum, Madrid

40 STUDIES, TOROS Y TOREROS, 2 March 1959

41 MAN CARRYING A SHEEP Indian ink 68×44, 20 August 1942

42 THE FACE OF PEACE Indian ink on Ingres paper 51×66, 5.12.50 XXIV

43 WAR AND PEACE Indian ink on Ingres paper 51×66, 9.8.52 XXII

44 WAR AND PEACE Indian ink on Ingres paper 51×66, 14.8.52 V

45 WAR AND PEACE Indian ink on Ingres paper 51×66, 15.8.52 IV

46 WAR AND PEACE Indian ink on Ingres paper 51×66, 19.8.52 XVIII

47 WAR AND PEACE Indian ink on Ingres paper 51×66, 5.10.51 I

48 WAR AND PEACE Indian ink on Ingres paper 51×66, 5.10.51 II

49 WAR AND PEACE Indian ink on Ingres paper 51×66, 5.10.51 III

50 WAR AND PEACE Indian ink on Ingres paper 51×66, 5.10.51 VI

51 MOTHERHOOD study on Ingres paper 51×66, 4.9.52 III

52 HEAD 15.9.64 I

53 HEAD 15.9.64 III

54 DONA CABEZA, 23.9.64 II

55 MAN AND WOMAN, 8.10.64 I

56 MAN AND WOMAN, 8.10.64 II

57 MAN AND WOMAN, 8.10.64 IV

58 MAN AND WOMAN, 8.10.64 VI

59 MAN AND WOMAN, 8.10.64 XV

60 MAN AND WOMAN, 8.10.64 XVII

61 MUSKETEER wash 65×50, 9.2.67 VI

62 MUSKETEER WITH PIPE wash 65×50, 10.2.67 IV

63 MUSKETEER wash 65×50, 11.2.67 II

64 MUSKETEER wash 60.5×49.5, 5.6.67 II and 8.6.67 (the small heads in the margins)

65 MAN WITH LAMB AND WATERMELON EATER wash 50×65, 9.2.67 III

66 THE CIRCUS wash 49.5×75.2, 11.3.67

67 MYTHOLOGICAL SCENE pencil 56.5×75, 30.8.67

68 MYTHOLOGICAL SCENE pencil 56.5×75, 31.8.67 I

69 COURTSHIP SCENE pencil 56.5×75, 1.9.67 I

70 THE THREE GRACES pencil and gouache 75×56.5, 3.9.67 II and 4.9.67

71 THE KISS pencil 33×50.5, 7.10.67 II

72 SIX NUDE FIGURES Indian ink and gouache 65×58, 8.11/14.11.67 and 25.12.67

73 THE SWIMMING POOL pencil 23.8×29.4, 27.1.68 VII

74 THE SWIMMING POOL pencil 48×59, 16.2.68 IV

75 FIGURES AT THE WINDOW pencil 49.2×75.5, 8.3.68 IV

76 HORSEWOMAN WITH BALL pencil 49.2×76, 8.3.68 II

77 TWO WOMEN coloured pencil 44×31.5, 4.2.69 III

78 MAN AND WOMAN Indian ink 50.8×65.2, 31.5.69

79 RECLINING WOMAN charcoal 50.57×65.5, 11.7.69

80 RECLINING WOMAN pencil 50.57×65.5, 11.8.69 I

81 RECLINING WOMAN coloured pencil 50.57×65.5, 11.8.69 II

82 RECLINING WOMAN pencil, Sunday 10.8.69 III

83 RECLINING WOMAN pencil and chalk 48×63.5, 20.9.69 III

84 COUPLE EMBRACE (sketchbook page) pencil 21×30.5, 26.11.69 II

85 COUPLE EMBRACE (sketchbook page) pencil 21×30.5, 26.11.69 III

86 COUPLE EMBRACE (sketchbook page) pencil 21×30.5, 26.11.69 IV

87 COUPLE EMBRACE (sketchbook page) pencil 21×30.5, 26.11.69 V

88 COUPLE EMBRACE (sketchbook page) pencil 21×30.5, 26.11.69 VI

89 COUPLE EMBRACE (sketchbook page) ink 21×30.5, 26.11.69 VII

90 COUPLE EMBRACE (sketchbook page) ink 21×30.5, 26.11.69 VIII

91 COUPLE EMBRACE (sketchbook page) ink 21×30.5, 26.11.69 IX

92 COUPLE EMBRACE (sketchbook page) ink 21×30.5, 26.11.69 X

93 COUPLE EMBRACE (sketchbook page) ink 21×30.5, 26.11.69 XI

94 SELF-PORTRAIT pencil and coloured pencil 65.7×50.5, 30.6.72, Fuji Television Gallery collection, Tokyo

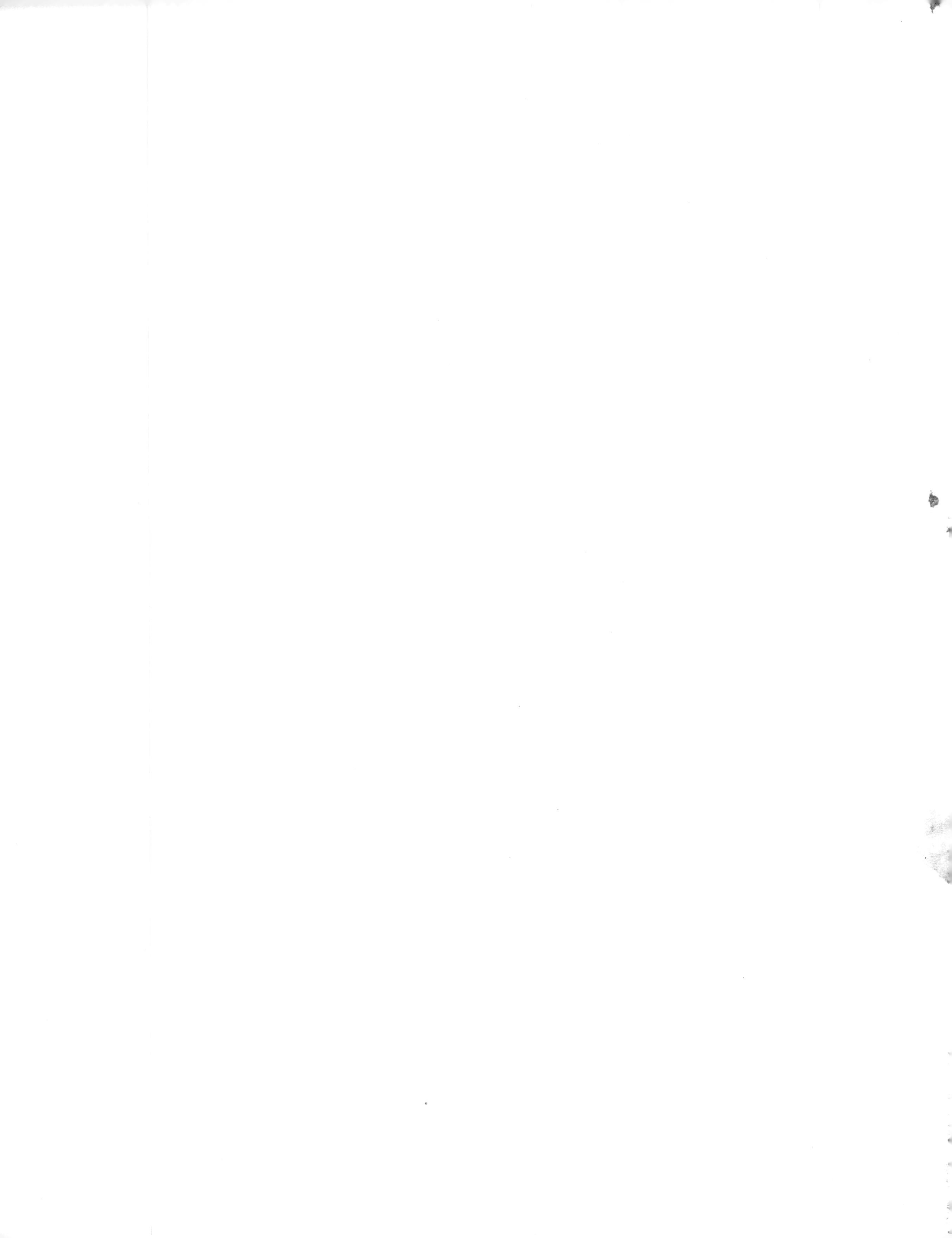